DESIGNING FOR
AUTISM SPECTRUM DISORDERS

Designing for Autism Spectrum Disorders explains the influence of the natural and man-made environment on individuals with autism spectrum disorders (ASD) and other forms of intellectual/developmental disabilities (IDD). Drawing on the latest research in the fields of environmental psychology and education, the authors show how architecture and interior spaces can positively influence individuals with neurodiversities by modifying factors such as color, lighting, space organization, textures, acoustics, and ventilation. Now you can design homes, therapeutic environments, work environments, and outdoor spaces to encourage growth and learning for the projected 500,000 children with ASD (in the United States alone) who are expected to reach adulthood by 2024.

Topics discussed include:

- Environmental design theories
- Symptoms of ASD
- Sensory processing deficits
- Design needs of individuals on the spectrum at all ages
- Design methods and solutions for spaces, including residential, learning, work, and therapeutic environments encompassing a wide range of budgets
- Designing for self-actualization, well-being, and a high quality of life for the duration of an individual's life
- Avenues for healthy living and aging in place
- Biophilic design
- Environmental impact on well-being
- Strategies to promote active living as an integral part of the welfare focus.

Kristi Gaines is the Director of the Graduate Programs in Interior and Environmental Design at Texas Tech University. She received her PhD in Environmental Design with collaterals in Architecture and Special Education. Dr. Gaines has a combined 20 years of professional interior design and teaching experience.

Angela Bourne is an Interior Designer and Educator at Fanshawe College in Canada. Over her 30 plus years in the profession, she has kept current by regularly practicing interior design and most recently combined her PhD research in Environmental Design with her practice to form her holistic company, "Nero-Considerate Environments."

Michelle Pearson is an Assistant Professor in the Interior Design Program at Texas Tech University. She received her PhD in Interior and Environmental Design. Her research focuses on built environments that promote health and wellness in children.

Mesha Kleibrink graduated from Texas Tech University with a Bachelor of Interior Design and Master of Science in Environmental Design. She is an associate member of IIDA and currently works as an interior designer and analyst at the Texas Tech University Health Sciences Center.

DESIGNING FOR
AUTISM SPECTRUM DISORDERS

Kristi Gaines, Angela Bourne,
Michelle Pearson, and Mesha Kleibrink

Routledge
Taylor & Francis Group

LONDON AND NEW YORK

First published 2016 by Routledge

2 Park Square, Milton Park, Abingdon, Oxfordshire OX14 4RN
52 Vanderbilt Avenue, New York, NY 10017

*Routledge is an imprint of the Taylor & Francis Group,
an informa business*

First issued in paperback 2018

Library of Congress Cataloguing in Publication Data
Names: Gaines, Kristi, author.
Title: Designing for autism spectrum disorders / Kristi Gaines,
    Angela Bourne, Michelle Pearson and Mesha Kleibrink.
Description: New York : Routledge, 2016. | Includes
    bibliographical references and index.
Identifiers: LCCN 2015046509| ISBN 9780415725279 (hardback :
    alk. paper) | ISBN 9781315856872 (ebook)
Subjects: LCSH: Senses and sensation in architecture. |
    Architecture—Psychological aspects. | Design—Human
    factors. | Autism spectrum disorders.
Classification: LCC NA2543.S47 G35 2016 | DDC 720/.47—dc23
LC record available at http://lccn.loc.gov/2015046509

ISBN: 978-0-415-72527-9 (hbk)
ISBN: 978-0-367-03046-9 (pbk)

Acquisition Editor: Wendy Fuller
Editorial Assistant: Grace Harrison
Production Editor: Hannah Champney

Designed and typeset by Alex Lazarou

Contents

DEDICATIONS

KRISTI GAINES

To Taylor, for his positive attitude and "can-do" approach to life that makes the world a better place.

To Bruce, Constance, Brandon, Matthew, Brian, Natalie, Connor, and Carson for their love, support, and encouragement.

To my mother, Jo Scott. Throughout her life she modeled a hard work ethic and a desire for excellence. She believed that I could do anything. This book is part of her legacy.

ANGELA BOURNE

To my brother Ted, and all his friends, who made me aware of the needs of people with intellectual and developmental disabilities.

To Greg, my husband, who was always there for me while I spent many hours working on this book and my dissertation.

To Donnie and Vanessa, our children, who also were behind me all the way during the book writing process.

To many supportive friends and family members who accepted me back into their lives after I missed many events to fulfill this challenge.

I love you all.

~Angie and Mom

MICHELLE PEARSON

To Derik for being my biggest supporter and best friend.

To my family, new and old, for all the love and encouragement.

To Capri and Madison for being there through it all. I couldn't have done this without you.

MESHA KLEIBRINK

To Jack, thank you for the impact you made so many years ago. This book is for you.

To Kyler, thank you for your overwhelming amount of support and love. I couldn't do it without you.

To Mom and Dad, thank you for teaching me to believe in myself. Your love and sacrifice have made everything in my life possible.

I love you all.

Illustration credits

5.7	Designed by Baskervill, Architects & Engineers; Photography by Lee Brauer
5.8	Designed by Baskervill Architects & Engineers; Photography by Lee Brauer
5.9	Designed by Baskervill Architects & Engineers; Photography by Lee Brauer
5.10	Designed by Baskervill, Architects & Engineers; Photography by Lee Brauer

CHAPTER 6

Table 6.1	Part of the Teaching students with autism: A resource guide for schools Victoria: British Columbia Ministry of Education, Special Programs Branch, British Columbia, 2003
Table 6.2	Adapted from Statistics for the Decibel (Loudness) Comparison Chart taken from a study by Marshall Chasin, M.Sc., Aud(C), FAAA, Center for Human Performance & Health, Ontario, Canada
6.1	Designed by Design Plus LLC, Albuquerque, NM
6.2	Adapted from Seep, B., Glosemeyer, R., Hulce, E., Linn, M., & Aytar, P. (2000), Classroom Acoustics: A Resource for Creating Environments with Desirable Listening Conditions
6.3	Adapted from Seep, B., Glosemeyer, R., Hulce, E., Linn, M., & Aytar, P. (2000), Classroom Acoustics: A Resource for Creating Environments with Desirable Listening Conditions
6.4	Adapted from Seep, B., Glosemeyer, R., Hulce, E., Linn, M., & Aytar, P. (2000), Classroom Acoustics: A Resource for Creating Environments with Desirable Listening Conditions
6.5	Adapted from Seep, B., Glosemeyer, R., Hulce, E., Linn, M., & Aytar, P. (2000), Classroom Acoustics: A Resource for Creating Environments with Desirable Listening Conditions
6.6	Adapted from Seep, B., Glosemeyer, R., Hulce, E., Linn, M., & Aytar, P. (2000), Classroom Acoustics: A Resource for Creating Environments with Desirable Listening Conditions <FM.

CHAPTER 7

Table 7.1	From Part of the Teaching students with autism: A resource guide for schools Victoria: British Columbia Ministry of Education, Special Programs Branch, British Columbia, 2000
7.1	Photo courtesy of The Brookwood Community, Brookshire, Texas
7.2	Copyright: In Green; Image ID 196276397 from Shutterstock
7.3	Image ID 198150539; Copyright: OSORIOartist
7.4	Copyright: WorldWide; Image ID 275107637 from Shutterstock
7.5	Image ID 97794683; Copyright: Ronstik from Shutterstock
7.6	Copyright: Mariusz S Jurgielewicz; Image ID 128799082 from Shutterstock
7.7	Copyright: ZouZou; Image ID 247008373 from Shutterstock

CHAPTER 8

Table 8.1	From Part of the Teaching students with autism: A resource guide for schools Victoria: British Columbia Ministry of Education, Special Programs Branch, British Columbia, 2000
8.1	Copyright: Iriana Shiyan
8.2	Copyright: ChameleonsEye
8.3	Copyright: Shvaygert Ekaterina
8.4	Copyright: Iriana Shiyan
8.5	Image courtesy of The Brookwood Community, Brookshire, Texas

CHAPTER 9

9.1	Illustrated by Elizabeth Johnston-Howard, Copyright: Angela Bourne
9.2	Illustrated by Elizabeth Johnston-Howard, Copyright: Angela Bourne
9.3	Illustrated by Elizabeth Johnston-Howard, Copyright: Angela Bourne
9.4	Illustrated by Elizabeth Johnston-Howard, Copyright: Angela Bourne
9.5	Illustrated by Elizabeth Johnston-Howard, Copyright: Angela Bourne
9.6	Illustrated by Elizabeth Johnston-Howard, Copyright: Angela Bourne
9.7	Illustrated by Elizabeth Johnston-Howard, Copyright: Angela Bourne
9.8	Illustrated by Elizabeth Johnston-Howard, Copyright: Angela Bourne
9.9a	Illustrated by Elizabeth Johnston-Howard, Copyright: Angela Bourne
9.9b	Illustrated by Elizabeth Johnston-Howard, Copyright: Angela Bourne
9.10	Illustrated by Elizabeth Johnston-Howard, Copyright: Angela Bourne
9.11	Illustrated by Elizabeth Johnston-Howard, Copyright: Angela Bourne

CHAPTER 10

10.1	Copyright: Locke Science Publishing Company, Inc; Reproduced with permission Gaines K. S., Curry Z., Shroyer J., Amor C., Lock, R. H. (2014), The perceived effects of visual design and features on students with autism spectrum disorder, Journal of architectural and planning research 31 no. 4 (2014):282–298.

10.2	Designed by GA Architects
10.3	Steelcase, Inc.
10.4	Steelcase, Inc.
10.5	Steelcase, Inc.
10.6	Steelcase, Inc.
10.7	Designed by Design Plus LLC, Albuquerque, NM. Photographed by Kirk Gitttings Photography
10.8	Designed by Design Plus LLC, Albuquerque, NM
10.9	Designed by Design Plus LLC, Albuquerque, NM
10.10	Symbol Chart Developed by Design Plus LLC, Albuquerque, NM
10.11	Designed by Design Plus LLC, Albuquerque, NM
10.12	Specialized Design Consultant – Design Plus LLC, Albuquerque, NM, Architect of Record – Vigil & Associates, Albuquerque, NM
10.13	Designed by GA Architects, London, UK, in collaboration with the Borough Architect

CHAPTER 11

11.1	Illustration by Kathryn Lopez
11.2	Illustration by Kathryn Lopez
11.3	Illustration by Kathryn Lopez
11.4	Illustration by Kathryn Lopez
11.5	Illustration by Kathryn Lopez
11.6	Illustration by Kathryn Lopez
11.7	Designed by GA Architects, London, UK
11.8	Designed by GA Architects, London, UK
11.9	Designed by GA Architects, London, UK
11.10	Designed by McBride, Kelley & Baurer Architects, Chicago and GA Architects, London, UK
11.11	Designed by GA Architects, London, UK
11.12	Courtesy of The Brookwood Community in Brookshire, Texas
11.13	Courtesy of The Brookwood Community in Brookshire, Texas
11.14	Courtesy of The Brookwood Community in Brookshire, Texas
11.15	Copyright: Angela Bourne
11.16	Copyright: Angela Bourne

CHAPTER 12

12.1	Courtesy of The Brookwood Community in Brookshire, Texas
12.2	Copyright: Paladjai
12.3	Copyright: Mirexon
12.4	Courtesy of The Brookwood Community in Brookshire, Texas
12.5	Courtesy of Bittersweet Farms in Whitehouse, Ohio
12.6	Courtesy of Bittersweet Farms in Whitehouse, Ohio

CHAPTER 13

13.1	Designed by ARK (Architecture, Research and Knowledge), Toronto, Canada; Photographed by Tom Arban
13.2	Designed by ARK (Architecture, Research and Knowledge), Toronto, Canada; Photographed by Tom Arban
13.3	Designed by ARK (Architecture, Research and Knowledge), Toronto, Canada; Photographed by Tom Arban
13.4	Designed by ARK (Architecture, Research and Knowledge), Toronto, Canada; Photographed by Peter Sellar
13.5	Designed by ARK (Architecture, Research and Knowledge), Toronto, Canada; Photographed by Tom Arban
13.6	Jarrott, Kwack, & Relf, 2002
13.7	Designed by HGA (Minneapolis, MN) and interior design consultant A. J. Paron-Wildes
13.8	Designed by HGA (Minneapolis, MN) and interior design consultant A. J. Paron-Wildes
13.9	Designed by HGA (Minneapolis, MN) and interior design consultant A. J. Paron-Wildes
13.10	Designed by HGA (Minneapolis, MN) and interior design consultant A. J. Paron-Wildes
13.11	Designed by HGA (Minneapolis, MN) and interior design consultant A. J. Paron-Wildes
13.12	Designed by HGA (Minneapolis, MN) and interior design consultant A. J. Paron-Wildes

CHAPTER 14

14.1	Designed by Virginia Burt Designs, Ontario, Canada; Photography by Brad Feinknopf
14.2	Designed by Virginia Burt Designs, Ontario, Canada
14.3	Illustrated by: Elizabeth Johnston-Howard
14.4	Designed by Virginia Burt Designs, Ontario, Canada; Photography by Brad Feinknopf
14.5	Designed by Christine Reed, RLA, ASLA, landscape architect and Associate Principal at OICB, San Francisco
14.6	Designed by Christine Reed, RLA, ASLA, landscape architect and Associate Principal at OICB, San Francisco
14.7	Designed by Christine Reed, RLA, ASLA, landscape architect and Associate Principal at OICB, San Francisco
14.8	Designed by Christine Reed, RLA, ASLA, landscape architect and Associate Principal at OICB, San Francisco
14.9	Designed by Christine Reed, RLA, ASLA, landscape architect and Associate Principal at OICB, San Francisco
14.10	Designed by Reed Associates Landscape Architects, Sunnyvale, California
14.11	Illustrated by Virginia Burt Designs, Ontario, Canada

Acknowledgements

Funding Sources/Grants
American Society of Interior Designers Foundation
Organization for Autism Research
Office of the Vice President for Research, Texas Tech University
College of Human Sciences, Texas Tech University

Advisors
Ghasson Shabha, PhD
    Birmingham School of the Built Environment, Birmingham City University,
    Birmingham, UK

Joann Shroyer, PhD
    Professor Emeritus, College of Human Sciences, Texas Tech University,
    Lubbock, Texas

Zane Curry, PhD
    Professor Emeritus, College of Human Sciences, Texas Tech University,
    Lubbock, Texas

Robin Lock, PhD
    Professor, College of Education, Texas Tech University, Lubbock, Texas

Sherry Sancibrian, MS CCC-SLP
    Professor Department of Speech, Language, and Hearing Sciences,
    Health Sciences Center, Texas Tech University, Lubbock, Texas

Debajyoti Pati, PhD
    Professor, College of Human Sciences, Texas Tech University, Lubbock,
    Texas

Lee S. Duemer, PhD
    Professor, College of Education, Texas Tech University, Lubbock, Texas

Katy Lopez, MS
    Designer

Lupe Zermeno, MS
    Furniture Account Manager

Graduate Research Assistants
Nizar Haddad
Rachita Patel
Ahdab Mahdaly

Contributors

Architects

ARK (Architecture, Research and Knowledge), Toronto, Canada
Design Plus LLC. Architects, Albuquerque, NM
Baskervill (Architecture, Engineering and Interior Design Firm), Richmond , VA
GA Architects, London, UK
HGA, Architects and Engineers, Minneapolis, MN
Vigil & Associates Architectural Group P.C., Albuquerque, NM

Interior Designers

Lennie Scott-Webber, PhD, Owner/Principal of INSYNC: Education Research + Design
A. J. Paron-Wildes, National A&D Manager, Allsteel, Stillwater, Minnesota
Katy Lopez, MS, Houston, TX

Landscape Architects

Virginia Burt, FCSLA, ASLA, Visionscapes Landscape Architects Inc. Campbellville, ON, Canada
Christine Reed, RLA, ASLA, OlCB in San Francisco, CA
Paul Reed, Reed Associates Landscape Architects, Sunnyvale, CA

Schools

Rio Grande High School, Intensive Support Program (ISP) & School Based Health Clinic (SBHC), Albuquerque, NM
Highland High School, Albuquerque, NM, Design Plus, Architects, Albuquerque, NM
Faison School for Autism, Richmond, VA
Intensive Support Hub District Prototype, Albuquerque, NM
Whitton School Kingston Upon Thames, London Borough of Richmond, in London, UK
Acland Burghley School, London Borough of Camden, in London, England
Newmark School, Scotch Plains, NJ
Sunfield 24-Hour Residential School for Children with Severe Learning Disabilities and Autism, London, UK
Little City Foundation, Palatine, IL
Nottingham Regional Society for Autistic Children and Adults, Langley Mill, Nottingham, UK

Housing Communities Designed for People with ASD

Brookwood Community, Berkshire, TX
Bittersweet Farms, Whitehouse, OH
Camphill Village, Copake, NY
Marbridge Foundations, Manchaca, TX
TERI Inc., Oceanside, CA

PART 1

Beginnings

Introduction to Autism Spectrum Disorders (ASD)

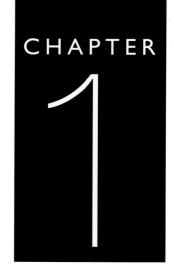

CHAPTER 1

Individuals with Autism Spectrum Disorders are part of a growing population that is usually ignored in design. The needs of those with ASD are excluded entirely from all building codes and design guidelines.[1] This is a serious concern, since these individuals are more sensitive to their physical surroundings than the average person. When an individual is unable to understand or adapt to their environment, negative behaviors typically ensue.[2] Although the surrounding environment has such a strong influence over people with ASD, there is very little information on how to design spaces for these individuals.

Another prominent challenge involved in designing spaces for individuals with ASD is that no two cases are alike. ASD is referred to as a spectrum disorder because each individual has different symptoms, different sensitivities, and a different level of functioning.[3] Symptoms vary from mild to severe; some children on the spectrum have intellectual disabilities or impaired speech, while others do not.[4] Ideally, spaces would be designed for each individual case and the space would accommodate each unique symptom but also help individuals with ASD build a tolerance to environmental stimuli. McCallister states that environments for individuals on the spectrum should prepare them for the challenges and problems they will face in everyday life: "Cocooning the ASD pupil from all external factors will not necessarily help them reach their full potential in life."[5] Therefore, designers should not overly cater to users with ASD and create unrealistic environments that will leave them unprepared to face other environments.

Individuals with Autism Spectrum Disorders (ASD) are particularly sensitive to the surrounding environment, primarily because of sensory processing deficits. For many, sensory processing deficits, such as sensitive eyesight or hearing, can make the built environment a distracting and even frightening place. In her autobiography, Temple Grandin described autism as "seeing the world through a kaleidoscope and trying to listen to a radio station that is jammed with static at the same time. Add to that a broken volume control, which causes the volume to jump erratically from a loud boom to inaudible."[6] Many individuals on the spectrum employ coping mechanisms in the form of rigid and repetitive behaviors to deal with incoming sensory stimuli. To an outsider, these behaviors appear like an inappropriate tantrum when in actuality, they are the result of an "imbalance between the environment and an individual's ability to adapt to it."[7] Architecture and interior spaces can be modified to positively influence the behavior individuals with ASD often exhibit by modifying factors such as color, texture, sense of closure, orientation, acoustics, ventilation, etc.[8]

Background/History

Autism is a developmental disorder that affects the functioning of the brain. Individuals with ASD are identified as having difficulty with social interaction, communication skills, and as having a small range of interests.[9] IQ levels of individuals on the spectrum can vary in range from gifted to severe mental disabilities. At the mild end of the spectrum, ASD may be nearly indistinguishable from the general public. These individuals are commonly referred to as high functioning. Others with ASD exhibit severe or life-threatening behaviors. Self-injurious behavior is uncommon in individuals with ASD, but may include head banging or biting oneself.[10]

According to recent reports, cases of Autism Spectrum Disorders are on the rise. Some of the more recent statistics indicate that one in 68 children is diagnosed with ASD.[11] This number has risen from approximately three per 1,000 children in the 1990s.[12] Similar increases have also been documented in Japan, Europe, and the UK.[13, 14] Whether the increase is due to ASD becoming more prevalent or because autism awareness and detection has broadened is unknown. Some researchers believe the rise is because the diagnostic criteria for ASD now include pervasive developmental disorder (PDD) and Asperger's syndrome.[15] Whatever the reason, the increase in reported cases qualifies as a serious public health concern.[16] Some fear the rise in cases could lead to an ASD epidemic.[17] There are a variety of treatments but, at present, no known cure. Experts do not yet fully understand how or why the disorder even occurs.

Sensory Processing

Individuals with ASD often have abnormal responses to incoming sensory information from the surrounding environment. Typically, people receive information about a space based on all of their senses collectively: smell, sight, taste, sound, and touch. This ability is known as sensory integration and is essential to achieve a coherent perception of a situation and to decide how to act.[18] However, people with ASD have deficits in sensory integration due to the inability to process information from several senses at once. This may be manifested through being hyper-sensitive to stimuli or being hypo-sensitive (under-reactive) to stimuli. Rapid shifting of attention between two different stimuli is difficult, and abnormal sensory processing can cause individuals with ASD to demonstrate unusual behaviors. Additionally, a dysfunction in this sensory integration may result in language delays and academic under-achievement.[19, 20, 21] There are some reports of sensory perception deficits in which sounds are perceived as smells or colors.[22]

Hypo- and Hyper-sensitivity

Generally, individuals with ASD are either hypo-sensitive or hyper-sensitive to certain information pertaining to smell, sight, taste, sound, or touch. There are also instances of hyper- or hypo-sensitivities in vestibular movement and proprioception, or the ability to sense the position of the body in space. Hypo-sensitive cases appear to be under-responsive, as if certain sensory information goes unnoticed or certain senses are impaired. Young children who were later diagnosed with ASD and had hypo-sensitive auditory tendencies were often thought to be deaf as infants.[23] Hypo-sensitive cases are often qualified as "sensory-seeking," meaning they often create or generate their own sensory experiences either for pleasure or to block out other unpleasant stimuli. Conversely, hyper-sensitive cases are over-responsive to sensory stimuli. Children with hyper-sensitivity can be easily overwhelmed by incoming sensory information. The environment can be terrifying at times because loud or sudden noises feel physically painful to hyper-sensitive individuals.[24] Some experts believe that this kind of sensory overload is experienced more among individuals with Asperger's syndrome than other individuals on the spectrum.[25] A common occurrence among people with ASD is the inability to use all of the senses at one time and when attempting to use more than one sense, sensory overload occurs. Sometimes these individuals need an "anchor" for their environment: "I had to feel something that stood still, something anchored, in a world that had suddenly become totally unpredictable."[26] Individuals with ASD are often slow in shifting focus between visual stimuli and auditory stimuli.[27] One individual on the spectrum reported a similar dilemma in that he was unable to use more than one sense at a time: "Most people have a mind like a flashlight, with an area of high focus, and a larger area of partial awareness; my mind is more like a laser pointer, that highlights only a single small dot." [28]

Table 1.1 lists examples of symptoms that individuals with autism may face related to sensory processing and whether the symptoms qualify as hypo-sensitive or hyper-sensitive. Out of the list of sensory processing deficits in Table 1.1, children with ASD appear to exhibit auditory and tactile processing difficulties the most.[29]

Repetitive and Restricted Behaviors

Individuals with ASD also exhibit repetitive, rigid behaviors. These kinds of behaviors are defined as repetitive, sometimes self-injurious body movements, compulsive behaviors, and limited, almost obsessive interests.[30] Self-injurious behaviors, like head banging, are also called "stimming." These can be dangerous both to the individual and to other individuals nearby.[31, 32] Other examples of

Table 1.1 Hyper- and Hypo-Sensitive Symptoms of ASD.

Sense	Hypo-sensitive	Hyper-sensitive
Auditory (Sound)	Does not respond when name is called; Enjoys strange noises; Enjoys making loud, excessive noises	Overly sensitive to loud noises; Appears to hear noises before others; Cannot function well with background noise
Tactile (Touch)	Touches people and objects unnecessarily; Has abnormally high pain threshold (does not appear to be hurt after a hard fall); Does not appear to feel extreme temperatures	Avoids wearing certain fabrics; Becomes distressed during grooming; Does not like being wet or going barefoot; Reacts negatively to being touched
Visual (Sight)	Disregards people or objects in environment; Can see only outlines of certain objects; Likes bright colors and bright sunlight	Bothered by bright lights (covers eyes or squints); Easily distracted by movement; Stares at certain people or objects
Vestibular (Motion)	Moves around unnecessarily; Enjoys spinning in circles; Becomes excited about any task involving movement	Seems unbalanced; Becomes distressed when upside-down or when feet leave the ground
Smell/Taste (Olfactory)	Some reports of Pica or eating non-food substances; "Feels" objects with mouth; Seeks out strong smells; Oblivious to some scents	Picky eater; Will only eat foods with certain textures, with particular smells, or at a certain temperature
Proprioception (Sense of body's location)	Unaware of body position in space and body sensations like hunger; Often lean against people or objects	Odd bodily posture; Uncomfortable in most positions; Difficulty manipulating small objects

these kinds of repetitive behaviors are finger and hand flicking, rocking, or tapping objects.[33] Many children with high-functioning autism or Asperger's syndrome seem to exhibit more repetitive, self-injurious behaviors and tantrums than other individuals on the autism spectrum.[34] One study found that children who exhibit unusual sensory responses were much more likely to also have repetitive behaviors. These behaviors could be the child's attempt to either generate a sensory experience or to try to maintain control over their environment after sensory overload has taken place.[35] Often, these behaviors are comforting to the child when an environment is overwhelming.[36] In Asperger's syndrome, where difficulty with auditory processing is a common occurrence, repetitive behaviors may be the child's way of staying in control or keeping a grip on their environment when they miss an important auditory clue and become distressed.[37] Also quite common among individuals on the spectrum is the desire for a predictable environment. Stimming is repetitive and predictable and may be a way to block out complex and confusing sensory stimuli.[38]

Narrow interests also fall under the category of repetitive behaviors. A fascinating occurrence is that children with ASD sometimes show remarkable talent and mastery of particular interests, including music, math, or chess.[39] Younger children or children that are on the lower functioning end of the spectrum may show an almost obsessive preference for a particular object such as dinosaurs, trains, or baseball. Though these interests can often be a distraction, they can also be used to calm a child or used as a reward for successfully completing homework or doing a chore. Repetitive, rigid behaviors also include insistence on sameness in routine and physical environment. This involves adherence to certain routines or rituals, insistence on the same foods, and wearing only certain types of clothing.[40] Insistence on sameness can translate to details as small as the order of items on a bookshelf.

Individuals with ASD can become quite upset if their routine is disrupted. Like communication problems, these strong preferences for predictability may also be caused by sensory processing abnormalities. People on the spectrum may dislike being touched or trying new foods because it is uncertain or unreliable but might enjoy touching others or eating only foods with certain textures because it is predictable and familiar.[41] Similarly, younger children might have strong preferences for theme songs, certain melodies, or other sounds and desire to hear them repeatedly.[42] One explanation for this insistence on sameness and other rigid thinking is the Theory

of Executive Function. Executive functions have to do with cognitive processes like concentration, planning, and attention, and most individuals with ASD are thought to have a lack of control over their executive functions.[43] Executive dysfunction in ASD is the reason many individuals on the spectrum have trouble reorienting attention from one task to another and become distressed when routine is disrupted. Poor executive functions lead to poor impulse control, disorganized and inflexible thoughts or actions, and inappropriate, out-of-context behavior.[44]

Difficulties in Communication and Social Interaction

Difficulties with communication and social interactions are another problem experienced by individuals with ASD. Struggles can begin as early as infancy when babies begin communicating with their parents. Signs of ASD in babies can be the delay of speech or babbling and a lack of early uses of gesture, as well as failure to respond to their own name.[45] Parents of babies later diagnosed with ASD might feel dejected because of the non-communicative behaviors of their infant, which may lead to further complications in teaching and learning communication between parents and children.[46] Children learn social norms and cultural norms, such as intimacy and the appropriate distance to keep from others, primarily through social play.[47] Without positive friendships or appropriate play, even more communication and social deficits arise, since having friends provides benefits for all children with or without ASD. Having close friendships can be important for future development, building self-esteem, and helping a child better cope with stressful events.[48] Children with ASD may struggle to make friends because their play does not attract or engage others, usually due to their highly structured and inflexible nature.[49] Children often shy away from social interaction, and without consistent, sustained interactions with others, social skills fall even more behind. Frequently, communication deficits lead to extreme isolation or loneliness.[50]

Individuals with ASD may experience problems with social interactions partly because of their repetitive behaviors, as they do not welcome social interaction from others. These kinds of difficulties are more common among individuals with Asperger's syndrome who have additional difficulty with social and emotional responsiveness.[51] There is also evidence that social engagement is made even more difficult by sensory processing deficits. Some individuals with ASD have revealed that a sensory distraction in the environment has caused them to miss a social cue, making the current situation more confusing and stressful.[52] Often, children may avoid social interaction, especially in larger groups, because they fear unwanted tactile contact or want to avoid uncomfortable volume levels if they have auditory sensitivities. However, one study disagreed, stating that there was no relationship between sensory deficits and social and communicative symptoms of autism.[53]

Despite their struggles, individuals on the spectrum can be taught social skills step by step. Most people learn social norms and practices intuitively or through observation; however, individuals with ASD do not easily pick up hidden meanings or unspoken social cues. Many higher functioning individuals learn some social norms and rules for interacting with others, but they do not work for every situation, since other people break these rules or change them.[54] Children with ASD who have more play dates in their homes then show more initiative and success in social situations at school.[55] For some children, practicing during play dates can help develop and fine tune social skills.

Many higher functioning individuals, such as those with Asperger's syndrome, are more aware of their own behaviors and more readily notice differences between themselves and others.[56] Some individuals describe this awareness in autobiographical accounts as a "wide, unbridgeable gap between themselves and other people."[57] These same autobiographical accounts also describe how individuals on the spectrum feel as if they are outsiders observing the actions of others and trying to understand.[58] Some individuals with ASD feel lonelier and have lower quality relationships with others because they are more aware of their social limitations and therefore shy away from social communication.[59] Awareness of being different is not necessarily negative for some of these individuals. Some describe some of their abilities and symptoms, such as picking up on small details that go unnoticed by others or strong memory and recall, with pride.[60]

The Importance of Designing for Autism Spectrum Disorders and Other Developmental Disabilities

ASD is a complicated neurological disorder, and there may never be a time where it is completely understood. Individuals on the spectrum are part of a growing population that is usually ignored in design, even though architects and designers are responsible for accommodating the needs of all users.[61] This book applies evidence-based design methods to a wide range of everyday environments. Designing spaces for individuals with Autism Spectrum Disorders (ASD) can be a way to improve quality of life, foster independence, and ensure safety. The methods outlined in this book will help individuals on the spectrum despite their level of functioning or prevalence of particular symptoms and make the environment safer, more organized, and more comfortable for the user. These symptoms of ASD should not be stifled by parents and designers. These symptoms do not necessarily need to be embraced, but accepted and, if possible, turned into something positive. For example, individuals that are sensory-seeking should not always be discouraged. Instead they should be well-supervised and allowed to play, touch, feel, taste, and smell. Individuals with ASD can be taught what is safe and appropriate and still be allowed to be themselves.

Design professionals, educators, and parents must be aware of the sensory dysfunction experienced by individuals with ASD in order to provide appropriate environments. The underlying premise of this book is that systemic, empirical research combined with pragmatic approaches to design development can contribute to the planning and management of environments that enhance organizational effectiveness. This book will serve as a valuable tool for professionals involved in designing, building, developing, and administering the design of physical environments for individuals with ASD throughout the lifecycle. Educators and parents will also benefit from the contents. Environmental design theories, symptoms of ASD, and design solutions for a variety of spaces will be addressed. Chapters will focus on sensory processing deficits and the design needs of individuals on the spectrum. The remainder of the book will outline a variety of design methods and solutions for spaces, including residential, learning, work, therapeutic, and outdoor environments.

Notes

1. Khare, Rachna, and Abir Mullick. "Incorporating the behavioral dimension in designing inclusive learning environment for autism." *ArchNet-IJAR* 3, no. 3 (2009): 45–64.

2. Sánchez, Pilar Arnaiz, Francisco Segado Vázquez, and Laureano Albaladejo Serrano. *Autism and the built environment.* INTECH Open Access Publisher, 2011.

3. National Institutes of Health. "Autism spectrum disorders (ASDs)." Eunice Kennedy Shriver: National Institute of Child Health and Human Development, November 15, 2011. http://www.nichd.nih.gov/health/topics/asd.cfm.

4. Landrigan, Philip J. "What causes autism? Exploring the environmental contribution." *Current opinion in pediatrics* 22, no. 2 (2010): 219–225.

5. McAllister, Keith. "The ASD-friendly classroom: design complexity, challenge and characteristics." In *Design research society conference.* Retrieved from http://www.designresearchsociety. org/docs-procs/DRS2010/PDF/084.pdf. 2010.

6. Grandin, Temple. *Thinking in pictures: My life with autism* (expanded edition). New York: Vintage, 2006.

7. Sánchez, Pilar Arnaiz, Francisco Segado Vázquez, and Laureano Albaladejo Serrano. *Autism and the built environment.* INTECH Open Access Publisher, 2011.

8. Mostafa, Magda. "An architecture for autism: Concepts of design intervention for the autistic user." *Archnet-IJAR: International Journal of Architectural Research* 2, no. 1 (2008): 189–211.

9. Scott, J., C. Clark, and M. Brady. *Students with autism.* Canada: Thompson Wadsworth, 2000.

10. Scott, J., C. Clark, and M. Brady. *Students with autism.* Canada: Thompson Wadsworth, 2000.

11. Centers for Disease Control and Prevention. "Diagnostic criteria." November 1, 2011. Accessed August 1, 2014. http://www.cdc.gov/ncbddd/autism/hcp-dsm.html.

12. Blaxill, Mark F. "What's going on? The question of time trends in autism." *Public health reports* 119, no. 6 (2004): 536.

13. Landrigan, Philip J. "What causes autism? Exploring the environmental contribution." *Current opinion in pediatrics* 22, no. 2 (2010): 219–225.

14. Scott, Fiona J., Simon Baron-Cohen, Patrick Bolton, and Carol Brayne. "Brief report: Prevalence of autism spectrum conditions in children aged 5–11 years in Cambridgeshire, UK." *Autism* 6, no. 3 (2002): 231–237.

15. Scott, Fiona J., Simon Baron-Cohen, Patrick Bolton, and Carol Brayne. "Brief report: Prevalence of autism spectrum conditions in children aged 5–11 years in Cambridgeshire, UK." *Autism* 6, no. 3 (2002): 231–237.

16. Lin, Ling-Yi, Gael I. Orsmond, Wendy J. Coster, and Ellen S. Cohn. "Families of adolescents and adults with autism spectrum disorders in Taiwan: The role of social support and coping in family adaptation and maternal well-being." *Research in autism spectrum disorders* 5, no. 1 (2011): 144–156.

17. Maenner, Matthew J., and Maureen S. Durkin. "Trends in the prevalence of autism on the basis of special education data." *Pediatrics* 126, no. 5 (2010): e1018–e1025.

18. Iarocci, Grace, and John McDonald. "Sensory integration and the perceptual experience of persons with autism." *Journal of autism and developmental disorders* 36, no. 1 (2006): 77–90.

19. Freed, Jeffrey, and Laurie Parsons. *Right-brained children in a left-brained world: Unlocking the potential of your ADD child.* Simon and Schuster, 1998.

20. Grandin, Temple. *Thinking in pictures: My life with autism* (expanded edition). New York: Vintage, 2006.

21. Hatch-Rasmussen, Cindy. "Sensory integration." Center for the Study of Autism at www.autism.org/si.html. 1995.

22. O'Neill, Meena, and Robert S. P. Jones. "Sensory-perceptual abnormalities in autism: A case for more research?" *Journal of autism and developmental disorders* 27, no. 3 (1997): 283–293.

23. Tomchek, Scott D., and Winnie Dunn. "Sensory processing in children with and without autism: A comparative study using the short sensory profile." *American journal of occupational therapy* 61, no. 2 (2007): 190–200.

24. Jones, Robert, Ciara Quigney, and Jaci Huws. "First-hand accounts of sensory perceptual experiences in autism: A qualitative analysis." *Journal of intellectual and developmental disability* 28, no. 2 (2003): 112–121.

25. Myles, Brenda Smith, Winnie Dunn, Louann Rinner, Taku Hagiwara, Matthew Reese, Abby Huggins, and Stephanie Becker. "Sensory issues in children with Asperger syndrome and autism." *Education and training in developmental disabilities* 39, no. 4 (2004): 283–290.

26. Baumers, Stijn, and Ann Heylighen. "Beyond the designers' view: How people with autism experience space." In *Design and complexity. Proceedings of the Design Research Society Conference 2010.* 2010.

27. Courchesne, Eric, Jeanne Townsend, Natacha A. Akshoomoff, Osamu Saitoh, Rachel Yeung-Courchesne, Alan J. Lincoln, Hector E. James,

Richard H. Haas, Laura Schreibman, and Lily Lau. "Impairment in shifting attention in autistic and cerebellar patients." *Behavioral neuroscience* 108, no. 5 (1994): 848.

28. Jones, Robert, Ciara Quigney, and Jaci Huws. "First-hand accounts of sensory perceptual experiences in autism: A qualitative analysis." *Journal of intellectual and developmental disability* 28, no. 2 (2003): 112–121.

29. Tomchek, Scott D., and Winnie Dunn. "Sensory processing in children with and without autism: A comparative study using the short sensory profile." *American journal of occupational therapy* 61, no. 2 (2007): 190–200.

30. Gabriels, Robin L., John A. Agnew, Lucy Jane Miller, Jane Gralla, Zhaoxing Pan, Edward Goldson, James C. Ledbetter, Juliet P. Dinkins, and Elizabeth Hooks. "Is there a relationship between restricted, repetitive, stereotyped behaviors and interests and abnormal sensory response in children with autism spectrum disorders?" *Research in autism spectrum disorders* 2, no. 4 (2008): 660–670.

31. Vogel, Clare L. "Classroom design for living and learning with autism." *Autism Asperger's digest* 7 (2008).

32. Cascio, Carissa, Francis McGlone, Stephen Folger, Vinay Tannan, Grace Baranek, Kevin A. Pelphrey, and Gregory Essick. "Tactile perception in adults with autism: A multidimensional psychophysical study." *Journal of autism and developmental disorders* 38, no. 1 (2008): 127–137.

33. Leekam, Susan R., Margot R. Prior, and Mirko Uljarevic. "Restricted and repetitive behaviors in autism spectrum disorders: A review of research in the last decade." *Psychological bulletin* 137, no. 4 (2011): 562.

34. Myles, Brenda Smith, Winnie Dunn, Louann Rinner, Taku Hagiwara, Matthew Reese, Abby Huggins, and Stephanie Becker. "Sensory issues in children with Asperger syndrome and autism." *Education and training in developmental disabilities* 39, no. 4 (2004): 283–290.

35. Gabriels, Robin L., John A. Agnew, Lucy Jane Miller, Jane Gralla, Zhaoxing Pan, Edward Goldson, James C. Ledbetter, Juliet P. Dinkins, and Elizabeth Hooks. "Is there a relationship between restricted, repetitive, stereotyped behaviors and interests and abnormal sensory response in children with autism spectrum disorders?" *Research in autism spectrum disorders* 2, no. 4 (2008): 660–670.

36. Ashburner, Jill, Jenny Ziviani, and Sylvia Rodger. "Sensory processing and classroom emotional, behavioral, and educational outcomes in children with autism spectrum disorder." *American journal of occupational therapy* 62, no. 5 (2008): 564–573.

37. Myles, Brenda Smith, Winnie Dunn, Louann Rinner, Taku Hagiwara, Matthew Reese, Abby Huggins, and Stephanie Becker. "Sensory issues in children with Asperger syndrome and autism." *Education and training in developmental disabilities* 39, no. 4 (2004): 283–290.

38. Ashburner, Jill, Jenny Ziviani, and Sylvia Rodger. "Sensory processing and classroom emotional, behavioral, and educational outcomes in children with autism spectrum disorder." *American journal of occupational therapy* 62, no. 5 (2008): 564–573.

39. Heaton, Pamela, Beate Hermelin, and Linda Pring. "Autism and pitch processing: A precursor for savant musical ability?" *Music perception* 15, no. 3 (1998): 291–305.

40. Leekam, Susan R., Margot R. Prior, and Mirko Uljarevic. "Restricted and repetitive behaviors in autism spectrum disorders: A review of research in the last decade." *Psychological bulletin* 137, no. 4 (2011): 562.

41. Ashburner, Jill, Jenny Ziviani, and Sylvia Rodger. "Sensory processing and classroom emotional, behavioral, and educational outcomes in children with autism spectrum disorder." *American journal of occupational therapy* 62, no. 5 (2008): 564–573.

42. Talay-Ongan, Ayshe, and Kara Wood. "Unusual sensory sensitivities in autism: A possible crossroads." *International journal of disability, development and education* 47, no. 2 (2000): 201–212.

43. Sánchez, Pilar Arnaiz, Francisco Segado Vázquez, and Laureano Albaladejo Serrano. *Autism and the built environment.* INTECH Open Access Publisher, 2011.

44. Davies, Fran and S. Clayton. "Even the ants are noisy: Sensory perception in people with autism spectrum disorder." Presentation at NAS Regional Conference in London, 2008.

45. Mitchell, Shelley, Jessica Brian, Lonnie Zwaigenbaum, Wendy Roberts, Peter Szatmari, Isabel Smith, and Susan Bryson. "Early language and communication development of infants later diagnosed with autism spectrum disorder." *Journal of developmental & behavioral pediatrics* 27, no. 2 (2006): S69–S78.

46. Talay-Ongan, Ayshe, and Kara Wood. "Unusual sensory sensitivities in autism: A possible crossroads." *International journal of disability, development and education* 47, no. 2 (2000): 201–212.

47. Jordan, Rita. "Social play and autistic spectrum disorders: A perspective on theory, implications and educational approaches." *Autism* 7, no. 4 (2003): 347–360.

48. Frankel, Frederick D., Clarissa M. Gorospe, Ya-Chih Chang, and Catherine A. Sugar. "Mothers' reports of play dates and observation of school playground behavior of children having high-functioning autism spectrum disorders." *Journal of child psychology and psychiatry* 52, no. 5 (2011): 571–579.

49. Jordan, Rita. "Social play and autistic spectrum disorders: A perspective on theory, implications and educational approaches." *Autism* 7, no. 4 (2003): 347–360.

50. Sánchez, Pilar Arnaiz, Francisco Segado Vázquez, and Laureano Albaladejo Serrano. *Autism and the built environment*. INTECH Open Access Publisher, 2011.

51. Myles, Brenda Smith, Winnie Dunn, Louann Rinner, Taku Hagiwara, Matthew Reese, Abby Huggins, and Stephanie Becker. "Sensory issues in children with Asperger syndrome and autism." *Education and training in developmental disabilities* 39, no. 4 (2004): 283–290.

52. Williams, Emma. "Who really needs a 'theory' of mind? An interpretative phenomenological analysis of the autobiographical writings of ten high-functioning individuals with an autism spectrum disorder." *Theory & psychology* 14, no. 5 (2004): 704–724.

53. Rogers, Sally J., Susan Hepburn, and Elizabeth Wehner. "Parent reports of sensory symptoms in toddlers with autism and those with other developmental disorders." *Journal of autism and developmental disorders* 33, no. 6 (2003): 631–642.

54. Williams, Emma. "Who really needs a 'theory' of mind? An interpretative phenomenological analysis of the autobiographical writings of ten high-functioning individuals with an autism spectrum disorder." *Theory & psychology* 14, no. 5 (2004): 704–724.

55. Frankel, Frederick D., Clarissa M. Gorospe, Ya-Chih Chang, and Catherine A. Sugar. "Mothers' reports of play dates and observation of school playground behavior of children having high-functioning autism spectrum disorders." *Journal of child psychology and psychiatry* 52, no. 5 (2011): 571–579.

56. Myles, Brenda Smith, Winnie Dunn, Louann Rinner, Taku Hagiwara, Matthew Reese, Abby Huggins, and Stephanie Becker. "Sensory issues in children with Asperger syndrome and autism." *Education and training in developmental disabilities* 39, no. 4 (2004): 283–290.

57. Williams, Emma. "Who really needs a 'theory' of mind? An interpretative phenomenological analysis of the autobiographical writings of ten high-functioning individuals with an autism spectrum disorder." *Theory & psychology* 14, no. 5 (2004): 704–724.

58. Grandin, Temple. *Thinking in pictures: My life with autism* (expanded edition). New York: Vintage, 2006.

59. Frankel, Frederick D., Clarissa M. Gorospe, Ya-Chih Chang, and Catherine A. Sugar. "Mothers' reports of play dates and observation of school playground behavior of children having high-functioning autism spectrum disorders." *Journal of child psychology and psychiatry* 52, no. 5 (2011): 571–579.

60. Jones, Robert, Ciara Quigney, and Jaci Huws. "First-hand accounts of sensory perceptual experiences in autism: A qualitative analysis." *Journal of intellectual and developmental disability* 28, no. 2 (2003): 112–121.

61. Mostafa, Magda. "An architecture for autism: Concepts of design intervention for the autistic user." *Archnet-IJAR: International journal of architectural research* 2, no. 1 (2008): 189–211.

Foundational Theories for ASD

Over the last century, research relating to autism has been concentrated in the fields of medicine, psychology, and psychiatry. However, there has been limited research on how environments may affect behavior and be designed to meet the needs of those with ASD. This is unfortunate, as there is a considerable amount of evidence demonstrating that one's surroundings can positively contribute to well-being. When developing spaces that meet the needs of people with ASD, architects, planners, and designers need to understand the characteristics of the population so they can design spaces that support the learning process, nurture the development of independence, and preserve the dignity of this group of people.

It is often necessary to utilize multiple theories, models, or perspectives to inform design solutions. For example, the designer of a hospital in the United States would firstly need to gain an understanding of established societal norms (social learning theory) such as expected privacy levels. The designer would also want to understand the interrelationship between the different areas within the hospital (integral theories), and the design elements that lead to perceptions of control (control theories).

Theories of the Environment and Behavior

Environment Behavior Theory is a conceptual model recognizing the relationship between an individual and his or her environment.[1] Kurt Lewin, a psychologist, formulated an ecological equation to quantify this relationship between his or her environment: $B = f(P, E)$. The formula states that behavior is a function of the person and his or her environment, where B is the behavior, P is the person, and E is the environment.

This was an innovative concept that suggested that behavior not only comes from within an individual, but is also influenced by the environment. Unfortunately Lewin's model had little impact on the field because the term "environment" was such a broad term. Further development by Lawton gained greater attention as he added the notion that more than just the objective environment, E, should be considered. He argued that an individual's perception of their environment $(P \times E)$ should also be considered.

Environmental Preference Theory

Environmental Preference Theory is based on the idea that people prefer scenes that are engaging and involving rather than simple and boring.[2] The study of the human–environment experience is complex and may involve research from a variety of perspectives in order to understand how individuals perceive their environment. The Environmental Preference Theory is an appropriate theory to use when "studying well-being through the development of self-actualization because it offers a broad practical method for designing engaging environments."[3] Engaging environments are important for the self-actualization of individuals with ASD. In addition, engaging environments help sustain skill sets, aptitudes, and talents and help increase self-esteem.

Notable research includes studies on landscape environments and the effects on nursing home residents.[4,5,6,7] Each of these studies identified a resident's needs for change and variety in the everyday situations for the sustainment and development of mental clarity. Collectively they termed this approach an inspiring design. Similarly, Scott used environmental preference theory in interior settings to study the validity of complexity and mystery as predictors of interior preferences and sought to identify design attributes associated with their perception in an indoor setting.[8] The results showed that both complexity and mystery were positively related to preference as well as to each other. Characteristics of interior features associated with complexity included the quantity and variety of architectural and interior components in a scene, the scene's spatial geometry, and the overall composition of the setting. Perceptions of mystery included physical accessibility to the promised information in the scene, distance of view to the nearest point of interest, spatial definition, screening of the promised information, and lighting that offered dramatic contrasts in brightness.

The Environmental Preference Theory has several constructs, some of which are more commonly referenced in environmental design studies than others. The four principles of the theory are complexity, coherence, legibility, and mystery. The following descriptions explain the Environment Preference Theory constructs:[9]

1. Complexity is defined in terms of the degree of visual information that is available in the environment, level of detail of the information (i.e. is the design intricate or simple?), diversity of the scene, and the richness of the environment.[10] Complexity reflects how much is going on in a particular environment.[11]
2. Coherence refers to features in the environment that help in organizing and understanding the space, including features that direct our attention.[12] Spatial organization, patterns of brightness, size, texture, line, shape, and color can enhance coherence by organizing the scene to provide redundant cueing.[13]
3. Legibility is defined as a space that is easy to understand and to remember.[14] A legible space contains distinct features that aid in wayfinding, making it easy both to find a desired location and to return to the point of origin.[15,16]
4. Mystery refers to features in the environment that invite or encourage further exploration of the environment with the promise that one could learn more.[17, 18]

The Environmental Preference Theory[19] is an appropriate theory to use when studying well-being. The principles examine the relationship between people and how they perceive the environment. This framework positions the designer to be cognizant of how design can help create "preferred environments" or environments that stimulate and comfort the user.

Therapeutic Environment Theory

The Therapeutic Environment theory stems from the fields of environmental psychology (the psycho-social effects of environment), psychoneuroimmunology (the effects of environment on the immune system), and neuroscience (how the brain perceives architecture).[20, 21, 22, 23, 24, 25]

The design of therapeutic environments has been well researched in the study of designing for an aging population. Cohen and Weiseman developed a conceptual framework for therapeutic environments that assumes that the nature and needs of residents define therapeutic goals, which in turn helps shape the physical setting indirectly through their cultural relationships with the social organizational context.[26] Their concept, Therapeutic Goals: Focus on Continuing of the Self, includes:

1. Maximizing safety and security
2. Maximizing awareness and orientation
3. Supports of functional abilities

4. Facilitation of social context
5. Provision of privacy
6. Provision of opportunities for personal control
7. Regulation of stimulation
8. Provision of continuity of self

Many of the philosophies of therapeutic environments are based on whether or not architectural features make a home more adaptable. Thompson, Robinson, Dietrich, and Sinclair studied architectural features and perceptions of community residences.[27] They introduced the idea that architectural features such as doors, windows, stairs, and ceiling heights serve as architectural interventions that contribute therapeutic qualities to a space. In their work they refer to elements of the built environment as a prosthesis and diathesis. Prosthetic interventions include elements that serve as an aid and allow for greater autonomy, whereas diathesis hinders access. Examples of architectural prosthesis could be clear wayfinding, adequate lighting for a task, and acoustical regulation. Examples for architectural diathesis might be drafts caused from poor insulation, veiling reflections from inappropriate lighting, and excessive odors, all of which could diminish the safety and/or well-being of a person. Lawton and Simon stress the need for design interventions that are prosthetic, as they support people with low functional capacity to use the environment.[28] Due to advancements in design for diversity and the implementation of building codes, most dwellings are designed to prevent placing individuals at physical risk. Unfortunately, little has been done to address the psychological consequences of architectural elements for populations with sensory sensitivities and low cognitive abilities.

Gestalt Theory

The Gestalt Theory is used to understand how individuals organize the stimuli they are presented with. Perception of an environment is a combination of senses (sight, smell, touch, or sound). The Gestalt Theory emphasizes that the whole of anything is greater than the sum of its parts. The principles and rules that form the foundation of the Gestalt Theory help people to understand how humans and environments interact. The fundamental goal of the Gestalt Theory is to understand how one organizes their perceptions into a coherent whole.

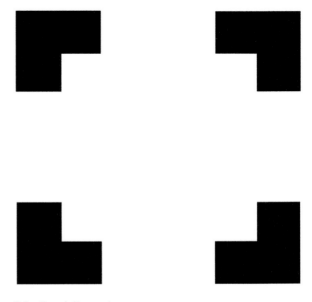

2.1 Gestalt Perception.

The ability to look at an object as a whole, not just as individual pieces, poses another cognitive processing issue for people with ASD in particular. For example, in the diagram above (Figure 2.1), a neurotypical (NT) individual would be able to see four smaller, black squares with a white, large square overlapping. By comparison, an individual with ASD may not see squares at all or only see the black outside squares.

According to Bogdashina, a typical brain "'fills in the gaps' and 'predicts' the final picture."[29] When an individual with ASD is expected to process a large amount of stimuli simultaneously, he or she may find it difficult to "break" the whole image or situation into meaningful parts. In contrast, the individual may focus on the pieces that grab their attention the most. Put simply, they may not see the forest for the trees. This theory provides a background to explain some of the social deficits (noted below) associated with ASD. For example, as without central coherence, individuals lack the ability to interpret emotions based on facial expressions.[30]

- A weak central coherence involves the inability to integrate details into a meaningful whole.[31]

- Focus on parts rather than the whole.[32]
- Memory is often stored as an unprocessed, un-interpreted image.[33]

Sensory Integration Theory

Sensory Integration Theory is the process that refers to the detection, integration, organization, and use of the sensory information that helps a person interact with his or her environment.[34] People whose sensory input is not organized or integrated in the brain have sensory integrative dysfunction (SID). As a result, the environment often causes the individual to feel confusion, irritation, or an inability to participate and act in manners similar to non-ASD individuals. Sensory Integration (SI) Theory was developed from the work of Jean Ayres and expanded by Fisher, Murray, and Bundy. The foundation of SI Theory is that proper integration of the sensory systems allows for the development of language, attention, organization, motor abilities, interpersonal relationships, and academic learning.

The three major premises of Sensory Integration were developed through the work of Fisher, Murray, and Bundy (1991). The three postulates include:[35]

- Neurotypical (NT) individuals gain sensory information from the environment. They process this information within the central nervous system and organize their behavior based on the sensory input.
- A deficit in the integration of sensory information leads to difficulty with conceptual and motor learning.
- Appropriate intervention of enhanced sensory activity with the production of adaptive behavior results in improved sensory integration, which leads to enhanced learning.

The senses of hearing, vision, taste, smell, and touch respond to external stimuli outside the body. The vestibular, proprioceptive, and tactile senses are functions of the body that assist an individual to find their self in the world.[36] Research from a variety of fields, including neuropsychology, neurology, physiology, child development, and psychology, have helped caregivers and designers develop intervention strategies and understand the Sensory Integration Theory. Treatment of symptoms is provided through a variety of activities and equipment to teach directionality, coordination, balance control, vestibular and sensory stimulation, and fine motor control.[37]

Elements of Legibility

The Theory of Legibility helps provide direction for accommodating wayfinding deficits. Wayfinding refers to the process of organizing spatial and environmental information to help users find their way.[38] Designers are often put to task to enhance the wayfinding of individuals in order to keep them safe and diminish their frustration. While working with the city of Boston's planning department in the late 1950s, Kevin Lynch, an urban planner, identified and described five predominate elements that lead to the legibility and image of a city: paths, edges, districts, nodes, and landmarks. In his classic book, *The Image of the City*, Lynch stated, "Districts are structured with nodes, defined by edges, penetrated by paths, and sprinkled with landmarks. Elements regularly overlap and pierce one another."[39] Lynch coined his elements to describe cities, but they also apply to micro-communities such as malls, resorts, hospitals, airports, and even homes. The following describe the elements:

- Paths are channels people use as they travel from one area to another; examples include walkways, roads, and transit lines. Paths should be clearly identified and continuous. The strongest form of a path clearly indicates the start point and the end point.
- Edges, such as shorelines and fences, preclude travel and may appear to be boundaries. The strongest form of an edge is one that is constant and continuous.
- Districts, the largest elements, are regions having a particular character that people can readily identify: commercial, residential, artistic, and so on.
- Nodes are well-known points within the environment to and from which people travel; they are often places where paths converge such as a bank of elevators or an airport.
- Landmarks, easily seen and singular components within an environment, are used for location orientation, and are often found within districts and nodes.

Like Lynch's theory, Gibson's Affordance Theory refers to spaces as containing arrangements of materials, furnishings, and finishes that afford detectable functions.[40] Substances and surfaces can also help provide cognitive clarity for one to be able to build their connections and their cognitive comprehension.

Prospect and Refuge Theory

Appleton was the first to propose the Prospect-refuge theory.[41] The prospect-refuge theory built on an idea originally conceptualized by Lorenz, which said "to see without being seen" is an intrinsically human trait.[42] According to Appleton, it is human nature to claim territory and to defend that territory when necessary.[43] Our ancestors claimed territory for survival. They needed to attain food, water, and shelter. In many ways, we continue to carry out these traits, although they may be presented in a subtler manner. In order to understand the theory, it is helpful to first look at the name itself. Prospect, by definition, is the ability to survey the environment, have unimpeded view of the space before entering or "previewing."[44] Refuge is the ability to hide if necessary escape routes should be provided.

According to Appleton, humans subconsciously desire the ability to be able to see into a room before entering and also desire areas in which to hide inside that room. Other theorists, Stewart-Pollack and Menconi Pollock, claim that the opportunity for prospect and refuge offer one of the most satisfying experiences in residential privacy by providing feelings of safety and of being inside and looking out.[45] The challenge in interacting with other people is the desire to maximize control of contact. This includes the desire to be with others as well as the desire to avoid others. Being able to see into a room before making a commitment to enter can satisfy this need for control. Regnier and Denton label this as "previewing."[46]

The concept of previewing can be accomplished by sidelights, windows in doors, and subdividing spaces so one has a view from a distance. Previewing methods also help to make entrances and exits more visible once inside a space. This can be helpful for individuals, particularly children, who feel the need to escape from a stressful social situation. Exits that are made more visible by a sidelight or window will help inhabitants to clearly see an escape route.

Spaces that provide for prospect and refuge also encourage social interaction. The theory, based on man's evolutionary past of living on the savannah, refers to prospect as something good such as weather, food, and company of loved ones or people who care

for you. Refuge is a place free from predators and harsh weather. Large areas divided into smaller areas, or areas with lower ceilings that permit looking out to more open spaces, are positive, as they provide refuge and the opportunity to look for prospect.[47, 48]

Additional Theoretical Work

Other early theoretical work includes studies by Asperger, which deducted ASD as a psychodynamic etiology.[49] It wasn't until more than a decade later that autism was considered due to a neurological origin and conceptualized as a cognitive "disarrangement" rather than an emotional disorder. Today, autism has come to be considered as a developmental disorder. Hence, it is included among the Pervasive Developmental Disorders (PDDs) and includes individuals with Asperger's syndrome, Rett syndrome, and childhood disintegrative disorder. The most influential theories developed to date that inform the design of space for people with ASD include: 1) theory of executive function; 2) theory of mind; and 3) Weak Central Coherence Theory.

Theory of Executive Function

Many individuals with ASD are thought to lack certain executive functions that control cognitive processes such as concentration, planning, and attention.[50] Poor executive functions lead to trouble reorienting attention from one task to another, poor impulse control, disorganized and inflexible thoughts or actions, and inappropriate, out-of-context behavior.[51] This impairment would also be the origin of stereotyped and repetitive behaviors, "which would not be correctly governed by an executive or supervisory system."[52]

Theory of Mind

Thought to explain some of the difficulties with social interaction among individuals with autism, Theory of Mind refers to the ability of an individual to recognize the mental states of others, including deciphering beliefs, desires, intentions, imagination, and emotions.[53] Theory of Mind includes "the capacity to interpret acts of motion as a consequence of volitional mental states and… for the capacity to perceive that someone is sensorially engaged in the same way as oneself."[54] In other words, the individual may have difficulty reading and relating to others. The behavior of others may come off as confusing and unpredictable because without a Theory of Mind, individuals with ASD do not understand that other people have thoughts and that those thoughts may be different from their own.[55] With mind-blindness, all verbal messages are taken literally, which demonstrates why individuals on the spectrum often treat people like inanimate "objects."[56] Unlike neurotypical (NT) children, children with ASD do not understand the concept of deception, the idea that someone might possess incorrect information or false beliefs, or that a person's expression or body language can indicate how they are feeling.[57] Mind-blindness would also account for individuals with ASD treating others "like objects," since the individual is not able to recognize a mind in them, and may indicate a lack of self-consciousness.[58]

Weak Central Coherence Theory

One of the theories thought to explain unusual attention to details, a common symptom among individuals with ASD, weak central coherence refers to a bias toward local or piecemeal information rather than global or configurational processing.[59] Weak central coherence involves the inability by people with ASD to integrate details into a meaningful whole.[60] Some of the earliest studies of classic autism confirm this unusual focus on parts rather than the whole.[61] This is why individuals with ASD often focus on extraneous details and are unable to think about things cohesively.[62] Put simply, weak central coherence is the failure to see the big picture. This theory helps to explain some of the social deficits associated with ASD. Without central coherence, individuals lack the ability to interpret emotions based on facial expressions.[63] Without processing someone's facial expressions or body language as a whole, individuals on the spectrum might be fixated on a seemingly extraneous detail on the face or process a face feature by feature.[64] Weak central coherence may also explain some of the other symptoms associated with ASD. Abnormal attention to detail may also explain distress over even the smallest changes in the physical environment.[65] In language, some higher-functioning individuals with ASD understand the meanings of individual words

but struggle to understand the meaning of complete sentences.[66] Weak Central Coherence Theory may also provide insight to the sometimes amazing ability of some individuals with autism to focus on details, but also still be unable to consolidate numerous pieces into a meaningful whole. In addition, this theory would explain why some individuals with ASD have issues discerning irony, metaphors, or mere jokes.[67] Bogdashina talks about Gestalt perception, meaning the act of grasping all the details in a single, sensory image.[68] The term "Gestalt," then, tries to refer to an holistic perception, but not, as it may seem, to the integration of all the details in a whole.

Notes

1. Lewin, Kurt. *Field theory in social science.* Harper, 1951.

2. Kaplan, Rachel, Stephen Kaplan, and Terry Brown. "Environmental preference: A comparison of four domains of predictors." *Environment and behavior* 21, no. 5 (1989): 509–530.

3. Kopec, David Alan. *Environmental psychology for design.* New York: Fairchild, 2006.

4. Kaplan, Stephen. "The restorative benefits of nature: Toward an integrative framework." *Journal of environmental psychology* 15, no. 3 (1995): 169–182.

5. Kaplan, Rachel, and Eugene J. Herbert. "Cultural and sub-cultural comparisons in preferences for natural settings." *Landscape and urban planning* 14 (1987): 281–293.

6. Scott, Suzanne C. "Visual attributes related to preference in interior environments." *Journal of interior design* 18, no. 1–2 (1993): 7–16.

7. Bengtsson, Anna, and Gunilla Carlsson. "Outdoor environments at three nursing homes: Focus group interviews with staff." *Journal of housing for the elderly* 19, no. 3–4 (2006): 49–69.

8. Scott, Suzanne C. "Visual attributes related to preference in interior environments." *Journal of interior design* 18, no. 1–2 (1993): 7–16.

9. Kaplan, S., and R. Kaplan. *Cognition and environment: Functioning in an uncertain world.* Praeger, 1982.

10. Scott, Suzanne C. "Visual attributes related to preference in interior environments." *Journal of interior design* 18, no. 1–2 (1993): 7–16.

11. Kaplan, Rachel, and Stephen Kaplan. *The experience of nature: A psychological perspective.* CUP Archive, 1989.

12. Herzog, Thomas R., and Olivia L. Leverich. "Searching for legibility." *Environment and behavior* 35, no. 4 (2003): 459–477.

13. Kaplan, Rachel, and Stephen Kaplan. *The experience of nature: A psychological perspective*. CUP Archive, 1989.

14. Kaplan, Rachel, and Stephen Kaplan. *The experience of nature: A psychological perspective*. CUP Archive, 1989.

15. Kaplan, Rachel, and Stephen Kaplan. *The experience of nature: A psychological perspective*. CUP Archive, 1989.

16. Herzog, Thomas R., and Olivia L. Leverich. "Searching for legibility." *Environment and behavior* 35, no. 4 (2003): 459–477.

17. Kaplan, Rachel, and Stephen Kaplan. *The experience of nature: A psychological perspective*. CUP Archive, 1989.

18. Herzog, Thomas R., and Olivia L. Leverich. "Searching for legibility." *Environment and behavior* 35, no. 4 (2003): 459–477.

19. Kaplan, S., and R. Kaplan. *Cognition and environment: Functioning in an uncertain world*. Praeger, 1982.

20. Cohen, Uriel, and Gerald D. Weisman. *Holding on to home: Designing environments for people with dementia*. Johns Hopkins University Press, 1991.

21. Regnier, Victor. *Design for assisted living: Guidelines for housing the physically and mentally frail*. John Wiley & Sons, 2003.

22. Kaplan, Rachel, Stephen Kaplan, and Robert Ryan. *With people in mind: Design and management of everyday nature*. Island Press, 1998.

23. Ulrich, Roger S. "Effects of gardens on health outcomes: Theory and research." In C. C. Marcus and M. Barnes, *Healing gardens: Therapeutic benefits and design recommendations* (pp. 27–86). New York: John Wiley & Sons, 1999.

24. Ulrich, Roger S. "Effects of healthcare environmental design on medical outcomes." In *Design and health: Proceedings of the second international conference on health and design* (pp. 49–59). Stockholm, Sweden: Svensk Byggtjanst, 2001.

25. Zeisel, John. *Inquiry by Design: Environment/behavior/neuroscience in architecture, interiors, landscape and planning*. New York: WW Norton & Company, 2006.

26. Cohen, Uriel, and Gerald D. Weisman. *Holding on to home: Designing environments for people with dementia*. Johns Hopkins University Press, 1991.

27. Thompson, Travis, Julia Robinson, Mary Dietrich, Marilyn Farris, and Valerie Sinclair. "Architectural features and perceptions of community residences for people with mental retardation." *American journal of mental retardation: AJMR* 101, no. 3 (1996): 292–314.

28. Lawton, M. P., and B. Simon. "The ecology of social relationships in housing for the elderly." *The gerontologist* 8, no. 2 (1968): 108–115.

29. Bogdashina, Olga. *Sensory perceptual issues in autism and Asperger Syndrome: Different sensory experiences, different perceptual worlds*. Jessica Kingsley Publishers, 2003.

30. Burnette, Courtney P., Peter C. Mundy, Jessica A. Meyer, Steven K. Sutton, Amy E. Vaughan, and David Charak. "Weak central coherence and its relations to theory of mind and anxiety in autism." *Journal of autism and developmental disorders* 35, no. 1 (2005): 63–73.

31. Sánchez, Pilar Arnaiz, Francisco Segado Vázquez, and Laureano Albaladejo Serrano. *Autism and the built environment*. INTECH Open Access Publisher, 2011.

32. Kanner, Leo. *Autistic disturbances of affective contact*. Publisher not identified, 1943.

33. Bogdashina, Olga. *Sensory perceptual issues in autism and Asperger Syndrome: Different sensory experiences, different perceptual worlds*. Jessica Kingsley Publishers, 2003.

34. Ayres, A. J. *Sensory integration and learning disabilities*. Los Angeles: Western Psychological Services, 1972.

35. Fisher, A. G., E. A. Murray, and A. C. Bundy. *Sensory integration: Theory and practice*. F. A. Davis, 1991.

36. Ferguson, J. "Sensory integration therapy." 2003. Retrieved June 3, 2003. http://memorialhospital.org/sensoryintegration.htm.

37. Ferguson, J. "Sensory integration therapy." 2003. Retrieved June 3, 2003. http://memorialhospital.org/sensoryintegration.htm.

38. Brandon, Kelly C. "Wayfinding." *Issues in graphic design*. 2014. http://www.kellybrandondesign.com/IGDWayfinding.html.

39. Lynch, Kevin. *The image of the city*. Vol. 11. MIT press, 1960.

40. Gibson, James J. "The concept of the stimulus in psychology." *American psychologist* 15, no. 11 (1960): 694.

41. Appleton, Jay. *The experience of landscape*. New York: John Wiley & Sons, 1975.

42. Lorenz, Konrad. *Man meets dog*. Baltimore, MD: Penguin Books, 1964.

43. Appleton, Jay. *The experience of landscape*. New York: John Wiley & Sons, 1975.

44. Regnier, Victor, and Alexis Denton. "Ten new and emerging trends in residential group living environments." *Neurorehabilitation* 25, no. 3 (2008): 169–188.

45. Stewart-Pollack, Julie, and Rosemary Menconi. *Designing for privacy and related needs*. Fairchild Books, 2005.

46. Regnier, Victor, and Alexis Denton. "Ten new and emerging trends in residential group living environments." *Neurorehabilitation* 25, no. 3 (2008): 169–188.

47. Hildebrand, Grant. *Origins of architectural pleasure*. University of California Press, 1999.

48. Regnier, Victor, Jennifer Hamilton, and Suzie Yatabe. *Assisted living for the aged and frail: Innovations in design, management, and financing.* Columbia University Press, 1995.

49. Asperger, H. "Die Bautistischen Psychopathen" [im Kindesalter.] Archiv fur Psychiatrie und Nervenkrankheiten, 117, 76–136. Translated by U. Frith in U. Frith (Ed.) (1991) *Autism and Asperger syndrome,* pp. 36–92. Cambridge, 1944.

50. Sánchez, Pilar Arnaiz, Francisco Segado Vázquez, and Laureano Albaladejo Serrano. *Autism and the built environment.* INTECH Open Access Publisher, 2011.

51. Davies, Fran, and S. Clayton. "Even the ants are noisy: Sensory perception in people with autism spectrum disorder." Presentation at NAS Regional Conference in London, 2008.

52. Frith, Uta. *Autism: Explaining the enigma.* Wiley-Blackwell, 1989.

53. Williams, Emma. "Who really needs a 'theory' of mind? An interpretative phenomenological analysis of the autobiographical writings of ten high-functioning individuals with an autism spectrum disorder." *Theory & psychology* 14, no. 5 (2004): 704–724.

54. Talay-Ongan, Ayshe, and Kara Wood. "Unusual sensory sensitivities in autism: A possible crossroads." *International journal of disability, development and education* 47, no. 2 (2000): 201–212.

55. Burnette, Courtney P., Peter C. Mundy, Jessica A. Meyer, Steven K. Sutton, Amy E. Vaughan, and David Charak. "Weak central coherence and its relations to theory of mind and anxiety in autism." *Journal of autism and developmental disorders* 35, no. 1 (2005): 63–73.

56. Sánchez, Pilar Arnaiz, Francisco Segado Vázquez, and Laureano Albaladejo Serrano. *Autism and the built environment.* INTECH Open Access Publisher, 2011.

57. Baron–Cohen, S. "Autism: the empathizing-systematizing (ES) theory, cognitive neuroscience." *New York: New York Academy of Sciences,* no. 1156 (2009): 68–80.

58. Frith, Uta, and Francesca Happé. "Theory of mind and self-consciousness: What is it like to be autistic?" *Mind & language* 14, no. 1 (1999): 82–89.

59. Brock, Jon, Caroline C. Brown, Jill Boucher, and Gina Rippon. "The temporal binding deficit hypothesis of autism." *Development and psychopathology* 14, no. 2 (2002): 209–224.

60. Sánchez, Pilar Arnaiz, Francisco Segado Vázquez, and Laureano Albaladejo Serrano. *Autism and the built environment.* INTECH Open Access Publisher, 2011.

61. Kanner, Leo. *Autistic disturbances of affective contact.* Publisher not identified, 1943.

62. Davies, Fran, and S. Clayton. "Even the ants are noisy: Sensory perception in people with autism spectrum disorder." Presentation at NAS Regional Conference in London, 2008.

63. Burnette, Courtney P., Peter C. Mundy, Jessica A. Meyer, Steven K. Sutton, Amy E. Vaughan, and David Charak. "Weak central coherence and its relations to theory of mind and anxiety in autism." *Journal of autism and developmental disorders* 35, no. 1 (2005): 63–73.

64. Brock, Jon, Caroline C. Brown, Jill Boucher, and Gina Rippon. "The temporal binding deficit hypothesis of autism." *Development and psychopathology* 14, no. 2 (2002): 209–224.

65. Happé, Francesca, and Uta Frith. "The weak coherence account: detail-focused cognitive style in autism spectrum disorders." *Journal of autism and developmental disorders* 36, no. 1 (2006): 5–25.

66. Brock, Jon, Caroline C. Brown, Jill Boucher, and Gina Rippon. "The temporal binding deficit hypothesis of autism." *Development and psychopathology* 14, no. 2 (2002): 209–224.

67. Frith, Uta. *Autism: Explaining the enigma.* Wiley-Blackwell, 1989.

68. Bogdashina, Olga. *Theory of mind and the triad of perspectives on autism and asperger syndrome: A view from the bridge.* Jessica Kingsley Publishers, 2006.

Human–Environment Interaction

CHAPTER

3

Most of the research in the field of human–environment interaction has been produced by environmental psychologists who focus on the psychological aspects relative to one's environment rather than the influence of the physical setting. This chapter expands on the suggested psychological response and addresses the physical space. The physical environment is a relatively stable assembly of shapes and forms that make up a volume of space. In architectural interior spaces, shapes and forms can include doors, walls, floors, ceilings, furniture, and fixtures that may or may not be adorned with a variety of patterns, textures, and colors. The physical environment also includes outside spaces (discussed in Chapter 14) such as gardens and playgrounds and the built structures within them such as pathways, arbors, and gazebos. In this chapter, the interior of a building is discussed from a therapeutic perspective to accommodate people with Autism Spectrum Disorders. Individuals on the spectrum process their environment much differently than neurotypical (NT) individuals. An awareness of these characteristics is vital for designing environments for people with ASD.

The therapeutic environment focuses on a user's needs and their environmental fit. An integral part of therapeutic spaces are that they provide for restoration, or they are *restorative*[1,2,3,4] and *instorative*.[5,6] A restorative environment allows for recovery through "being away."[7,8] Ulrich's theory of supportive gardens[9,10] describes a nurturing environment that has the ability to improve physical and mental health. This philosophy emphasizes positive distractions through a sense of control, access to privacy, social support, physical movement, exercise, and access to nature.

An instorative environment strengthens identity and self-esteem. The drive for health and well-being are promoted when the experiences and activities in the environment correspond with the user's background and disposition.[11,12] Providing for both restorative and instorative opportunities is relative to the creation of environments that meet the needs of people with autism. Even though these individuals may or may not be clinically ill, the rejuvenation properties of restoration may help a person with autism cope with their sensory sensitivities. Likewise, the concept of instorative-ness increases the possibilities of gaining something more than a sensory–environmental balance. When planned well, an instorative space provides opportunities for the user to participate in activities that help them become more self-reliant, self-confident, acquire new skills, or gain in physical fitness.[13] Instorative features

3.1 (right) Detailed famous Maslow pyramid describing all essential needs for each human being

3.2 (facing page, left) Hall's Theories of Proxemics

3.3 (facing page, right) ASD Personal Space Zones

SELF-ACTUALIZA-TION
morality, creativity, spontaneity, acceptance, experience purpose, meaning and inner potential

SELF-ESTEEM
confidence, achievement, respect of others, the need to be a unique individual

LOVE AND BELONGING
friendship, family, intimacy, sense of connection

SAFETY AND SECURITY
health, employment, property, family and social abilty

PHYSIOLOGICAL NEEDS
breathing, food, water, shelter, clothing, sleep

can be attained by giving a person with autism control over their personal space and a say in their daily schedule.

Maslow proposed a hierarchy of needs, shown in Figure 3.1, that identifies the various needs motivating human behavior. In this pyramid shape, the lowest levels represent basic needs of mankind, and the more complex needs are located at the top of the pyramid. At the peak of this hierarchy is self-actualization, where the need for privacy exists. The need for privacy, personal space, territory, and control of crowding is becoming a universal concern for designers, architects, and facility managers. This includes meeting other human needs such as security, affiliation, and esteem.

In this chapter, a variety of human–environmental interaction concepts are examined relative to the design of spaces for people with autism. They include territoriality, personal space, privacy, crowding, and stress. This focus is based on the premise that the ability to have privacy and control one's space is integral to a person's well-being.

An overview of privacy aspects of the environmental behavior theory and conscientious implementation of design principles are discussed and inform the development of a design prototype for a group living home. The evidence based design concept outlined in this chapter provides designers, architects, facility developers, caregivers, families, and individuals with autism tools to understand the human–environment interaction and to design spaces that are restorative and instorative and enhance their well-being throughout their life course.

Human–Environmental Interaction Concepts

Territoriality

Territory can be as big as a geographical space and as small as a personal space. Regardless of the scope, territoriality is usually based on having control over an area of space. In the case of an individual's space, territory is an invisible bubble that surrounds him or her. Definitions of territorial space are varied. Generally, territoriality in humans is at least partly driven by learned factors such as culture, social values, religion, technology, etc. Delaney states that territoriality involves "ways of world-making informed by beliefs, desires, and culturally and historically contingent ways of knowing."[14] For people with autism, their "world making" is complicated by their sensory inhibitions, making the entire sense-making process complex. The various forms/levels of territory are partly focused on the way our built environment is designed and functions. Four types include (1) personal space; (2) primary territory; (3) secondary territory; and (4) public territory.

Personal Space
Among all four types of territories, personal space is a territory that humans carry with themselves and is not related to a particular physical place. Robert Sommer calls personal space a portable territory that every human owns and carries wherever he or she goes.[15] Edward T. Hall, in his "Theories of Proxemics,"[16] explains that personal space is influenced by social and cultural values. In another addition, he "examines the spacing or distance that we

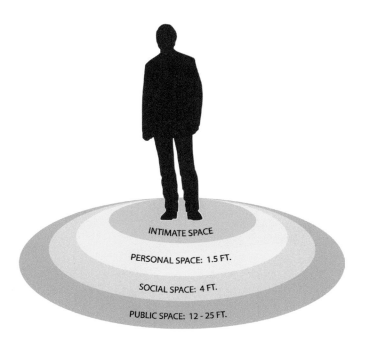

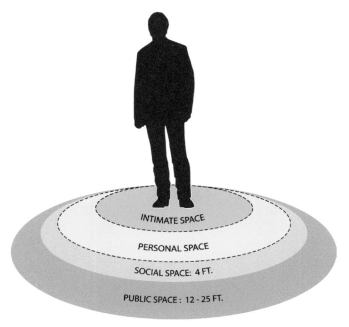

naturally place between ourselves and others in different situations."[17] Hall (1966) defines four basic zones of interpersonal distance[18] (see Figure 3.2) including:

1. Intimate distance: less than 6 inches to 18 inches
2. Personal distance for interactions among good friends or family members: 1.5 to 4 feet
3. Social distance for interactions among acquaintances: 4 to 7 feet to 12 feet
4. Public distance used for public speaking: 12 to 25 feet to 25 feet or more.

These personal space zones may differ among individuals with ASD and with children. Children may not begin to develop body boundaries until age three or four. Typically, personal space grows as a child does. Sommer defined personal space as the invisible boundary where intruders are not allowed.[19] This bubble, however, is flexible and differs depending on the situation. For example, a larger bubble will exist in the company of strangers or in unfamiliar places. Personal space and intimate space may be larger for individuals on the spectrum. Often, individuals with ASD that have tactile sensitivities fear coming in physical contact with others and may require more personal space than others. Conversely, individuals with under-sensitive proprioception have difficulty determining the location of their body in space and may lean on objects or people to help orient themselves. Similarly, the social and communication deficits associated with ASD often ensure that individuals on the spectrum do not learn appropriate distances to keep from others or when and how it is safe to touch others.

The ring representing space for social interaction is not the same among ND populations either. Many individuals on the spectrum avoid social interactions with others. For people with ASD, human interaction can be challenging because individuals on the spectrum are unable to recognize that people have thoughts and ideas different from their own, an idea known as lacking a Theory of Mind.[20, 21, 22] Human behavior, therefore, is incredibly unpredictable and confusing. Most individuals with ASD prefer interaction with inanimate objects, as the behavior is easy to understand and entirely predictable.

Figure 3.3 depicts a smaller social space for individuals with ASD than for NT individuals. The dashed lines around personal and intimate space indicate how these areas can fluctuate for ND people.

Primary Territory

Unlike personal space, primary, secondary, and public territories are stationary, meaning they are related to a particular place over which one claims ownership. Primary territory is the primary place of retreat for its occupants and is considered a permanent territory. One's home and bedroom in particular are considered primary spaces. Porteous defines three purposes of primary territory: security, identity, and stimulation.[23] All three purposes are important for the development and well-being of an individual with autism and need to be accounted for in the design of the spaces they use and occupy. Spaces that individuals can claim as their own such as the bedroom are of particular importance, as they provide a person with autism a sense of autonomy and significance. Allowing them

3.4 Transparency through spaces allows for "previewing"

3.5 (facing page) Viewing from above to build confidence and establish a sense of control over one's environment

to claim territory such as a bedroom that they can personalize also provides a sense of control.

In addition to claiming personal territory, the idea of being able to live in and move throughout our territory comfortably is vital. Appleton's prospect-refuge theory speaks to this. He states, "at both human and sub-human levels the ability to see and the ability to hide are both important in calculating a creature's survival prospects ... Where he has an unimpeded opportunity to see we can call it a *prospect*. Where he has an opportunity to hide, a *refuge*."[24] According to Appleton, humans subconsciously desire the ability to be able to see into a room before entering it and also desire areas in which to hide inside that room.[25] Stewart-Pollack and Menconi state that prospect and refuge support feelings of privacy and safety.[26] The challenge in interacting with other people is the desire to maximize control of contact. This includes the desire to be with others as well as the desire to avoid others. Being able to see into a room before making a commitment to enter it can satisfy this need for control. Regnier and Denton label this as "previewing."[27]

The concept of previewing can be accomplished by providing transparency through a space. A spatial design that is laid out as an open-concept space can achieve this, as it enables one to view from one space to another and scan the terrain without interruption. Previewing can also be achieved by planning multi-level spaces in a manner that allows a person to view from above. Other design features that allow for previewing include incorporating architectural elements such as an upper-level balcony with open-style railing, floor-to-ceiling windows with transparent window treatments, sidelights beside doors, windows in doors, and subdividing spaces so one has a view from a distance (Figures 3.4 and 3.5). Providing opportunities for a person with ASD to easily see where entrances and exits are in a space can help relieve the stress a person with ASD might experience when they are confronted with too much information to compute in a space. This is especially helpful for individuals who feel the need to escape from the sensory overload from people, noise, architectural elements, and an interior's décor.

3.6 Sample 1 of resident's (Max) personalized bedroom

Appleton states that part of human nature is to claim and defend one's territory.[28] Throughout history, this has been a basic need for survival. In many ways, we continue to carry out these traits, although they may be presented in a more subtle manner. For people with autism, their territory is often based on items or material goods they own or like to interact with such as technology, computers, trains, and magazines. Most individuals with ASD, especially children, like to be in spaces that include personal items. Additionally, they feel comfortable when these items are arranged in their spaces in a systematic and orderly fashion. Neurodiverse children will often personalize or claim territory (their bedrooms for example) by displaying toys and objects in a very specific way, either by size, shape, or color (Figure 3.6).

Secondary Territories
Compared to primary territories, secondary territories do not permit permanent ownership. Stewart-Pollack and Menconi (2005) explain, "Occupancy in secondary territories is temporary."[29] A secondary territory would be one's office or work place, or schools that can be personalized to some degree.

In the classroom, a locker or cubby should be provided to allow students to express their self-identity and territorial behaviors. Having a personal territory reduces stressful feelings for individuals on the spectrum. Design characteristics can make substantial differences in social and cognitive development. Personalization of space helps to form individual identity and self-worth.[30] The physical design should create a sense of territoriality or ownership.

A study conducted by Killeen, Evans, and Danko (2003) offers information about school design and learning.[31] Sense of ownership, control, personalization, and territoriality contribute to engagement in the learning process. The study examined children's sense of ownership in a school whose walls were covered with permanent student artwork compared to a school with temporary student artwork. Permanent artwork consisted of ceramic tile displays installed in the school hallways throughout the building. The other school displayed temporary student artwork on walls and bulletin boards. The student's sense of ownership was significantly greater in the school with permanent artwork.

Public Territory

Public territories such as parks, restaurants, recreational areas, and shopping centers[32] cannot be personalized. These territories function according to formal regulations, customs, norms, and laws. In order to have a place of our own in a public territory, we need to mark it in some way: "Once we have placed our blanket or towel on the beach, we have marked our territory and expect that territory to be ours for as long as we have it marked."[33]

Privacy

Environmental behavioral theorists such as Rapoport[34] and Lang[35] suggest that privacy has to do with the ability of individuals or groups to control their visual, auditory, and olfactory interactions with others. Rapoport defines privacy as the ability to control interactions, to possess options, and to achieve desired interactions.[36]

Two discerning social psychologists, Westin and Altman, have written extensively on privacy.[37, 38, 39] Westin's theory speaks to ways that people protect themselves by temporarily limiting access to themselves by others.[40] Westin's theory is still applicable to populations with neurodiverse limitations because they still possess basic life needs: physiological, safety, belonging, esteem, and self-actualization.[41] Both neurotypical and neurodiverse people need to have the opportunity to choose their level of privacy, whether it be solitude, intimacy, anonymity, or reserve. This choice allows for personal autonomy, emotional release, self-evaluation, and protected communication.[42] Like NT populations, ND individuals need to live and learn in spaces that provide personal privacy from the time they are children into adulthood. As children, the most important and the most frequented spaces are the classroom and the home, and both can be modified to be more appropriate for the privacy needs of children with ASD. In the home, it is important for children to have a bedroom or an escape space that is theirs to personalize and retreat to during times of stress. The same goes for classrooms with ND students. A separate, isolated area where the student can have some privacy during sensory overload or frustration should be available. Giving adults with autism adequate privacy in their living environment is slightly more complicated. Many individuals with autism transition out of their parental/birth homes during early adulthood into semi-independent living accommodations such as group homes. They experience an escalated need for privacy when living with unrelated people. Stewart-Pollack and Menconi stress the impact of this change by stating that adjustment is required when individuals leave their family environment where territoriality has been clearly established within the structure of the family.[43] Living in a communal setting often means sharing spaces with more people with diverse intellectual abilities and behaviors. Hence, individuals with autism require help adjusting to their new space and may need to be provided with opportunities to escape and have some privacy.

Altman defines these levels of privacy as follows: [44, 45]

1. Solitude: when an individual is alone and free from observation or physically withdrawn from others
2. Intimacy: having a close, relaxed relationship with another person
3. Anonymity: the ability to be anonymous or "alone in a crowd"
4. Reserve for Personal Autonomy: putting up a psychological barrier in order to withhold personal information from others
5. Emotional Release: having privacy to relax from social roles
6. Protected Communication: private communication with close friends, spouses, and confidantes
7. Self-Evaluation: the ability to reflect privately, integrating experiences and thoughts for future action

Crowding/Public Spaces

Because of the inhibitions many individuals with ASD experience, they usually enter a room (especially an unfamiliar one) with caution, as they may experience a sensory overload. In response, they look for opportunities to attain privacy. Quite frequently they choose to stand or sit in locations where they can hug the wall or are translucent as an act to attain privacy. Doing this may set them as outsiders, and their acquisition of information is restricted.

Many design approaches can be used to create privacy. Acoustical/auditory and visual privacy have the biggest impact on well-being. Modular, repetitive built-in units may serve to provide opportunities for personalization and territorial marking. Additionally, the desire to have choice and control over one's environment is a precursor for optimum privacy. Generous amounts of natural light controlled by adjustable window treatments allow for personal choice as does the opportunity to personalize private spaces with personal memorabilia.

School and class size correspond to crowding and personal space. In 1930, there were 262,000 public schools in the United States. Today, there are only about 91,000 although the population has grown from 25 million in 1950 to 47 million. Small schools provide benefits of participation in leadership and extracurricular activities. Schools with 500 or fewer students have lower crime levels and less serious student misconduct. Children in classrooms of 13–17 students outperform those in classes of 22–25 students.[46] Additionally, public circulation areas are typically crowded and the most difficult school spaces to prevent illicit activity. Shortening hallways and corridors is a way to reduce unwanted social behaviors.[47]

Stress

According to Kopec, stress is defined as a "psychological or physiological response to a stimulus or stressor."[48] He further explains that stress may come from internal or external sources. External sources of stress for individuals with ASD may include physical environmental features such as crowding, noise, fluorescent lights, spatial disorganization, and others.[49] Individuals with ASD may be more prone to external stressors due to greater sensitivity to environmental stimuli.

Internal sources of stress may be reduced through choice and control. Several theorists believe that when people have the opportunity to make choices and control their daily lives they experience greater well-being.[50, 51, 52] Due to impaired adaptive behaviors, ND individuals often do not have as much control over their lives as NT people. As a result, they are at risk for negative consequences from stressful experiences. Cohen, Glass, and Phillips (1977) have called groups with diminished control over their environments "susceptible populations."[53] In creating spaces for this population, well-being and feelings of control may be enhanced through design interventions.[54]

Providing choice and control for children is more difficult since they require more guidance and supervision by a caregiver. Specific spaces in the home and the classroom should be provided for the child to retreat to in times of stress when there is a need for privacy. Allowing a child to use and personalize these spaces provides a feeling of choice and control. In the home, allowing a child with ASD to personalize his or her bedroom is crucial to their well-being and the development of self-determination. The child should be free to choose the color of the walls, some of the furnishings, and the decorations in their bedroom. Specific design interventions and methods for children in a home environment are discussed in later chapters.

There will be times when a child is disruptive, for any number of reasons, and there are ways to address this through design. Installing an "escape space" could be very beneficial in reducing disruptive behaviors and tantrums. This area is a place for students to retire, for example, when they are experiencing sensory overload and feel stressed. In the escape space they can calm down and regain control, away from an academic task, and then return to the task refocused. The user will have solitude in order to collect his or her thoughts, calm down, and rejoin the other students.[55] Many individuals on the spectrum reported feeling a sense of control and release when they had a designated place for relaxation.[56] Ideally, the escape space should be placed inside the classroom for teachers to be able to continue observing students when they retreat there.[57] In this case, the space can be divided from the rest of the classroom using screens, bookcases and other pieces of furniture. The following describes a study by Mostafa in which an escape space was implemented in a classroom:

> Before implementation, the student with ASD often removed herself from the group to sit in a corner and after several minutes would rejoin the group. After the escape space was added to the classroom, the student initially retreated to the space quite frequently. Over time, the student used the space less and less. The teachers did note that the student would look over her shoulder at the space but could stay focused on the task at hand as if knowing the escape space was there if needed was sufficient for her to continue.[58]

This space should be equipped with minimal furnishings, soft lighting, soothing music, and comfortable pillows to sit on (Figure 3.7).[59] A few outside items can be provided in the space for sensory stimulation, if they are not overwhelming to the child and will be a source of comfort. Items should be small, like a piece of fabric or sandpaper. Escape spaces can be stress-reducing interventions for individuals with ASD at school or home.

3.7 A window seat nestled between bookcases can provide an area to escape from daily stresses

Hall's Perceptions of Space

In Hall's research, he examined the distances people keep from one another and their environment while performing different activities like conversing, greeting, and other forms of human discourse.[60] Additionally, Hall proposed that different cultures have different personal space requirements. He identified one's perception of their surroundings as various perceptions of space—*thermal space, tactile space, olfactory space, auditory space,* and *visual space*—all of which are related to the sensory sensitivity categories people with autism are known to have.

In discussing *thermal space,* he describes how NT humans regulate their body temperature and react to higher and lower temperatures. Thermal distance plays a major role in how most people experience crowding. Individuals with autism may be hypersensitive or hypo-sensitive to temperature and therefore will need opportunities to adjust their thermostats and or have the ability to close off or let in outside air. Hall also refers to *tactile space,* which separates us from the objects around us. Tactile, or the touchy-feel sense, is a very important sense to consider in designing spaces for autism, as tactile hyper- or hypo-sensitivity is said to be one of the most common symptoms among ND individuals. Many people with autism prefer touch in the form of deep therapeutic pressure or prefer not to be touched at all. They have also been known to be sensitive to even the slightest amount of material touching the skin, such as clothing tags.

Olfactory stimuli (smells) can also trigger unfavorable responses for an ND individual with a more pronounced sense of smell. Hall also discusses auditory space and how it is experienced differently from culture to culture. Some cultures depend on thick walls in order to screen sounds, but other cultures are more amenable to sounds and open spaces. Typically NT people can adjust to diverse acoustics, but for ND individuals, a slight variation of decibel may send them into a panic. In most cultures, vision is the most developed sense and has become the sense people rely on to gather information about their surroundings. People with autism, on the other hand, have a tendency to fixate on visual details and have difficulty with Gestalt Theory, i.e. not seeing the forest for the trees, or the inability to see a cohesive whole. Through his study of sensuous spaces, Hall developed a model of proxemics or "distance in man" (see Figure 3.2), displayed earlier in this chapter. Hall's research on sensual spaces

and spatial relationships prompted the examination of personal space relative to how people with ASD use and experience their space. In a study completed by Bourne, a personal space zone hypothesis was formulated that represents the personal zone behaviors typical of people with ASD. This theory forms a fundamental basis for the design of a sample group living home identified below.

The following suggested prototype recommends best practices for the design of group living environments for adults with autism and is sensitive to individuals' territorial and privacy needs. Personal space and various levels of territorial needs are addressed and delineated through interventions to promote comfort and well-being for the individuals with autism. Ways to combat stress through providing opportunities for choice and control are also addressed as a therapeutic means to self-actualization.

A prominent characteristic of people with autism is their need for predictability. Kopec describes how to provide spaces that deliver clear messages through architectural delineation.[61] He refers to the separation of one area from another via architectural elements or features, e.g. "thresholds, walls, or variation in ceiling height and floor depth."[62] In the next section, the suggested prototype recommends, architectural delineation is used as a prosthetic and therapeutic intervention to promote well-being, comfort, and independence through interdependence.

Privacy-Control and Choice

Choice and control are key interrelated concepts of privacy for people with autism. The susceptible population this book focuses on who live in group settings often do not have the opportunity to make choices or control their physical space and their interactions within it due to their behavioral idiosyncrasies. Stewart-Pollack and Menconi explain that "choice involves the ability to decide how much interaction we have with others and under what circumstances; control involves the ability to adjust the physical environment or regulate exposure to surroundings."[63] Providing opportunities for choice and control in the physical space of group homes is a challenge given the range of behavioral diversities people on the autism spectrum elicit. One way to meet this challenge is to provide individual bedrooms that can be personalized. Another method is to provide options in wayfinding, furniture layout, and a variety of public and private spaces.

Giving residents in a group home an opportunity to decide when, where, and how much they want to mix with others in their group living situation is one way to respond to their need for control.

Practical Applications for Designers

A Group Home Design Prototype

This design prototype (Figure 3.8 overleaf) for a group home provides suggestions for the integration of architectural elements, finishes, materials, and spatial layouts that maximize the need for privacy and control over the environment of a person with ASD. In this group home design, control is incorporated in the positioning and layout of architectural forms and shapes and the juxtaposing of public, semi-public, and private spaces.

Privacy-Control and Choice—*Public Spaces*

The challenge in living with other people in general, for most people, is finding a balance between public and private space. Providing opportunities for one to have choice and gain control in their environment can be achieved by providing opportunities for prospect and refuge. Choice is achieved in this design proposal by allowing individuals with ASD opportunities to preview and scan their terrain (prospect) or to sit back and view from a distance in a more enclosed environment (refuge). In this design recommendation, architectural and spatial interventions have been created to optimize opportunity for prospect and refuge. Being able to view into the great room in the group home, for example, from a variety of vantage points—i.e. the dining area, kitchen, sunroom, and foyer—allows one to survey and digest the various zones within the space prior to settling in and taking part in group gatherings. The physical layout (the architectural forms, shapes and colors, patterns and textures) of this main room and the adjacent rooms have been carefully laid out to accommodate the resident privacy. The design affords both extroverted and introverted people with ASD to relate to the space in a manner that allows them to get comfortable in their own time and manner. The expansive, open-concept family room allows social individuals

to meet as a large group and be seen, and allows more reserved individuals to view from the sidelines and scan the terrain or environment (prospect) before they enter. Many individuals with ASD fall into the more reserved category, finding close contact with others stressful.

Rooms with a variety of fenestrations such as doorways, windows, etc. make "previewing" a space simpler (Figure 3.9 overleaf). The smaller, more intimate, subdivided, and anchored seating with "comfortable lounge chairs placed at right angles where two people can speak privately" also "offer choice and control and autonomy in a public space"[64] and reinforce the opportunity for refuge.

The intentional symmetrical floor plan centers around the hearth, the gathering place for social activity. This neuro-sensitive design intervention reinforces Perreault, Gurnsey, Dawson, Mottron, and Bertone's research, which found that people with autism have a heightened sensitivity to vertical, horizontal, or diagonal symmetry.[65] They came to this conclusion after several experiments on spatial preference. This favorable response is believed to be due to a keen ability to isolate detailed, local information, while still processing global information. Their preference for symmetry and predictability could also be why they like spaces and items laid out in an orderly fashion.

The discrete circular forms in the outline of the perimeter architecture (spaces, bulkhead, transoms and formations on the floor and hall) connect the smaller adjacent rooms (sunroom and den/office), and serve as cognitive calculation spots for one to gather their thoughts and carry on maneuvering through the space. The great living area affords plenty of opportunity for one to sit/be where they choose. The niches and nooks (Figure 3.10 overleaf) in the various rooms that emerge off the great room provide claimable private areas for everyone, reinforcing Jacobson, Silverstien, and Wislow's ideas that even if the spaces are tiny private niches, desk window seats, or alcoves, they offer an opportunity for privacy.[66]

Additionally, the free-flowing lines of the circular form dictating the perimeter of the great room enable one to transition smoothly from public areas to private by creating an unobtrusive, natural, life-like path.[67] This is especially appropriate for people who might have proprioceptive sensory deficits (common in individuals with autism and Parkinson's disease), as it permits them to find their way in a discrete manner by allowing them to hug a wall as they maneuver through the space.[68]

3.8 (below) Group Home Design Concept: Floor plan (six residents)

3.9 (facing page, top) Group Home Design Concept: Symmetrical floor plan with variety of fenestrations

3.10 (facing page, bottom) Group Home Design Concept: Niches and Nooks

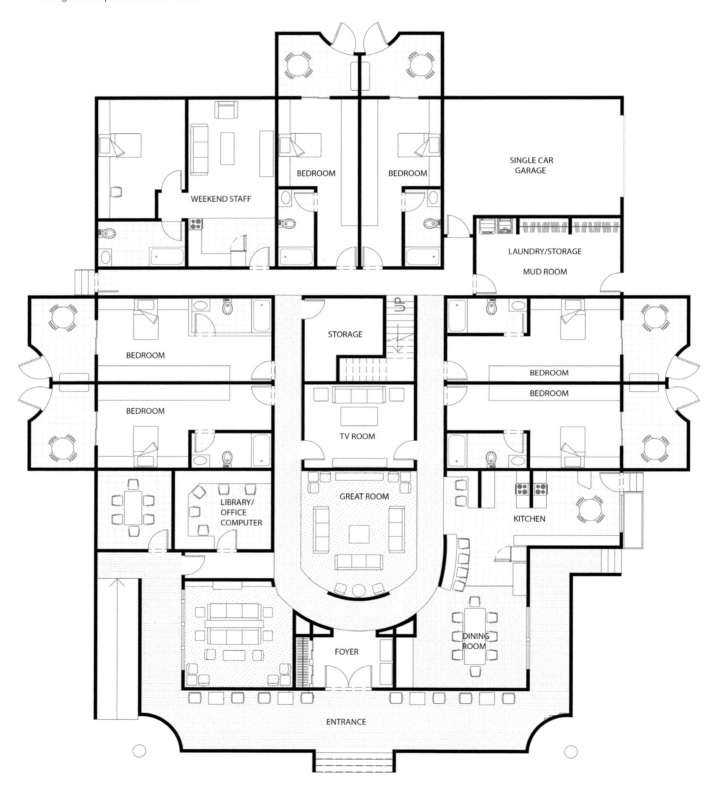

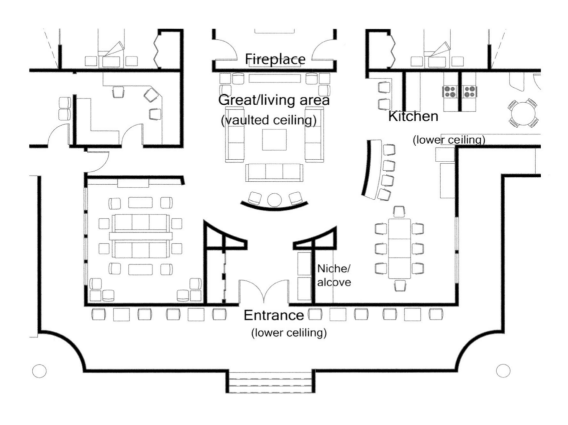

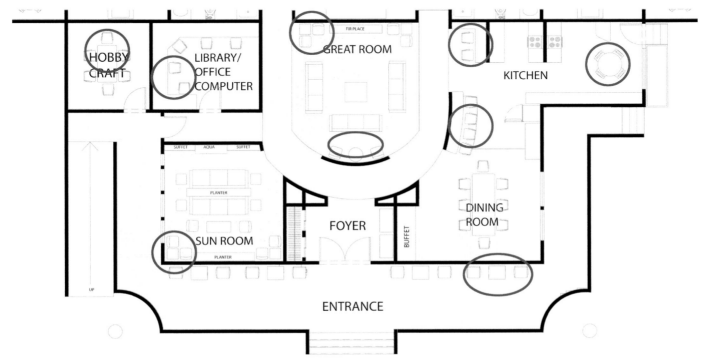

3.11 Use of window coverings to provide flexibility

The expansive vaulted ceiling height in the public space creates an uplifting feeling and encourages those with autism to break their habit of often looking down and focusing on minute objects or patterns. By looking up, they also see diffused light cascading from the clerestory windows, which provides a connection to what's happening outside, time of day, season, etc. Important note: proper shading devices are required to prevent unwanted glare and excess light. Figure 3.11 illustrates the use of window coverings that provide flexibility. The blinds may be opened, closed, raised, or lowered to control lighting and heat gain.

The small seating area near the fireplace, flanked by a library of shelved books and furnished with winged-back chairs, provides an area of intimacy and allows one to claim personal space as well as an opportunity to have discrete views to the surrounding spaces (Figure 3.12).

Privacy-Control and Choice—*Semi-Public Spaces*

Design interventions that promote privacy through choice and control have also been intentionally incorporated into semi-public spaces. The various escape areas including "snoezelen" rooms, craft/hobby rooms, and sun/porch areas where residents can retreat to help decrease stress levels and reduce anxiety.[69] Escaping to these areas can also help enable an individual with ND to choose their level of privacy and control the amount of interaction they have with their house mates. The fact that the rooms have views to nature (biophilia design) reinforces Ulrich's, and Kaplan and Dana's, seminal research on the benefits of nature as being both a therapeutic and restorative experience in attaining a quality of well-balanced privacy.[70, 71]

The implementation of corner windows in each of these rooms also enhances the privacy experience, as they allow one to appreciate the full views because windows located in these positions "dissolve the corner and carry the eye in an unbroken line to the outside

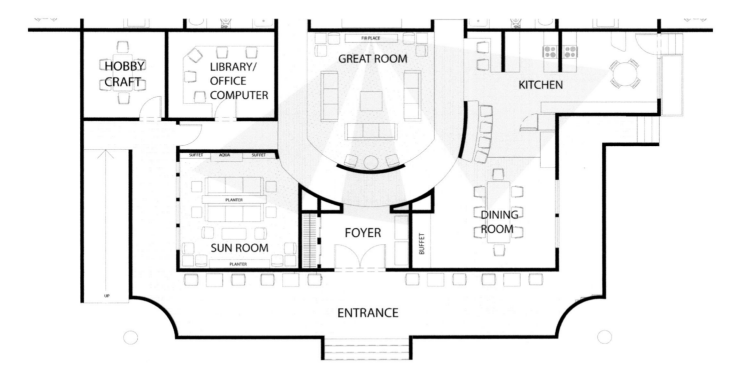

3.12 Group Home Design Concept: Great Room Visibility Study

world."[72] The visual feeling of a window goes almost exclusively from inward to outward: it is therefore "looking out not seeing in,"[73] enabling the "inhabitants to have the outside world at their visual disposal and at the same time provides control over their accessibility to the world."[74]

Additionally, the positioning of the sunroom, dining, kitchen, and laundry room also maximize views to the gardens and activity beyond the interior. Rooms like these where an inhabitant can see out are known as "interstitial edge conditions,"[75] where residents can feel part of the activities taking place outside even if they are not comfortable being outside—i.e. because of natural elements like extreme heat, cold, wind, insects, etc. Simmel and Wolff describe this as "having the outside world at their visual disposal" while maintaining control.[76] Schwartz also reported that an important part of residential privacy is the feeling of safety by being inside and looking out.[77] This idea is reinforced in the space created by the covered porch, with its low, wood-clad ceiling, ceiling fans, and rocking chairs where residents can sit and gaze out. This design is also sensitive to the placement of public and semi-public spaces (Figure 3.13 overleaf).

According to Jacobson, Silberstein, and Winslow, to protect privacy, "place rooms along a privacy gradient with most public areas near the entry and the most private and more remote rooms furthest from the entry."[78] The location of the private bedrooms also concurs with this recommendation as does the transition space, or the hallways leading to the residents' private bedrooms. The fact that the bedrooms can also be accessed from secondary entrances and exits also helps with the feeling of control, an important concept for individuals with autism who find approaching and interacting with groups of people stressful. Furthermore, placing the bedrooms in pods of two (Figure 3.14) also aids in privacy, as the residents only have two bedroom doors to remember and choose from (cognitive privacy) rather than several doors along a corridor, which is often the case in group living situations. The short corridors leading to these rooms also provide spatial privacy for residents who may have proprioception deficits (common in individuals with autism and

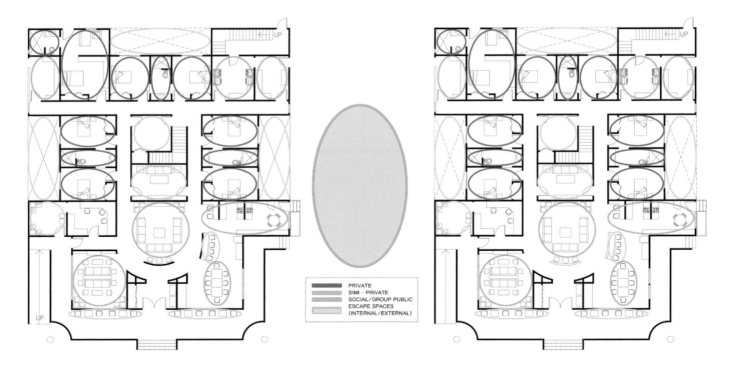

PRIVATE
SIMI - PRIVATE
SOCIAL / GROUP PUBLIC
ESCAPE SPACES
(INTERNAL / EXTERNAL)

3.13 Group Home Design Concept: Privacy—Escape Spaces

Parkinson's disease) to make connections and stabilize themselves. Collectively the bedroom access design interventions reinforce Baum and Davis' recommendations that "dorms be designed with short corridors to the individual resident units with smaller subunits—rooms off of them as they produce more positive behaviors, as well as less withdrawal due to a less crowded feeling of rooms aligned along a long corridor."[79]

Privacy-Control and Choice—*Private Spaces—Resident Bedrooms*

One of the most controversial concerns in group housing is whether to provide single or double bedrooms for residents. The premise is that double rooms encourage interaction and social development and can sometimes minimize loneliness, but in some cases can limit privacy. Stewart, Pollock, and Menconi advocate for private rooms and state, "they afford opportunities for personalization of the space; a crucial need of young adults in transition."[80] Likewise, Morgan and Stewart believe privacy reduces aggression and agitation and improves sleep.[81] Having the opportunity to personalize one's space enhances feelings of privacy as well as reinforcing ownership of primary territory. Giving a resident the opportunity to bring in or purchase their own furniture and decorate their room also helps provide them with connections to express their personality. Ensuring there is ample room for personal trinkets and sentimental items to be displayed helps to trigger memories, contributing to their sense of control and autonomy, in the same way that seeing or holding

a favorite stuffed animal or gadget would help them remember.

In this design proposal, private rooms are recommended for optimum privacy. The fact that single rooms mean more space and more services also means the units would accommodate fewer residents. This is a positive outcome in most cases, as according to Day, Carren, and Stump's research, "units with fewer residents may reduce overstimulation among people by controlling noise and by limiting the number of people each resident encounters."[82] Single units are also important given a "majority of people in this group come out of a family environment in which territory has been clearly defined by the cultural norms and practices within the structure of the family."[83]

Many design approaches can be used to create privacy. Acoustical-auditory and visual privacy have been proven to have the biggest impact on well-being. Acoustical privacy in the residents' personal space has been incorporated in the design for this proposed community by: locating the bathroom on the corridor wall (as a buffer from the public spaces), incorporating acoustical-rated, sound-absorbent ceiling tiles into the ceiling design, securing sound-absorbing panels and built-in units along the shared bedroom walls (rather than the head of the bed), and by the use of soft goods such as carpeting, bedding, window treatments, and upholstery to absorb sound. Another intervention for providing privacy is the opportunity for personalization and territorial marking. This form of privacy is provided by the modular repetitive built-in units, which also accommodate many ND individuals' tendency to hoard, a compulsive disorder to hang on to their past lives, claim territorial control, and fulfill basic human needs of identity, stimulation, security,

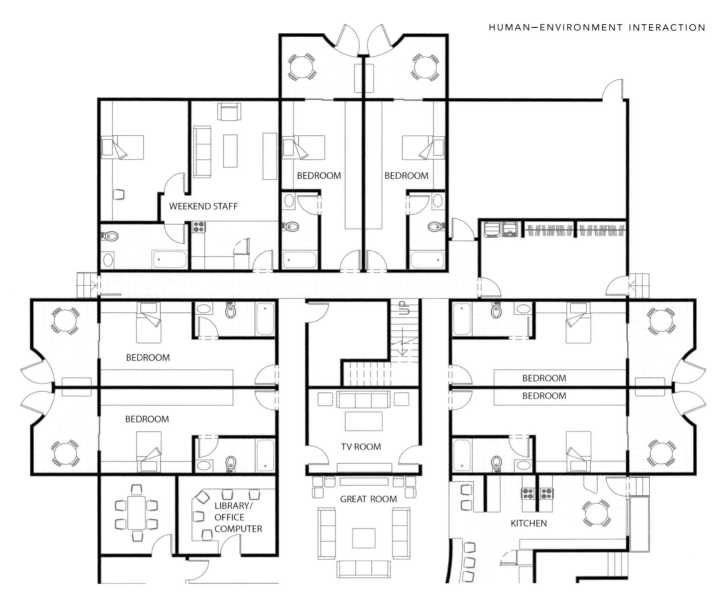

3.14 Group Home Design Concept: Privacy—Bedroom Entrances

and a frame of reference.[84] Additionally the desire to have choice and control over one's environment is a precursor for optimum privacy. Generous amounts of natural light controlled by adjustable window treatments provide personal choice as does the opportunity to personalize private spaces with personal memorabilia, favorite hobbies, etc.

Scale, orientation adjacencies, and size of space also contribute to the ability to personalize one's bedroom. The fact that each room includes an expansive closed-in porch with large windows where one can view nature and socialize with friends and family reinforces Evans, Lepore, and Shroeder's research that found resident rooms receiving more light are perceived as larger and less crowded than the same size rooms that have artificial light.[85] Additionally the side light at each resident's bedroom door provides a sense of control and visual privacy and heightens their sense of autonomy

by promoting a level of environmental privacy where one can be free from unauthorized intrusion.[86]

Collectively, research in the environmental behavior themes of privacy, sound practices in architecture/interior design, and the case study have contributed to the development of this proposed model. The various sensory sensitivities this population experiences were also considered, including auditory, sight, olfactory, tactile, and proprioceptive-spatial. These sensitivities were assessed relative to environmental design theories on privacy-choice, control, territory, and personal space.

The design concept also considers the group homes as part of a collection of homes that could form a community. Figures 3.13 and 3.14 illustrate how the buildings might be configured to promote socializing and at the same time afford residents opportunities to access private areas or "escape spaces."

The evidence-based design interventions developed in this study from research undertaken by Bourne respond to a growing need for an holistic housing plan for this population.[87, 88] The recommendations echo the premise of Kellert, Heerwagen, and Mandor that "therapeutic, restorative environments equipped with prosthetic architectural and design interventions are important to intellectual development and well-being"[89] and serve as an effective and responsible way to accommodate the sensory sensitivities and cognitive processing of people with ASD.

This archetype is unique in that it responds to the therapeutic needs of aging ND individuals like similar studies, and it also offers interventions to facilitate the therapeutic *instorative* and *restorative* needs of this population. The fact that privacy interventions have been developed through the strategic design and development of forms and shapes, volume of space, spatial agencies, colors, textures, patterns, and light as an instorative measure is especially distinctive given this approach has not been used before or recorded in research literature as a best practice in designing for ND populations. However, there is no "one-size-fits-all" design method. Both NT and ND individuals have personal preferences that will dictate the way they experience a space. The design methods outlined in this chapter are backed by research but will not necessarily benefit everyone. Herein lies the reason for the implementation of common themes such as predictability, clarity, repetition of form, shape, pattern, and materials used throughout. This building design model will not only benefit most ND users, but it will also provide professionals who design and develop environments for this population and developers and administrators with a resource that nurtures, develops, and sustains the intellectual, social, and physical health of this population throughout their life course.

Notes

1. Kaplan, Rachel, and Stephen Kaplan. *The experience of nature: A psychological perspective.* CUP Archive, 1989.

2. Kaplan, Rachel, Stephen Kaplan, and Robert Ryan. *With people in mind: Design and management of everyday nature.* Island Press, 1998.

3. Ulrich, Roger S. "Effects of gardens on health outcomes: Theory and research." In C. C. Marcus and M. Barnes, *Healing gardens: Therapeutic benefits and design recommendations* (pp. 27–86). New York: John Wiley & Sons, 1999.

4. Ulrich, Roger S. "Effects of healthcare environmental design on medical outcomes." In *Design and health: Proceedings of the second international conference on health and design* (pp. 49–59). Stockholm, Sweden: Svensk Byggtjanst, 2001.

5. Ottosson, Johan, and Patrik Grahn. "Measures of restoration in geriatric care residences: The influence of nature on elderly people's power of concentration, blood pressure and pulse rate." *Journal of housing for the elderly* 19, no. 3–4 (2006): 227–256.

6. Grahn, Patrik, and Ulrika A. Stigsdotter. "Landscape planning and stress." *Urban forestry & urban greening* 2, no. 1 (2003): 1–18.

7. Kaplan, Rachel, and Stephen Kaplan. *The experience of nature: A psychological perspective.* CUP Archive, 1989.

8. Kaplan, Rachel, Stephen Kaplan, and Robert Ryan. *With people in mind: Design and management of everyday nature.* Island Press, 1998.

9. Ulrich, Roger S. "Effects of gardens on health outcomes: Theory and research." In C. C. Marcus and M. Barnes, *Healing gardens: Therapeutic benefits and design recommendations* (pp. 27–86). New York: John Wiley & Sons, 1999.

10. Ulrich, Roger S. "Effects of healthcare environmental design on medical outcomes." In *Design and health: Proceedings of the second international conference on health and design* (pp. 49–59). Stockholm, Sweden: Svensk Byggtjanst, 2001.

11. Ottosson, Johan, and Patrik Grahn. "Measures of restoration in geriatric care residences: The influence of nature on elderly people's power of concentration, blood pressure and pulse rate." *Journal of housing for the elderly* 19, no. 3–4 (2006): 227–256.

12. Grahn, Patrik, and Ulrika A. Stigsdotter. "Landscape planning and stress." *Urban forestry & urban greening* 2, no. 1 (2003): 1–18.

13. Kellert, S. R., J. Heerwagen, and Martin Mador. *Biophilic design: The theory, science, and practice ofbringing buildings to life.* Chichester, UK: John Wiley & Sons Ltd., 2008.

14. Delaney, David. *Territory: a short introduction.* John Wiley & Sons, 2008.

15. Sommer, Robert. *Personal space. The behavioral basis of design.* Prentice-Hall, 1969.

16. Hall, Edward T. *The hidden dimension.* Garden City, NY: Doubleday, 1966.

17. Stewart-Pollack, Julie, and Rosemary Menconi. *Designing for privacy and related needs.* Fairchild Books, 2005. p. 23.

18. Hall, Edward T. *The hidden dimension.* Garden City, NY: Doubleday, 1966.

19. Sommer, Robert. *Personal space. The behavioral basis of design.* Prentice-Hall, 1969.

20. Williams, Emma. "Who really needs a 'theory' of mind? An interpretative phenomenological analysis of the autobiographical writings of ten high-functioning individuals with an autism spectrum disorder." *Theory & psychology* 14, no. 5 (2004): 704–724.

21. Burnette, Courtney P., Peter C. Mundy, Jessica A. Meyer, Steven K. Sutton, Amy E. Vaughan, and David Charak. "Weak central coherence and its relations to theory of mind and anxiety in autism." *Journal of autism and developmental disorders* 35, no. 1 (2005): 63–73.

22. Talay-Ongan, Ayshe, and Kara Wood. "Unusual sensory sensitivities in autism: A possible crossroads." *International journal of disability, development and education* 47, no. 2 (2000): 201–212.

23. Porteous, John Douglas. *Environment & behavior: Planning and everyday urban life.* Reading, MA: Addison-Wesley, 1977.

24. Appleton, Jay. *The experience of landscape.* New York: John Wiley & Sons, 1975.

25. Appleton, Jay. *The experience of landscape.* New York: John Wiley & Sons, 1975.

26. Stewart-Pollack, Julie, and Rosemary Menconi. *Designing for privacy and related needs.* Fairchild Books, 2005.

27. Regnier, Victor, and Alexis Denton. "Ten new and emerging trends in residential group living environments." *Neurorehabilitation* 25, no. 3 (2008): 169–188.

28. Appleton, Jay. *The experience of landscape.* New York: John Wiley & Sons, 1975.

29. Stewart-Pollack, Julie, and Rosemary Menconi. *Designing for privacy and related needs.* Fairchild Books, 2005.

30. Lackney, Jeffery A. "33 principles of educational design." Retrieved in 2008. http://schoolstudio.engr.wisc.edu.html.

31. Killeen, Jennifer Platten, Gary W. Evans, and Sheila Danko. "The role of permanent student artwork in students' sense of ownership in an elementary school." *Environment and behavior* 35, no. 2 (2003): 250–263.

32. Oldenburg, Ray. *The great good place: Café, coffee shops, community centers, beauty parlors, general stores, bars, hangouts, and how they get you through the day.* Paragon House Publishers, 1989.

33. Stewart-Pollack, Julie, and Rosemary Menconi. *Designing for privacy and related needs.* Fairchild Books, 2005.

34. Rapoport, Amos. *The meaning of the built environment: A nonverbal communication approach.* University of Arizona Press, 1982.

35. Lang, Peter J. "The application of psychophysiological methods to the study of psychotherapy and behavior modification." In *Handbook of psychotherapy and behavior change: An empirical analysis* (pp. 75–125). New York: Wiley, 1971.

36. Rapoport, Amos. *The meaning of the built environment: A nonverbal communication approach.* University of Arizona Press, 1982.

37. Westin, A. F. *Privacy and freedom.* Atheneum, NY, 1967.

38. Altman, Irwin. "*The environment and social behavior: Privacy, personal space, territory, and crowding.*" Brooks/Cole Publishing, 1975.

39. Altman, Irwin. "Privacy regulation: Culturally universal or culturally specific?" *Journal of social issues* 33, no. 3 (1977): 66–84.

40. Westin, A. F. *Privacy and freedom.* Atheneum, NY, 1967.

41. Maslow, Abraham H., and Norbett L. Mintz. "Effects of esthetic surroundings: I. Initial effects of three esthetic conditions upon perceiving 'energy' and 'well-being' in faces." *The Journal of Psychology* 41, no. 2 (1956): 247–254.

42. Westin, A. F. "*Privacy and freedom.* Atheneum, NY, 1967.

43. Stewart-Pollack, Julie, and Rosemary Menconi. *Designing for privacy and related needs.* Fairchild Books, 2005.

44. Altman, Irwin. "*The environment and social behavior: Privacy, personal space, territory, and crowding.*" Brooks/Cole Publishing, 1975.

45. Altman, Irwin. "Privacy regulation: Culturally universal or culturally specific?"*Journal of social issues* 33, no. 3 (1977): 66–84.

46. Lackney, Jeffery A. "33 principles of educational design." Retrieved in 2008. http://schoolstudio.engr.wisc.edu.html.

47. Lackney, Jeffery A. "33 principles of educational design." Retrieved in 2008. http://schoolstudio.engr.wisc.edu.html.

48. Kopec, David Alan. *Environmental psychology for design.* New York: Fairchild, 2006.

49. Shabha, Ghasson, and Kristi Gaines. "A comparative analysis of transatlantic design interventions for therapeutically enhanced learning environments–Texas vs West Midlands." *Facilities* 31, no. 13/14 (2013): 634–658.

50. De Charms, Richard. *Personal causation: The internal affective determinants of behavior.* Academic Press, 1968.

51. Seligman, Martin E. P. *Helplessness: On depression, development, and death.* WH Freeman/Times Books/Henry Holt & Co, 1975.

52. White, Robert W. "Motivation reconsidered: the concept of competence." *Psychological review* 66, no. 5 (1959): 297.

53. Cohen, Sheldon, D. C. Glass, and Susan Phillips. "Environment and health." In H. Freeman, S. Levine, and L. G. Reeder, *Handbook of medical sociology* (pp. 134–149). Englewood Cliffs, NJ: Prentice-Hall, 1979.

54. Thompson, Suzanne C., and Shirlynn Spacapan. "Perceptions of control in vulnerable populations." *Journal of Social Issues* 47, no. 4 (1991): 1–21.

55. Humphreys, Lee. "Cellphones in public: Social interactions in a wireless era." *New media & society* 7, no. 6 (2005): 810–833.

56. Merritt, Edwin T. *Magnet and specialized schools of the future: A focus on change.* R&L Education, 2005.

57. McAllister, Keith. "The ASD-friendly classroom: Design complexity, challenge and characteristics." In *Design Research Society Conference.* Retrieved in 2010 from http://www.designresearchsociety.org/docs-procs/DRS2010/PDF/084.pdf.

58. Mostafa, Magda. "An architecture for autism: Concepts of design intervention for the autistic user." *Archnet-IJAR: International journal of architectural research* 2, no. 1 (2008): 189–211.

59. Polirstok, Susan Rovet, Lawrence Dana, Serafino Buono, Vita Mongelli, and Grazia Trubia. "Improving functional communication skills in adolescents and young adults with severe autism using gentle teaching and positive approaches." *Topics in language disorders* 23, no. 2 (2003): 146–153.

60. Bechtel, Robert B. *Environment and behavior: An introduction.* Sage, 1997.

61. Kopec, David Alan. *Environmental psychology for design.* New York: Fairchild, 2006.

62. Kopec, David Alan. *Environmental psychology for design.* New York: Fairchild, 2006: 106.

63. Stewart-Pollack, Julie, and Rosemary Menconi. *Designing for privacy and related needs.* Fairchild Books, 2005: p. 13.

64. Jacobson, Max, Murray Silverstein, and Barbara Winslow. *Patterns of home: The ten essentials of enduring design.* Taunton Press, 2002. p. 14.

65. Perreault, Audrey, Rick Gurnsey, Michelle Dawson, Laurent Mottron, and Armando Bertone. "Increased sensitivity to mirror symmetry in autism." *PLoS one* 6, no. 4 (2011): e19519–e19519.

66. Jacobson, Max, Murray Silverstein, and Barbara Winslow. *Patterns of home: The ten essentials of enduring design.* Taunton Press, 2002.

67. Day, Kristen, Daisy Carreon, and Cheryl Stump. "The therapeutic design of environments for people with dementia: A review of the empirical research." *The gerontologist* 40, no. 4 (2000): 397–416.

68. Bogdashina, Olga. *Sensory perceptual issues in autism and Asperger Syndrome: Different sensory experiences, different perceptual worlds.* Jessica Kingsley Publishers, 2003.

69. Regnier, Victor, Jennifer Hamilton, and Suzie Yatabe. *Assisted living for the aged and frail: Innovations in design, management, and financing.* Columbia University Press, 1995.

70. Ulrich, Roger S. "Effects of gardens on health outcomes: Theory and research." In C. C. Marcus and M. Barnes, *Healing gardens: Therapeutic benefits and design recommendations* (pp. 27–86). New York: John Wiley & Sons, 1999.

71. Kaplan, Rachel. "The nature of the view from home psychological benefits." *Environment and behavior* 33, no. 4 (2001): 507–542.

72. Jacobson, Max, Murray Silverstein, and Barbara Winslow. *Patterns of home: The ten essentials of enduring design.* Taunton Press, 2002: p. 14.

73. Simmel, Georg, and Kurt H. Wolff. *The sociology of Georg Simmel.* Vol. 92892. Simon and Schuster, 1950.

74. Schwartz, Barry. "The social psychology of privacy." *American journal of sociology* 73, no. 6 (1968): 741–752.

75. Regnier, Victor, Jennifer Hamilton, and Suzie Yatabe. *Assisted living for the aged and frail: Innovations in design, management, and financing.* Columbia University Press, 1995.

76. Simmel, Georg, and Kurt H. Wolff. *The sociology of Georg Simmel.* Vol. 92892. Simon and Schuster, 1950.

77. Schwartz, Barry. "The social psychology of privacy." *American journal of sociology* 73, no. 6 (1968): 741–752.

78. Jacobson, Max, Murray Silverstein, and Barbara Winslow. *Patterns of home: The ten essentials of enduring design.* Taunton Press, 2002.

79. Baum, Andrew, and Glenn E. Davis. "Reducing the stress of high-density living: An architectural intervention." *Journal of personality and social psychology* 38, no. 3 (1980): 471.

80. Stewart-Pollack, Julie, and Rosemary Menconi. *Designing for privacy and related needs.* Fairchild Books, 2005.

81. Morgan, Debra G., and Norma J. Stewart. "Multiple occupancy versus private rooms on dementia care units." *Environment and behavior* 30, no. 4 (1998): 487–503.

82. Day, Kristen, Daisy Carreon, and Cheryl Stump. "The therapeutic design of environments for people with dementia: A review of the empirical research." *The gerontologist* 40, no. 4 (2000): 397–416.

83. Stewart-Pollack, Julie, and Rosemary Menconi. *Designing for privacy and related needs.* Fairchild Books, 2005. p. 28.

84. Samuels, J., O. Joseph Bienvenu III, M. A. Riddle, B. A. M. Cullen, M. A. Grados, K-Y. Liang, R. Hoehn-Saric, and G. Nestadt. "Hoarding in obsessive compulsive disorder: Results from a case-control study." *Behaviour research and therapy* 40, no. 5 (2002): 517–528.

85. Evans, Gary W., Stephen J. Lepore, and Alex Schroeder. "The role of interior design elements in human responses to crowding." *Journal of personality and social psychology* 70, no. 1 (1996): 41.

86. Regnier, Victor, and Jon Pynoos. *Housing the aged: Design directives and policy considerations.* Elsevier Publishing Company, 1987.

87. Bourne, Angela. "Therapeutic environments for adults with intellectual developmental diversities." Master's Report, Texas Tech University, 2012.

88. Bourne, Angela. "Neuro-considerate environments for adults with intellectual developmental diversities: An integrated design approach to support wellbeing." PhD diss., Texas Tech University, 2013.

89. Kellert, S. R., J. Heerwagen, and Martin Mador. *Biophilic design: The theory, science, and practice of bringing buildings to life*. Chichester, UK: John Wiley & Sons Ltd., 2008.

Perception, Cognition, and Sensation

Understanding how people with ASD perceive their surroundings is crucial to creating environments that provide an optimal Quality of Life (QOL). The behaviors of these individuals demonstrate differentiated cognitive processing and sensory sensitivities that make them experience their environments differently than neurotypical (NT) people. Personal accounts of people with ASD and empirical research by psychologists, sociologists, and teachers confirm that people with ASD have challenges with environmental adaptation. Disengagement is one of the prominent signs of adaptation. This shortcoming stifles a child's development and, as a result, inhibits their ability to develop socially, which is a precursor for learning.[1]

The gathering and managing process within a person's brain to build meaning of the world is complex. The constant engagement of the senses, examining, re-examining, sifting, and filtering of external stimulus require an interface and interconnection between oneself and their environment. As the information comes into the brain, they organize the incoming information into patterns of recognition and develop their understanding of a particular situation (cognition).

Perception is the first stage in the thought process. "Perception is the interpretation of incoming sensory information and is influenced by a variety of factors which may include: the type and level of the stimulus, a person's past experiences, level of attention to detail, readiness to respond, level of motivation, and current emotional state.[2] To perceive a space or object, the sensory organs gather stimuli, then the brain interprets that information through the process we know as perception."[3] We perceive our external world by engaging all of our senses. "Senses are the gateway to our perception."[4]

Traditional behavior studies on how the physical environment affects behavior provide a context for understanding how one develops their ability to perceive their environment. People with ASD in particular receive information about a space based on all of their senses collectively: smell, sight, taste, sound, touch, vestibular, and proprioception. This ability to comprehend one's space is known as sensory integration (SI) and is essential to achieve a coherent perception of a situation and to decide how to act.[5] Sensory integration is the process of organizing incoming sensory information that allows an individual to interact effectively with the environment in daily activities.[6] Sensory Integrative Dysfunction (SID) occurs when sensory input is not organized or integrated in the brain. This dysfunction can be described as having a low[7] or

Table 4.1 Behavioral Characteristics Associated with Autism Spectrum Disorders.

Behavioral Characteristics of Population Autism Spectrum Disorders (ASD)

DEFINITION	Is a complex Neurobiological Disorder • defined by a "triad" of deficits (Volkmar, 2005) in: – communication, social interaction, and repetitive behavior. The signs vary enormously among individuals; hence the term *spectrum* is used to reflect the wide range of occurrence and severity of these difficulties. • Difficulties in sensory integration (Iarocci and McDonald, 2006), receive information about a space based on all of their senses collectively: smell, sight, taste, sound, touch, and proprioception—interference with comprehending how to act (Iarocci and McDonald, 2006). • Experience synesthesia—i.e. smelling a color.

BEHAVIOR	**COMMUNICATION** • Delayed or lack of ability to use speech for social communication or the use of speech in a non-functional manner. Sensory Integration: **GESTALT PERCEPTION** • A weak central coherence involves the inability to integrate details into a meaningful whole (Mostafa, 2008). • Focus on parts rather than the whole (Kanner, 1943). • Memory is often stored as an unprocessed, un-interpreted image (Bogdashina, 2003). **PERIPHERAL PERCEPTION** • Prefer indirect eye contact—mono-processing; forcing eye-contact may lead to sensory overload or system shutdown (Jackson, 2002, p70). **HYPO-SENSITIVE** • Appear to be under-responsive, as if certain sensory information goes unnoticed or certain senses are impaired. **HYPER-SENSITIVE** • Over-responsive to sensory stimuli and overwhelmed by incoming sensory information (Bogdashina, 2010); "the intense world syndrome." • Inability to regulate volume; difficulty using an appropriate speaking volume or volume when listening to music or watching television, either too loud or too quiet, regardless of the presence of background noise (Talay-Ongan and Wood, 2000). • Repetitive speech and excessive noises (Echolalia) (Grandin, 2006). • Delayed processing of stimuli from any sensory stimulus and misunderstanding true meaning; takes communication literally; misunderstands idioms.

high threshold for response to stimuli.[8] SID is responsible for self-injury, self-stimulation, and stereotypic behaviors among people with autism due to faulty integration of sensory information.[9] These maladaptive behaviors are used to counteract the restricted sensory input or to avoid over-stimulation. Sensory integration is also referred to as sensory processing.

People with ASD are sensitive to the environment they encounter, as they have difficulty with the process of managing the information they get from the world.[10] Often the manner in which they perceive or come to know and adjust to spaces is uncomfortable, and they are confronted by an ongoing battle to conform and adjust to spaces that are not considerate of their neurological abilities and sensory sensitivities. For many, their perceptions are challenges due to sensory processing. The sensory input they experience through

their eyes and ears, for example, can make the built environment a distracting and even frightening place. These sensory inhibitions are suspected to be the reason many people with ASD find social engagements challenging given "looking and listening remains the most important activities for exploring the physical and social environment."[11] Many individuals within the spectrum employ coping mechanisms in the form of rigid and repetitive behaviors to deal with incoming sensory stimuli. To an outsider, these behaviors appear like an inappropriate tantrum, when in actuality, they are the result of an "imbalance between the environment and an individual's ability to adapt to it."[12] Architecture and interior spaces can be modified to positively influence individuals with ASD by modifying factors such as color, texture, sense of closure, orientation, acoustics, ventilation, etc.[13]

BEHAVIOR	SOCIAL SKILLS
	• Difficulties with social interaction; experience a sort of "mind-blindness" in that they lack the ability to understand that others have thoughts and beliefs (Frith, 2003).
	• Avoid interaction in social settings because of a sensory overload and their inability to discern the whole from the parts.
	• Avoid social interaction especially in larger groups, because they fear unwanted tactile contact or want to avoid uncomfortable volume levels if they have auditory sensitivities. However, one study disagreed, stating that there was no relationship between sensory deficits and social and communicative symptoms of autism (Rogers, Hepburn, & Wehner, 2003).
	REPETITIVE
	• Stereotypical movements such as arm flapping, finger flicking, or ritualized pacing and a narrow range of interest (Leekam, Uljarevic, and Prior, 2011).
	• Often enacted to generate a sensory experience or to try to maintain control over their environment after sensory overload has taken place (Gabriels et al., 2008).
	• Self-injurious body movements, compulsive behaviors, and limited, almost obsessive interests (Gabriels, et al., 2008).
	• Self-injurious behaviors, such as head banging.
	• Stemming adherence to certain routines or rituals, insistence on the same foods and wearing only certain types of clothing (Leekam, Uljarevic, and Prior, 2011).
	• Having objects and items in order (i.e. personal treasure mementos in the same place in their bedrooms; hoarding).
PHYSICAL Characteristics/ Health	• Defensive when touched by others and prefer to initiate and control all physical contact themselves (Talay-Ongan and Wood, 2000).
PREVALENCE	• Complex neurobiological disorder—signs of ASD vary enormously among individuals—wide range of occurrence and severity of these difficulties.
	• Pervasive disorder—way of living.
	• 1 in 88, according to the Center for Disease Controls in the U.S.
DEMOGRAPHIC	• Boys are four to five times more likely than girls to have autism.

Environmental Perception in ASD

Perception is one of the disciplines within psychology that informs the design of space for people. The goal of perception studies is to understand how stimuli from the world interacts with sensory systems. Research in perception frequently focuses on the relations between environmental events and a subjective experience. Understanding perception is essential for all areas within design.

The study of space design is closely linked with psychology and sociology. Four notable discourses have influenced the theory of proxemics. These include Altman's Privacy Theories,[14] Hall's proxemics theories,[15] Sommer's work in social design and personal space,[16] and Appleton's research in territory.[17] How one perceives their environment is based on many factors associated with proxemics. Like

NT people, individuals with ASD develop a variety of perspectives on their environment. They know when it is a right fit for them and whether it is comfortable and homelike. Their caregivers also know when something in a space irritates a person with ASD as they often elicit behaviors that demonstrate their dissatisfaction. One of the biggest factors in discomfort and QOL is a lack of privacy, personal space, and a feeling of infringement on one's territory. Hall says it is "universal and contributes to the meeting of other human needs such as security, affiliation, and esteem."[18]

A detailed outline of the behavior characteristics of people with ASD are outlined in Table 4.1. This overview provides professionals who design spaces for these populations with a condensed account of common characteristics that need to be acknowledged to create environments that provide a person–environment fit.

Spatial Perception is one's ability to evaluate how built fixtures, structures, and objects are arranged in space, and translate the information to make up a comprehension of the whole environment. People with ASD are often challenged with spatial perception, and as a result, they may use their body to register where they are in time and space (proprioception) and to control their balance (vestibular). "Where am I? Where am I going? How do I get there?" are the questions all people ask themselves when developing their spatial perception. A study by Lind, Williams, Raber, and Bowler showed significantly diminished performance with a task related to theory of mind and episodic memory.[19] This study suggests that individuals with ASD have impaired survey-based navigation skills manifested in difficulties with generating cognitive maps of the environment. Similarly, Bourne observed that individuals with ASD living in residential/work communities with campus-like settings frequently adhered to regular pathways of travel when traveling by foot and had great hesitation with changing the route they regularly took.[20]

Environmental Cognition in ASD

Cognitive challenges frequently include substantial limitation in one's capacity to think, including conceptualizing, planning, and sequencing thoughts and actions, remembering and interpreting subtle social cues, and understanding numbers and symbols. In the United States, more than twenty million people have a cognitive disability. The number of individuals with cognitive disabilities is expected to increase rapidly as the nation's population ages.[21] Cognitive disabilities are sometimes noted as characteristics of people diagnosed with ASD. For individuals on the spectrum, the limitations are due to the manner in which the neurons in their brains are hardwired, and cause them to process information differently.

Interaction with the environment stimulates all senses and enables people to construct knowledge about the world. Perception of the world is constructed through "experiences, memories, and cognitive processes."[22] Hearing the sound of an ambulance horn, for example, stimulates the sensory nerves in the ear, but one's ears do not recognize it as an ambulance horn. The sound of an ambulance horn is recognized through previous experience of the sound or similar sounds and the cognitive processes. Interestingly,

for most NT people this happens naturally. Similarly, spaces, finishes, and materials can evoke perceptions that enhance memory and understanding. The memory stores a perception as an unprocessed, interpreted image, and a trigger may bring that memory to the forefront. NT individuals may smell a particular food cooking, for example, and momentarily think back to a time when exposed to the same aroma. However, for a person with ASD, no one particular moment is recalled due to the Gestalt perception they experience. According to Bogdashina, "autistic memory is often described as associative memory."[23] However, if an environmental stimulus was connected with something unpleasant or painful, a person may throw a tantrum, which might appear to be happening "out of the blue."[24]

The literality of people with autism with regard to understanding speech is well known. Literalism can apply to any of the senses. This means they use the sense but do not interpret it. For example, an individual with ASD may view a picture and be able to describe the picture, but may have no comprehension of what the picture may represent. Similarly, they may hear words and be able to regurgitate them with little effort, but not have a realization of what has been said.

All of the behavioral challenges noted in the Characteristics of ASD chart (Table 4.1) point to difficulties with cognition processing (neurological processing) and achieving the optimum quality of life (QOL). Intellectual disability is regarded as a condition of arrested cognitive growth commencing in the developmental years of early and young childhood.[25] People with ASD often appear like they have arrested cognitive growth, but in a lot of cases they do not. In fact, many people with ASD excel in areas of intelligence and are known to have "islands of intelligence," and several are known to have "multiple islands of intelligence."[26] The brain often resists making new connections and instead strengthens existing ones to the point where children with autism may become experts in one or more areas. This explains the "geek syndrome" of focusing on a small island of knowledge to the detriment of all other aspects of life. Many people with ASD are unable to generalize situations. Transfer of knowledge and experience occurs in isolation and is not necessarily applied to new and similar types of situations.

Cognitive processing or intelligence in people with ASD has recently been referred to as "differently knowing" and is now referred to as a neurodiversity (ND). One who is ND is not disordered; rather, they possess a different sort of ordering system. The brain of a person diagnosed with ND is wired differently, making it difficult for them to perceive and relate to situations and people in their environment. By using the concept of neurodiversity to account for individual neurological differences, we create a discourse whereby labeled people may be seen in terms of their strengths as well as their weaknesses.[27] In intentional communities, individuals with ND are celebrated and a concerted effort is made to match the individuals with jobs and training that match their aptitudes.

Environmental Sensation in ASD

The Perceptual Architecture Theory outlines the five main senses of sight, hearing, touch, smell, and taste plus two lesser known sensory systems, the vestibular system and the proprioceptive system. The vestibular system relates to the positioning of the head in relation to the body. The proprioceptive system relates to the position and movement of the body in relation to space and objects. People with ASD are sensitive to the environment they encounter due to a difficulty with the process of organizing the information they get from their bodies and from the world around them.[28]

Individuals with ASD are often described as having a low-hyper-sensitive[29] or high-hypo-sensitive threshold for response to stimuli.[30] If they are hyper-sensitive, they are over-reactive to stimuli pertaining to the five senses, and if they are hypo-sensitive, they are under-reactive to stimuli pertaining to the five senses. Many experience both extremes in the same sense; they may be hyper-sensitive at one point in time and hypo-sensitive at another. These limitations make it difficult for them to perceive their environment and develop spatial relationships and to orientate themselves relative to their surroundings. Table 2.2 (overleaf) summarizes commonly identified observable behaviors that can inform the design on spaces of the ASD sector of the population under study.

Hyper- and hypo-sensitivities may disrupt the QOL and disrupt the ability to live comfortably and learn. An individual can suffer from hyper-sensitivity in any particular sense. In fact, two extremes may occur. One can be disturbed by the stimulus or fascinated by the stimulus. The fascination appears to exert a calming effect.[31] Many individuals like to spin or gaze at certain items and lose themselves in the stimulus. Others are so sensitive to stimuli that it interferes with daily living. The feel of their clothing may be unbearable.

The typical method of treating hyper- and hypo-sensitivities would be by a course of either desensitization or stimulation. However, in individuals with ASD, the sensitivities may alternate between hyper or hypo. Often, this varies depending on their circumstances. These inconsistencies in responses to the environment pose many challenges for designers who design environments for people with ASD, as it is difficult to design for both sensitivities. The compromise is to find commonalities and address them in shared spaces and reserve specific accommodations/applications for their individual personal spaces.

Practical Applications for Designers

Gathering information and processing is a complex process. The procedure requires constant engagement of the senses as one has to go through the process of examining, re-examining, sifting, and filtering of external stimulus. The activity requires an interface and interconnection between a person and their environment. As the information comes into the brain, the information is organized into patterns of recognition and leads to understanding of a particular situation (cognition). An important part of this learning process is the development of spatial cognition/perception. This is developed through the proprioceptive system.

The field of cognitive psychology is an area of study that examines how people mentally represent their experience and then use these representations to function effectively. Neisser believed that people bring their past knowledge and their biases to understanding the environment they encounter and that cognitive exploration requires one to perceive, imagine, think, remember, form concepts, and solve problems to understand a setting and situation (spatial perception).[32]

Academic studies and anecdotal accounts of one's physical environment have demonstrated the importance of the aesthetic and physical properties on one's perception. The insights and findings can inform designers and architects on the organization of physical space. Accounts of the various ways one's environment has effects on the environmental experience, particularly how it affects people's perceptions, evaluations, and behavior in their surroundings, have been documented in a variety of ways. Lowenthal and Riel,[33] Bourassa,[34] Russel,[35] and Groat[36] stressed the importance aesthetic

Table 4.2 Common Difficulties with Sensory Systems: Observable Behaviors.

COMMON DIFFICULTIES WITH SENSORY SYSTEMS: OBSERVABLE BEHAVIORS

HYPER-REACTIVE BEHAVIOR INDICATORS	HYPO-REACTIVE BEHAVIOR INDICATORS
AUDITORY SYSTEM	
• easily distracted by background sounds	• does not respond to name being spoken
• overreacts to sounds	• seems oblivious to sounds of surrounding activities
• unpredictable reactions to sounds	• creates constant sounds as if to stimulate self
• holds hands over ears to block noise	• unsafe because does not react to sounds indicating potential danger
• screams or cries at sounds in the environment	• does not respond to any kind of sound
• responds physically as if sound is a threat	
VISUAL SYSTEM	
• disturbed by bright lighting	• unaware of the presence of other people
• avoids sunlight	• unable to locate desired objects, people
• follows any movement in the room with eyes	• loses sight of people or objects when they move
• blocks field of vision with eyes	• cannot distinguish figure–ground relationships
• covers part of visual field—puts hands over part of the page in a book	
• responds physically to appearance of certain objects or colors	
TACTILE SYSTEM	
• touch defensive—does not like to be touched	• does not seem to grasp concept of personal space
• avoids tasks with strong tactile element (clay, water play, paint, food preparation)	• does not seem to notice touch of others
• complains about discomfort of clothing	• frequently puts things into mouth
• refuses to wear certain items—tugs at clothes	• does not adjust clothing that would seem to be an irritant
• responds negatively to textures in foods, toys, furniture	• high pain threshold, unaware of danger because of low response to pain
VESTIBULAR SYSTEM	
• overreacts to movement activities	• seems to need constant movement
• has difficulties navigating on different surfaces (carpets, grass, etc.)	• rocks, travels in circles
• walks close to wall, clings to supports such as banisters	• seems to tire easily when engaged in movement activities
• seems to be fearful when movement is expected, muscles seem tense	• generally slow to move, lethargic in movement
• rigid about positioning of body, keeps head in same rigid angle	• takes long time to respond to directions to move
• seems to become physically disoriented easily	
GUSTATORY and OLFACTORY SYSTEMS	
• eats a limited variety of foods	• seems to be constantly wanting food
• gags, refuses foods	• licks objects in the environment
• difficulties with oral hygiene	• chews on objects inappropriately
• spits out foods, medications	• high threshold for bad tastes—dangerous substances are not avoided
• overreacts to smells in environment	• sniffs objects and people in unusual ways
• smell-defensive—will avoid places or people with strong odors	• does not seem to notice smells others notice

properties have on users of a space. Their work demonstrates that responses differ among groups of perceivers. Therefore, individuals with ASD should be consulted on their preferences and needs when designing spaces for them.

Notes

1. Ruble, Lisa A., and Dana M. Robson. "Individual and environmental determinants of engagement in autism." *Journal of autism and developmental disorders* 37, no. 8 (2007): 1457–1468.

2. May, Mike. *Sensation and perception.* Infobase Publishing, 2009.

3. Kopec, David Alan. *Environmental psychology for design.* New York: Fairchild, 2006.

4. Nanda, U. *Sensthetics: A crossmodal approach to sensory design.* Saarbrücken, Germany: Lighting Source, 2008, 48.

5. Iarocci, Grace, and John McDonald. "Sensory integration and the perceptual experience of persons with autism." *Journal of autism and developmental disorders* 36, no. 1 (2006): 77–90.

6. Ayres, A. J. *Sensory integration and learning disabilities.* Los Angeles: Western Psychological Services, 1972.

7. Kern, Janet K., Madhukar H. Trivedi, Carolyn R. Garver, Bruce D. Grannemann, Alonzo A. Andrews, Jayshree S. Savla, Danny G. Johnson, Jyutika A. Mehta, and Jennifer L. Schroeder. "The pattern of sensory processing abnormalities in autism." *Autism* 10, no. 5 (2006): 480–494.

8. Watling, Renee L., Jean Deitz, and Owen White. "Comparison of sensory profile scores of young children with and without autism spectrum disorders."*American journal of occupational therapy* 55, no. 4 (2001): 416–423.

9. Ayres, A. J. *Sensory integration and learning disabilities.* Los Angeles: Western Psychological Services, 1972.

10. Kranowitz, Carol, and Lucy Miller. *The out-of-sync child: Recognizing and coping with Sensory Processing Disorder.* Skylight Press, 2005.

11. Frith, Uta. Autism: Towards an explanation of the enigma (2nd ed.) Madrid: Alianza Editorial, 2006. p. 170.

12. Mostafa, Magda. "An architecture for autism: Concepts of design intervention for the autistic user." *Archnet-IJAR: International journal of architectural research* 2, no. 1 (2008): 189–211.

13. Mostafa, Magda. "An architecture for autism: Concepts of design intervention for the autistic user." *Archnet-IJAR: International journal of architectural research* 2, no. 1 (2008): 189–211.

14. Altman, Irwin. *The environment and social behavior: Privacy, personal space, territory, and crowding.* Brooks/Cole Publishing, 1975.

15. Hall, Edward T. *The silent language.* Garden City, NY: Doubleday, 1959.

16. Sommer, Robert. *Personal space. The behavioral basis of design.* Prentice-Hall, 1969.

17. Appleton, Jay. *The experience of landscape.* New York: John Wiley & Sons, 1975.

18. Hall, Edward T. *The silent language.* Garden City, NY: Doubleday, 1959.

19. Lind, Sophie E., David M. Williams, Jacob Raber, Anna Peel, and Dermot M. Bowler. "Spatial navigation impairments among intellectually high-functioning adults with autism spectrum disorder: Exploring relations with theory of mind, episodic memory, and episodic future thinking." *Journal of abnormal psychology* 122, no. 4 (2013): 1189.

20. Bourne, Angela. "Neuro-considerate environments for adults with intellectual developmental diversities: An integrated design approach to support wellbeing." PhD diss., Texas Tech University, 2013.

21. Braddock, D., R. Hemp, M. C. Rizzolo, E. S. Tanis, L. Haffer, and J. Wu. *The state of the states in intellectual and developmental disabilities: Emerging from the great recession.* Washington DC: American Association on Intellectual and Developmental Disabilities (AAIDD), 2015.

22. Bogdashina, Olga. *Sensory perceptual issues in autism and Asperger Syndrome: Different sensory experiences, different perceptual worlds.* Jessica Kingsley Publishers, 2003. p. 37.

23. Bogdashina, Olga. *Sensory perceptual issues in autism and Asperger Syndrome: Different sensory experiences, different perceptual worlds.* Jessica Kingsley Publishers, 2003. p. 108.

24. O'Neill, Jasmine Lee. *Through the eyes of aliens: A book about autistic people.* Jessica Kingsley Publishers, 1999.

25. Felce, David. *A comprehensive guide to intellectual and developmental disabilities.* Ivan Brown and Maire Ede Percy, eds. PH Brookes, 2007.

26. Treffert, D. A. *Islands of genius: The bountiful mind of the autistic, acquired, and sudden savant.* Jessica Kingsley Publishers, 2010.

27. Armstrong, Thomas. *The power of neurodiversity: Unleashing the advantages of your differently wired brain.* Da Capo Press, 2011.

28. Kranowitz, Carol, and Lucy Miller. *The out-of-sync child: Recognizing and coping with Sensory Processing Disorder.* Skylight Press, 2005.

29. Kern, Janet K., Madhukar H. Trivedi, Carolyn R. Garver, Bruce D. Grannemann, Alonzo A. Andrews, Jayshree S. Savla, Danny G. Johnson, Jyutika A. Mehta, and Jennifer L. Schroeder. "The pattern of sensory processing abnormalities in autism." *Autism* 10, no. 5 (2006): 480–494.

30. Watling, Renee L., Jean Deitz, and Owen White. "Comparison of sensory profile scores of young children with and without autism spectrum disorders."*American journal of occupational therapy* 55, no. 4 (2001): 416–423.

31. Bogdashina, Olga. *Sensory perceptual issues in autism and Asperger Syndrome: Different sensory experiences, different perceptual worlds.* Jessica Kingsley Publishers, 2003.

32. Neisser, U. *Cognitive psychology.* New York: Appleton-Century-Crofts, 1966.

33. Lowenthal, David, and Marquita Riel. "The nature of perceived and imagined environments." *Environment and behavior* 4, no. 2 (1972): 189–207.

34. Bourassa, Steven C. *The aesthetic of landscape.* London and New York: Belhaven Press, 1991.

35. Russell, Robert L. "Children's philosophical inquiry into defining art: A quasi-experimental study of aesthetics in the elementary classroom." *Studies in art education* 29, no. 3 (1988): 282–291.

36. Groat, L. "Contextual compatibility in architecture: An issue of personal taste." In *Environmental aesthetics: Theory, research, and applications* (pp. 228–254). Cambridge University Press, 1988.

PART 2

Designing for the Senses

Sight

Sight is the sensory system that one uses to see their surroundings, such as nature, objects, and people. Vision is the most widely used sense by the general population. Visual sensitivities are not as commonly exhibited as auditory or tactile sensitivities by individuals with ASD. However, symptoms can be incredibly disruptive and challenging to cope with for individuals that exhibit them. Like most sensory symptoms, visual sensitivities can mostly be categorized as hyper-sensitive or hypo-sensitive. Individuals on the spectrum may exhibit visual hyper-sensitivities by appearing to notice everything in the environment and intensely focusing on the most minute of visual details. Visual hyper-sensitivities may also be exhibited by a difficulty making eye contact because of the intolerance for the movement of another person's eyes.[1] Some symptoms can be demonstrated as early as infancy, though the child is not typically diagnosed until about age three. Early features include avoiding eye contact, using peripheral vision to examine objects or people, and "inefficient eye gaze."[2]

Contrary to the often overwhelming effects of visual hyper-sensitivity, visual hypo-sensitivity is almost like possessing a visual impairment. Those with visual hypo-sensitivity may disregard people and objects in the environment, as if they are not there at all, or only see the outlines of objects. Some individuals may also enjoy bright colors and bright lights, things that would be overwhelming, even terrifying for an individual with visual hyper-sensitivity. As with all sensory symptoms, both hyper- and hypo-sensitivities, occurrence and severity of visual sensitivities vary widely. Table 5.1 overleaf summarizes these symptoms.

Many individuals with ASD show heightened visual spatial functioning associated with right hemispheric dominance or right brain/global learning.[3, 4] A number of studies examining environmental preferences in right brain/global learners and left brain/analytic processors find that relationships exist between cognitive style and environmental preferences.[5, 6, 7, 8, 9] People with spatial strengths are able to visually manipulate images in their minds and understand complex patterns.[10] They have a high level of creativity, which is a prerequisite for unique problem solving and their ability to contribute to new knowledge. The fields of engineering, architecture, chemistry, physics, and medical surgery all rely on spatial skills.[11]

Table 5.1 Common Difficulties with Sensory Systems: Observable Behaviors.

COMMON DIFFICULTIES WITH SENSORY SYSTEMS: OBSERVABLE BEHAVIORS

HYPER-REACTIVE BEHAVIOR INDICATORS	HYPO-REACTIVE BEHAVIOR INDICATORS
VISUAL SYSTEM	VISUAL SYSTEM
• disturbed by bright lighting	• unaware of the presence of other people
• avoids sunlight	• unable to locate desired objects, people
• follows any movement in the room with eyes	• loses sight of people or objects when they move
• blocks field of vision with eyes	• cannot distinguish figure–ground relationships
• covers part of visual field—puts hands over part of the page in a book	
• responds physically to appearance of certain objects or colors	

LIGHTING

Lighting is one of the most important components of design and one of the factors that most greatly influences how a space will be perceived. This is partially because lighting allows various elements in an environment to be seen.[12, 13] All forms of light in an environment can be categorized as either natural or artificial light. Arguably, the most important aspect of lighting in design is control. For example, most people prefer ample amounts of natural light in a space. But a space with multiple windows that do not have any window treatments, or any means to control the light, would be useless and undesirable.

Natural Light

Lighting is a very important part of the built environment, especially for individuals with ASD, as research has shown that they could be more sensitive to light output changes, and repetitive behaviors sometimes increase under fluorescent light sources.[14] Environments that only have artificial illumination and lack natural light increase stress and discomfort.[15] Natural light is much more beneficial than artificial light for reducing stress and discomfort and improving attitude and performance.[16] Overall, natural light has a positive influence on people. However, designers should be considerate of views when incorporating windows in a space to allow for natural light, as some views may pose a distraction. For example, in the classroom, views of the playground from the windows can be a distraction.[17] Clerestory windows can be installed in some cases or draperies added to already existing windows in order to provide natural light but minimize distracting views from the window. Tufvesson and Tufvesson also found in their research that several windows and doors on all of the walls in an environment can be stressful, but several windows side by side on the same wall were positive and a good source of daylight.[18] This may be because with a variety of different views, too much information may be coming in from windows on opposite walls. Having too many windows in a space is also likely to result in an overabundance of natural light that is sometimes difficult to control.

Artificial Light

In terms of artificial light, most fluorescent light sources cause flicker.[19] Visual hyper-sensitivity and repetitive behaviors were noted in areas with fluorescent lighting.[20, 21] Even though some of this flicker is not consciously perceived by most people, it can still cause headaches and eye strain and reduce academic performance.[22] Eye strain can eventually negatively affect sleep patterns.[23] Kuller and Laike concluded that children may be more sensitive to flicker than adults, so high-frequency fluorescent ballasts that do not flicker should be used in classrooms.

In a pilot study, researchers at the Scottsdale Unified School District installed sixty 2x2-foot flat-panel LED fixtures in four special education classrooms.[24] They found that the use of LED lighting saved energy by 60 percent and prevented students with autism from being bothered by the flicker associated with fluorescent fixtures. The panels produced a color temperature of 3500K and emitted 3850 lumens of brightness. Winterbottom and Wilkins identified lamps with a color temperature of 3500 K as being preferred.[25] Teachers reportedly favor soft lighting because they observe more relaxed behavior and better academic focus under dim lighting. In addition, classrooms should be equipped with blinds or drapes that can be adjusted to allow the desired amount of natural light to enter the space. If possible, dimmer switches should also be provided in classrooms to control levels of light. Winterbottom and Wilkins and Shabha and Gaines found that an overwhelming majority of teachers desired more control of light in their classrooms.[26, 27]

Angela Bourne, PhD observed that in a home for seven men with autism, the men preferred to keep the light levels very low. They also kept their blinds closed in their bedrooms and partially closed in the living areas. It appeared that they did not like brightly lit spaces.[28] Additionally, Shabha and Gaines determined that visual triggers influence the behavior of students with ASD.[29] The source of light (flickering light, direct sunlight), intensity of light, and luminance (reflection, shine, fluorescent glare) were found to have the greatest effect on behavior. A variety of light sources, such as overhead (general) lighting, natural light, task lighting, and softer lamp light, allows easier control of light.

Glare and Reflection

Glare occurs when one area of the visual environment is brighter than the general brightness of the rest of the environment.[30] Glare can come from artificial or natural sources, and the reflection off of surfaces is also considered glare. Individuals with neurodiversities may be distracted by sunlight coming in through the windows. As individuals on the spectrum pass down hallways in public spaces, glare from the light reflecting off of surfaces may blur the lines of definition in the architecture and furnishings.

Using a glazed or frosted glass will allow natural light to enter the space without creating sharp shadows or glare and will also diminish visually distracting views.[31] Some window coverings, like blinds, create what is described as "pattern glare."[32] Other sources of glare can come from desks and other surfaces and even from the dry erase board. To reduce glare on wall-mounted white boards, Winterbottom and Wilkins recommend mounting the board so that it tilts away from the wall by five to ten degrees.[33] Using matte surfaces, such as matte paint, carpet, or wall coverings made of fabric, will also reduce glare.

COLOR

Color is one of the most influential aspects of an environment with both psychological and physiological reactions. Figure 5.1 illustrates a color wheel with primary, secondary, and tertiary colors. Visible colors are seen through the cones of the eye. Red, blue, and green cones translate millions of colors. As a result, an individual will experience emotional and psychological responses to color.[34]

Half of the color wheel is classified as warm and the other half as cool. Figure 5.2 illustrates color temperature. Colors associated with red and yellow are considered warm. Warm colors advance in a space. Cool colors are associated with blue and green and tend to recede. Visual temperature may also be affected by intensity.[35] Lighting also has an effect on color perception and temperature. Placing a blue object under a light with blue wavelengths such as a cool fluorescent will heighten the blueness of the object. However, if a red object is placed under this same light, it will appear gray since no red color waves are being made by the light. Dr. Albert Styne's research showed that a space painted cool colors under cool fluorescent lighting resulted in spaces that seemed larger, quieter, and cooler.[36] A space with warm colors under warm incandescent lighting resulted in a more active space that seemed smaller, warmer, and louder. Purity and contrast were found to be more important than color temperature in other studies. For example, an intense green may stimulate people as much as an intense red.[37] Quantity of color is another consideration in the design of the physical environment. Verghese stated that large amounts of color overstimulate individuals no matter the color temperature or preference.[38]

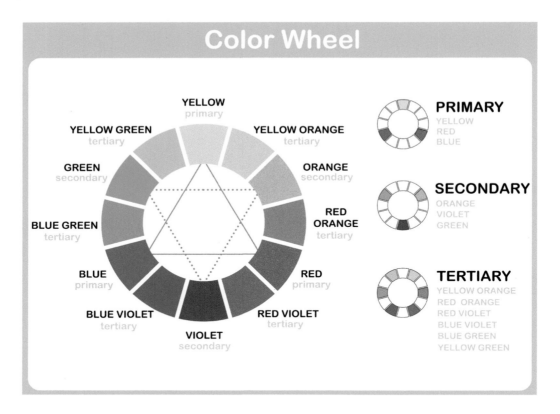

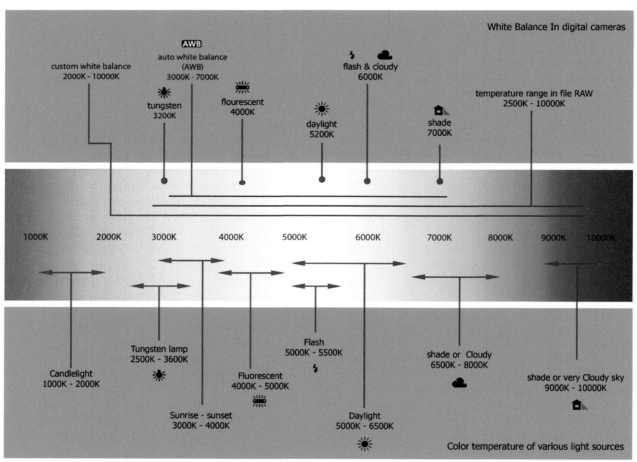

5.1 (facing page, top)
Color Wheel Worksheet—Red Blue Yellow color

5.2 (facing page, bottom)
Color temperature chart

People generally dislike both overly saturated colored spaces and monotone, colorless spaces.[39] Studies show that students strongly dislike stark white walls.[40] However, it is widely known that bright colors can be painful or distracting for the visually hypersensitive. Most research indicates that light, warm, neutral colors are best.[41] Other researchers suggest that one wall in particular, preferably the wall that will be in a student's immediate line of sight when they look up from their work, be painted a medium hue and the remaining walls in neutral hues.[42] In her autobiography, Temple Grandin reveals that she enjoyed having bright colors in her classrooms, but that they may be too stimulating for a "lower functioning" student.[43] When it comes to classroom settings, the use of color should primarily be for function.[44] For visually hyposensitive students, color can be used for wayfinding or as a tool to locate objects in the classroom. For example, colored tape can be used to delineate pathways around the room. Color can also be used in a controlled way as a reward or motivation. Benedyk, Woodcock, and Woolner conducted a study in which a lighting system was installed that floods the room with a student's favorite color.[45] A system such as this could be activated upon successful completion of a task. Another study identified students with ASD whose academic performance improved drastically when they used colored glasses or colored overlays on school papers.[46] Color choices for these kinds of alternative applications should be based on personal preference. Most environments for children reflect the color preferences of adults.[47]

Physiological Reactions to Color

The effects of color are far-reaching beyond aesthetics. Studies related to color effects have shown changes in blood pressure, eye strain, and brain development. The brain releases a hormone that affects our moods, mental clarity, and energy level when color is transmitted through the eyes.[48] Exposure to red causes the heart to beat faster, an increase in blood pressure, and heightened sense of smell. In contrast, blue causes the pulse rate to slow, and body temperature lowers. Pink has caused the suppression of aggressive behavior in prisoners.[49] A German study found that students with ADHD had "distorted color discrimination abilities."[50] Color could be a potential area for research for individuals on the spectrum to determine if their perception of color differs from the NT population.

Many individuals with ASD rely on their vision to make sense of their world. The use of visual aids such as used in TEACCH (discussed further in Chapter 10) are widely employed. The pictorial images help the people with ASD identify the steps and actions needed to complete a task. Individuals may carry wallet-sized, fold-up formats of their pictorial agendas and may post them in various areas in their personal space. Pictorial communication is widely used in kitchens and bathrooms.

Psychological Reactions to Color

Psychological responses to color include changes in mood and attention. The brain releases a hormone affecting moods, mental clarity, and energy level when color is transmitted through the eyes.[51] A study by Woodcock, Georgiou, Jackson, and Woolner[52] identified differences in "lower functioning" and "higher functioning" children on the spectrum. Their findings revealed that

- lower functioning children preferred the color red, round shapes, and sound/light equipment
- higher functioning children preferred the color blue and circular shapes

One proponent of providing subdued color schemes for children with autism is A. J. Paron-Wildes, Allied Member American Society of Interior Designers (ASID). She is the parent of a child with autism and has researched ways to make the environment more calming. She states that making environments appropriate for children on the spectrum benefits those with ADHD and that all children benefit from these environmental measures.[53]

SPACE ORGANIZATION

Legible Environment

Legible environments are simple and straightforward for navigation so that the user is not left wondering which activities and behaviors are most appropriate for that space. Designing truly legible spaces involves understanding that people with ASD think differently and

react differently to stimuli. Color and light are valuable wayfinding tools. "Color coded" buildings in which different floors have different color schemes would be an example.

A method called spatial sequencing reorganizes a space to promote routine.[54] When people begin to know what to expect in each space, transitions/routines become more predictable and less stressful. This is particularly true for individuals with ASD. Spatial sequencing involves dividing a classroom into different zones, with each zone having only one function or activity. The individuals will begin to associate an activity with a specific area or zone, which will then ease transitions between activities, protect routine patterns, and promote predictability.[55]

Sensory Integration and "Escape" Spaces

Sensory Integration spaces are based on sensory integration therapy, an idea that emphasizes the connection between sensory experiences and motor and behavioral performance.[56] Sensory integration therapy helps to calm children that are usually under-reactive to sensory stimulation and help build tolerance in children who are overly reactive. Sensory integration spaces are also called multi-sensory rooms or Snoezelen rooms. These rooms are the opposite of escape spaces. They are gently stimulating environments that are designed for interaction and to engage the senses. Multi-sensory rooms are beneficial to individuals not just with ASD,

but also with Alzheimer's, cerebral palsy, dementia, and patients with chronic pain or severe brain damage.[57] By providing spaces for children who are hypo-sensitive or sensory-seeking to play and engage their senses, they are less likely to try to generate unsafe sensory experiences elsewhere.[58, 59] These areas especially should be designed around an individual's unique symptoms and preferences. Installing expensive music or sound players in a sensory integration space for a child with primarily tactile sensitivity would be inappropriate and wasteful. The child's specific interests and hobbies should be taken into consideration as well. If the activities within the sensory integration space feel like play and not like therapy or work, the child will be more likely to willingly engage in them. As for what items and activities can take place in a sensory integration space, the ideas are endless. Many rooms have a tactile wall with three-dimensional objects with different textures and sizes to engage tactile senses. Projectors can be used to impose bright colors and patterns on a wall for visual stimulation. Equipment for multi-sensory spaces does not need to cost a fortune as long as it safely engages the child and the child has an interest in using the space. Activities for sensory integration can be as simple as a kiddie pool or box filled with balls.

More modern Snoezelen rooms have sophisticated technology, fiber optics, sound systems, and even an intentional aroma.[60] The sensory room shown in Figure 5.3 has a suspended ceiling that houses lighting designed and programed to change color and can be controlled to meet the needs of the students. The niche

between the wall and the suspended portion of the ceiling conceals the electrical and mechanical systems, thereby creating a less cluttered space. When in operation, the sensory room lighting emits a variety of colors and shapes that engage students' senses and enable them to manage their sensory sensitivities (Figure 5.4). The sensory space in Figure 5.5 allows the entire space to be flooded with a preferred color of light that may be changed based on individual preferences.

5.3 (facing page, top)
Sensory Room, Rio Grande High School, Intensive Support Program (ISP) and School Based Health Clinic (SBHC), Albuquerque, NM

5.4 (above)
Light, color, and shape engage students in sensory rooms. Rio Grande High School, Intensive Support Program (ISP) and School Based Health Clinic (SBHC), Albuquerque, NM. Designed by Design Plus LLC, Albuquerque, NM

5.5 (bottom)
Adjustable Color System, Highland High School, Albuquerque, NM

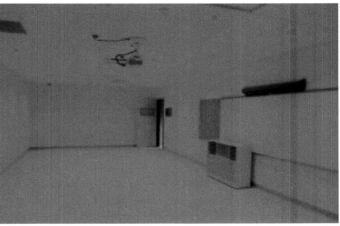

An "escape" space is different from a sensory integration space and is addressed in more detail in Chapter 3. Incorporating escape or break-out spaces into the interior environment may help reduce the impact of overwhelming environmental stimuli. This space may be a small room or a portion of a room. Bookcases and tents are two ways to integrate an escape space into a larger area. This space should have minimal soft furnishings such as bean bag chairs. Individuals with ASD may benefit from having a quiet space to retreat to when feeling overwhelmed with sensory overload from the environment.

DESIGNING FOR VISUAL SENSITIVITY

An individual with visual hyper-sensitivity is likely to be bothered by bright lights, easily distracted by movement, and stare at certain people or objects. Gaines, Curry, Shroyer, Sancibrian, Lock, and Amor identified color, light, and space organization as three visual factors impacting behavior for hyper-sensitive individuals with ASD.[61]

Visual hypo-sensitivity can be thought of as similar to having a visual impairment. Bourne observed that visually hypo-sensitive persons often disregard people or objects in the environment, can see only the outlines of certain objects, and might prefer bright colors and bright sunlight.[62] Designs should be planned accordingly. The participants with ASD frequently avoided eye contact with people and use their eyes more directly to examine objects. Deferential eye gaze and pointing is a prominent observed behavior. This differentiated vision appears to produce distorted perceptions, and individuals were often unaware of the presence of other people when they were involved in tasks such as drawing, painting, and working in a ceramics workshop.

Elements and Principles of Design

Applying the elements and principles of design into the environment may aid in environmental perception and provide visual appeal. The principles of design are abstract concepts that form the theory of design. These principles (scale, proportion, balance, rhythm, emphasis, and harmony) are universally accepted as the means by which we evaluate the elements of design (space, shape, form,

Table 5.2 Applications of the Principles of Design in the Built Environment.

Principle	Application
Scale	Furniture selections are the appropriate size for the user.
Proportion	The use of the golden mean/section (e.g. dado molding placed between 1/2 and 1/3 the height of the wall.
Balance	Symmetrical balance could be achieved by the placement of student desks as a mirror image on both sides of the room. Radial balance may be achieved using round tables with chairs for students. Asymmetrical balance may be achieved with objects of similar visual weight balanced form a central dividing line.
Rhythm	Repetition—Repetition of color, flooring, patterns, rows of seats, windows, doors. Progression—Shapes on floors, walls, and ceilings progressing from small to large or vice versa; shades of color; hallway with many doors. Transition—Crown or dado molding placed without interruption, floor borders. Opposition/contrast—Cabinetry, window frames, angular shapes placed next to rounded shapes. Radiation—Floor coverings, ceilings.
Emphasis	Chalk board or white board in the front of the classroom, workstations. Fireplace or bed in a residential space.
Harmony	Unity and variety are needed to achieve harmony. Unity is achieved through color scheme, consistent furniture styles, background materials have similar feeling. Use of pattern, value, textures are consistent with the master plan. Variety may bring diversity through differing colors, textures, and the contrast of materials. Variety must have order to prevent confusion.

Table 5.3 Applications of the Elements of Design in the Built Environment.

Element	Application
Space	Positive space is filled with color, texture, form, or mass through walls, furnishings, and graphics. Negative space is empty space surrounding positive space — the windows between walls, space between furniture pieces.
	Spaces should be closed off or divide up rooms with partition furnishings. Minimize visual distractions by avoiding open spaces.
	Use spatial sequencing or zoning.
	Provide opportunities to clean up clutter, remove from sight.
Shape and Form	Shape and form may be seen throughout the environment in furnishings, lighting, etc.
Mass	Massing is grouping components to give a more solid appearance.
Line	Lines form the walls, floors and ceiling of a room. Examples include a ceiling or floor pattern, or bookshelves.
Texture	Walls, floors, and furniture have rough or smooth texture.
	Finishes that reflect light and create glare should also be avoided such as matte paints, wall coverings and surfaces. For example: Carpet instead of highly polished tile.
Pattern	Pattern may be seen in fabric, carpet, wall, and floor coverings.
Light	Two sources: Natural and artificial light.
	Correctly placed windows and skylights are necessary to prevent undesirable solar heat gain and visual discomfort.
	Appropriate window coverings will also help to control harsh natural light and resulting glare/reflections.
	Lighting should be flexible (dimmers, multiple switches).
Color	Walls, floors, and decorative elements where color may be applied.
	Personal preference is important.
	For the visually hyper-sensitive bright colors and bold patterns can be distracting and painful.
	Softer hues, neutral colors, subtler patterns/textures.
	Most research indicates that light, warm, neutral colors are best (Vogel, 2008).
	Colors found in nature are most soothing.
	Visually hypersensitive individuals can focus on extraneous detail and become distressed by high amounts of color.
	For visually hypo-sensitive students, color can be used for wayfinding or as a tool to locate objects in the classroom. For example, colored tape can be used to delineate pathways around the room.

mass, line, texture, pattern, light, and color). Both elements and principles are primarily visual aspects of design. However, their use may be perceived through other senses (texture may be perceived through touch or sight, for example). Art, architecture, furniture, and materials have been evaluated using these concepts to determine good design for centuries. [63]

Possible applications of the elements and principles of design for individuals with ASD are summarized in Tables 5.2 and 5.3. Although this list provides practical recommendations, it is not all-inclusive. Additionally, when designing for individuals with ASD, all of the seven senses (hearing, sight, smell, taste, touch, vestibular, and proprioception) should be addressed, not just visual aspects.

Practical Applications for Design

In order to transform a 1950s international style office building into the new Faison School for Autism, Baskervill's design team embraced a research- and collaboration-based design approach. Using standard school requirements as a benchmark, the design team then explored the complexities of autism and its impact on the learning process and environment.

First, a series of "discovery" sessions were conducted, which included faculty, staff, and parents to ensure all points of view were represented. Consistent feedback requested design solutions that were functional, practical, safe, and supportive of the learning process while maintaining a fun, youthful spirit. Next, the collective team toured various schools, day care facilities, and even some unexpected sources of inspiration including restaurants, retail shops, and the Children's Museum of Virginia. Exploring a broad range of kid-friendly environments served as a creative catalyst, inspiring some of the alternative learning features in the final design, such as the exterior courtyard classrooms and caterpillar activity zones. In a focus group setting, color samples and patterns were evaluated and approved. The end result was a warm, residential-inspired palette with colorful accents that would appeal to all ages and sexes. Finally, in conjunction with Dr. Katherine Matthews of the Faison School, the design team hosted a screening and discussion of "Autism Every Day" to raise awareness amongst the design firm and community. The research and knowledge gained during the discovery phase became the conceptual foundation that inspired the final design solutions.

5.6 Lobby area illustrating the cheerful and inviting color palette of Faison School for Autism

The Faison School for Autism is a unique and welcoming learning environment that encompasses the needs of its students, staff, and families alike. The interior palette is bright, cheerful, and inviting. The color palette consists of warm wood floors, buttery yellow walls, and colorful accent glass tiles and paints in shades of blue, aqua, and green. Accent paint colors were assigned strategically throughout the school to assist with wayfinding and functional association. The interior design is a dynamic blend of layered color, texture, and patterns that invite students to explore (Figure 5.6).

Family friendly amenities such as a private play area for visiting siblings, community billboards, and a coffee lounge allow parents to feel at home and network with other families. Specially designed viewing windows were incorporated in classroom walls and doors to allow parental observation of their children's progress without interrupting the classroom routine.

The classroom design is divided into multiple activity zones, each with unique privacy, technology, and storage amenities. The classroom entrance contains custom-designed storage cubbies, a message center for parents, and a semi-private alcove to ease the transition tension before entering the classroom. The "classroom" environment is subdivided into three different teaching areas ranging from collaborative to private. Computer cafés and break-out space for play or special activities are incorporated into each classroom, which allows great flexibility in the daily routine without having to leave the classroom. Glass-walled teacher "workrooms" connect each classroom and offer added storage and staff workspace while constantly allowing staff to maintain visual connection with students.

Corridors were widened and asymmetrically designed to create a meandering, "main street" presence filled with special features to encourage spontaneous learning opportunities (Figures 5.7

5.7 Color used as a landmark in Faison School for Autism, Richmond, Virginia. Designed by Baskervill, Architects & Engineers. Photography by Lee Brauer

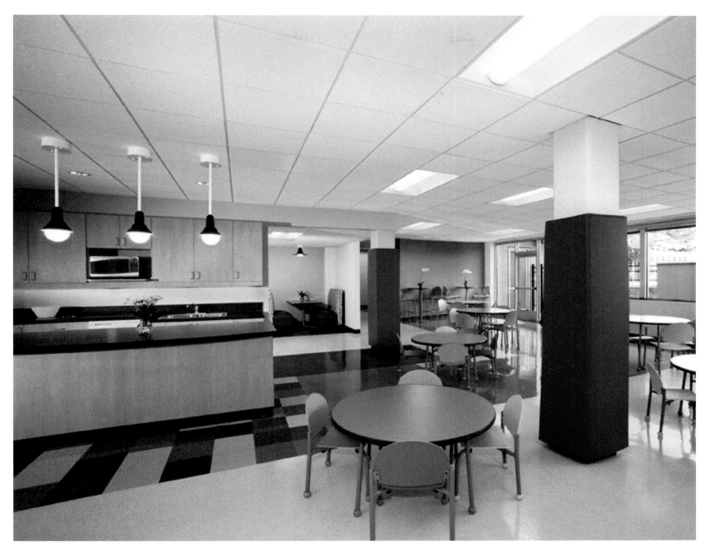

5.8 (facing page)
The inviting color scheme aids with wayfinding in Faison School for Autism, Richmond, Virginia

5.9 The use of accent colors and natural light is implemented into the student café in the Faison School, Richmond, Virginia

and 5.8). Each corridor contains a segmented, serpentine-shaped storage wall with built-in seating and display surfaces, affectionately termed "caterpillars." This unique element creates a collaborative activity center ideal for storytime, special activities, or small group meetings. Tackable display boards line the walls and are highlighted below by custom floor tile insets in multiple colors and shapes forming "learning sidewalks." Conversational "park benches," student artwork display windows, and abundant natural light were finishing touches to the corridor design concept.

The student café is a bright, hip alternative to a conventional cafeteria (Figure 5.9). Various furniture groupings allow students to dine in their choice of group dining tables, two-person bar tables with stools, or a semi-private TV lounge. A residential dining room alcove and a miniature restaurant complete with booths and a menu board creates teaching opportunities for life skills behavior training.

In addition to outdoor playgrounds, the school offers two secure exterior courtyards adjacent to the café and multi-purpose gym. The courtyards offer multiple benefits to the staff and students including outdoor dining, an amphitheater performance platform, herb and flower gardens, and sensory walls utilizing water and tactile objects for teaching purposes.

One of the primary goals of the learning process is comfort and acclimation of the student into everyday life. The Faison School is not intended to be drastically different from the real world. Students

5.10 Exterior view of the Faison School for Autism, Richmond, Virginia

learn through interaction with staff, peers, the environment, and infrastructure. With thoughtful and responsive design, the Faison School for Autism (Figure 5.10) offers the physical stage to support those daily interactions and experiences.

Notes

1. Grandin, Temple. *Thinking in pictures: My life with autism* (expanded edition). New York: Vintage, 2006.

2. Tomchek, Scott D., and Winnie Dunn. "Sensory processing in children with and without autism: A comparative study using the short sensory profile." *American Journal of occupational therapy* 61, no. 2 (2007): 190–200.

3. Mitchell, Peter, and Danielle Ropar. "Visuo-spatial abilities in autism: A review." *Infant and child development* 13, no. 3 (2004): 185–198.

4. Freed, Jeffrey, and Laurie Parsons. *Right–brained children in a left-brained world: Unlocking the potential of your ADD child.* Simon and Schuster, 1998.

5. Lovelace, Maryann Kiely. "Meta-analysis of experimental research based on the Dunn and Dunn model." *The Journal of educational research* 98, no. 3 (2005): 176–183.

6. Rayneri, Letty J., Brian L. Gerber, and Larry P. Wiley. "Gifted achievers and gifted underachievers: The impact of learning style preferences in the classroom." *Prufrock journal* 14, no. 4 (2003): 197–204.

7. Rita, Dunn, and Kenneth Dunn. "Learning styles/teaching styles: Should they… can they… be matched?" *Educational leadership* 36, no. 4 (1979): 238–244.

8. Dunn, Rita, Shirley A. Griggs, Jeffery Olson, Mark Beasley, and Bernard S. Gorman. "A meta-analytic validation of the Dunn and Dunn model of learning-style preferences." *The journal of educational research* 88, no. 6 (1995): 353–362.

9. Carbo, Marie, and Helene Hodges. "Learning styles strategies can help students at risk." *Teaching exceptional children* 20, no. 4 (1988): 55–58.

10. Mann, Rebecca Lyn. "The identification of gifted students with spatial strengths: An exploratory study." UMI ProQuest digital dissertations, 2005.

11. Mann, Rebecca Lyn. "The identification of gifted students with spatial strengths: An exploratory study." UMI ProQuest digital dissertations, 2005.

12. Fielding, Randall. "Learning, lighting and color: Lighting design for schools and universities in the 21st century." *Designshare (NJ1)*. 2006.

13. Lyons, John B. "Do school facilities really impact a child's education." *CEFPI brief, issue trak* (2001): 1–6.

14. Boyce, Peter R. "Review: The impact of light in buildings on human health." *Indoor and built environment* 19, no. 1 (2010): 8–20.

15. Kuller, Rikard, and Thorbjorn Laike. "The impact of flicker from fluorescent lighting on well-being, performance and physiological arousal." *Ergonomics* 41, no. 4 (1998): 433–447.

16. Edwards, L., and Paul A. Torcellini. *A literature review of the effects of natural light on building occupants.* Golden, CO: National Renewable Energy Laboratory, 2002.

17. Tufvesson, Catrin, and Joel Tufvesson. "The building process as a tool towards an all-inclusive school. A Swedish example focusing on children with defined concentration difficulties such as ADHD, autism and Down's syndrome." *Journal of housing and the built environment* 24, no. 1 (2009): 47–66.

18. Tufvesson, Catrin, and Joel Tufvesson. "The building process as a tool towards an all-inclusive school. A Swedish example focusing on children with defined concentration difficulties such as ADHD, autism and Down's syndrome." *Journal of housing and the built environment* 24, no. 1 (2009): 47–66.

19. Winterbottom, Mark, and Arnold Wilkins. "Lighting and discomfort in the classroom." *Journal of environmental psychology* 29, no. 1 (2009): 63–75.

20. Gabriels, Robin L., John A. Agnew, Lucy Jane Miller, Jane Gralla, Zhaoxing Pan, Edward Goldson, James C. Ledbetter, Juliet P. Dinkins, and Elizabeth Hooks. "Is there a relationship between restricted, repetitive, stereotyped behaviors and interests and abnormal sensory response in children with autism spectrum disorders?" *Research in autism spectrum disorders* 2, no. 4 (2008): 660–670.

21. Boyce, Peter R. "Review: The impact of light in buildings on human health." *Indoor and built environment* 19, no. 1 (2010): 8–20.

22. Kuller, Rikard, and Thorbjorn Laike. "The impact of flicker from fluorescent lighting on well-being, performance and physiological arousal." *Ergonomics* 41, no. 4 (1998): 433–447.

23. Boyce, Peter R. "Review: The impact of light in buildings on human health." *Indoor and built environment* 19, no. 1 (2010): 8–20.

24. Castle, S. "LED lighting creates nurturing environment for autistic students." 2014. http://www.k-12techdecisions.com/article/led_lighting_saves_one_school_money_and_creates_a_better_learning_environme.

25. Winterbottom, Mark, and Arnold Wilkins. "Lighting and discomfort in the classroom." *Journal of environmental psychology* 29, no. 1 (2009): 63–75.

26. Shabha, Ghasson, and Kristi Gaines. "A comparative analysis of transatlantic design interventions for therapeutically enhanced learning environments—Texas vs West Midlands." *Facilities* 31, no. 13/14 (2013): 634–658.

27. Winterbottom, Mark, and Arnold Wilkins. "Lighting and discomfort in the classroom." *Journal of environmental psychology* 29, no. 1 (2009): 63–75.

28. Bourne, Angela. "Neuro-considerate environments for adults with intellectual developmental diversities: An integrated design approach to support wellbeing." PhD diss., Texas Tech University, 2013.

29. Shabha, Ghasson, and Kristi Gaines. "A comparative analysis of transatlantic design interventions for therapeutically enhanced learning environments—Texas vs West Midlands." *Facilities* 31, no. 13/14 (2013): 634–658.

30. Winterbottom, Mark, and Arnold Wilkins. "Lighting and discomfort in the classroom." *Journal of environmental psychology* 29, no. 1 (2009): 63–75.

31. Humphreys, Lee. "Cellphones in public: Social interactions in a wireless era." *New media & society* 7, no. 6 (2005): 810–833.

32. Winterbottom, Mark, and Arnold Wilkins. "Lighting and discomfort in the classroom." *Journal of environmental psychology* 29, no. 1 (2009): 63–75.

33. Winterbottom, Mark, and Arnold Wilkins. "Lighting and discomfort in the classroom." *Journal of environmental psychology* 29, no. 1 (2009): 63–75.

34. Nielson, Karla J. and David A. Taylor. *Interiors: An introduction.* New York: McGraw–Hill, 2007.

35. Styne, A. F. "Making light and color work in office harmony." *The office* (1990): 77–78.

36. Styne, A. F. "Making light and color work in office harmony." *The office* (1990): 77–78.

37. Morton, Jill. *Color voodoo for the office.* Colorcom, 1998.

38. Verghese, Preeti. "Visual search and attention: A signal detection theory approach." *Neuron* 31, no. 4 (2001): 523–535.

39. Gaines, Kristi S., and Zane D. Curry. "The inclusive classroom: The effects of color on learning and behavior." *Journal of family & consumer sciences education* 29, no. 1 (2011): 46–57.

40. Maxwell, Lorraine E. "A safe and welcoming school: What students, teachers, and parents think." *Journal of architectural and planning research* 17, no. 4 (2000): 271–282.

41. Vogel, Clare L. "Classroom design for living and learning with autism." *Autism Asperger's digest* 7 (2008).

42. Engelbrecht, K. "The impact of color on learning." *NeoCON2003,* 2003.

43. Grandin, Temple. *Thinking in pictures: My life with autism* (expanded edition). New York: Vintage, 2006.

44. Gaines, Kristi S., and Zane D. Curry. "The inclusive classroom: The effects of color on learning and behavior." *Journal of family & consumer sciences education* 29, no. 1 (2011): 46–57.

45. Benedyk, R., A. Woodcock, and A. Woolner. "Applying the hexagon-spindle model for educational ergonomics to the design of school environments for children with autistic spectrum disorders." *Work journal* 32 (2009): 249–259.

46. Ludlow, Amanda K., and Arnold J. Wilkins. "Case report: color as a therapeutic intervention." *Journal of autism and developmental disorders* 39, no. 5 (2009): 815–818.

47. Read, Marilyn A., and Deborah Upington. "Young children's color preferences in the interior environment." *Early childhood education journal* 36, no. 6 (2009): 491–496.

48. Engelbrecht, K. "The impact of color on learning." *NeoCON2003,* 2003.

49. Walker, Morton. *The power of color.* Avery Publishing Group, 1991.

50. Banaschewski, Tobias, Sinje Ruppert, Rosemary Tannock, Björn Albrecht, Andreas Becker, Henrik Uebel, Joseph A. Sergeant, and Aribert Rothenberger. "Colour perception in ADHD." *Journal of child psychology and psychiatry* 47, no. 6 (2006): 568–572.

51. Engelbrecht, K. "The impact of color on learning." *NeoCON2003,* 2003.

52. Woodcock, A., D. Georgiou, J. Jackson, and A. Woolner. "Designing a tailorable environment for children with autistic spectrum disorders." *The Design Institute, Coventry School of Art and Design, Coventry University, UK.* n.d.

53. Clay, R. A. "No more Mickey Mouse design: Child's environments require unique considerations." *ASID ICON* (2004): 43–47.

54. Mostafa, Magda. "An architecture for autism: Concepts of design intervention for the autistic user." *Archnet-IJAR: International journal of architectural research* 2, no. 1 (2008): 189–211.

55. Khare, Rachna, and Abir Mullick. "Incorporating the behavioral dimension in designing inclusive learning environment for autism." *ArchNet-IJAR* 3, no. 3 (2009): 45–64.

56. Dawson, Geraldine, and Renee Watling. "Interventions to facilitate auditory, visual, and motor integration in autism: A review of the evidence." *Journal of autism and developmental disorders* 30, no. 5 (2000): 415–421.

57. International Interior Design Association (IIDA). "Multi-sensory environments for special populations—Live webinar." Healthcare Design Webinars. January 26, 2012.

58. Sánchez, Pilar Arnaiz, Francisco Segado Vázquez, and Laureano Albaladejo Serrano. *Autism and the built environment.* INTECH Open Access Publisher, 2011.

59. Polirstok, Susan Rovet, Lawrence Dana, Serafino Buono, Vita Mongelli, and Grazia Trubia. "Improving functional communication skills in adolescents and young adults with severe autism using gentle teaching and positive approaches." *Topics in language disorders* 23, no. 2 (2003): 146–153.

60. International Interior Design Association (IIDA). "Multi-sensory environments for special populations—Live webinar." Healthcare Design Webinars. January 26, 2012.

61. Gaines, Kristi S., Zane Curry, JoAnn Shroyer, Cherif Amor, and Robin H. Lock. "The perceived effects of visual design and features on students with autism spectrum disorder." *Journal of architectural and planning research* 31, no. 4 (2014): 282–298.

62. Bourne, Angela. "Neuro-considerate environments for adults with intellectual developmental diversities: An integrated design approach to support wellbeing." PhD diss., Texas Tech University, 2013.

63. Nielson, Karla J. and David A. Taylor. *Interiors: an introduction.* New York: McGraw-Hill, 2007.

Auditory

CHAPTER

6

Auditory sensitivity is experienced by a high percentage of children with ASD. Multiple studies have identified auditory processing difficulties as the most prevalent sensory trigger for individuals on the spectrum.[1,2,3,4] However, Quill argues that this oversensitivity to sound is experienced at certain pitches or types of sounds.[5] Each individual with ASD will vary in severity and presence of individual symptoms. Table 6.1 reviews common difficulties with the auditory system exhibited by individuals with ASD.

Table 6.1 Common Difficulties with Sensory Systems: Observable Behaviors.

HYPER-REACTIVE BEHAVIOR INDICATORS	HYPO-REACTIVE BEHAVIOR INDICATORS
AUDITORY SYSTEM	
• easily distracted by background sounds	• does not respond to name being spoken
• overreacts to sounds	• seems oblivious to sounds of surrounding activities
• unpredictable reactions to sounds	• creates constant sounds as if to stimulate self
• holds hands over ears to block noise	• unsafe because does not react to sounds indicating potential danger
• screams or cries at sounds in the environment	• does not respond to any kind of sound
• responds physically as if sound is a threat	

One symptom of auditory sensitivity not listed in the table is the inability to regulate volume. Children with ASD have difficulty using an appropriate speaking volume or volume when listening to music or watching television. They may be either too loud or too quiet regardless of the presence of background noise.[6] Another symptom that is not listed on the table is Echolalia. Echolalia is another term for the repetitive speech and excessive noises made by some auditory hypo-sensitive individuals.[7]

As discussed in Chapter 2, Hall states that acceptable levels of noise in the environment vary from culture to culture.[8] NT people are generally able to adapt to varying levels of acoustics. However, for ND individuals, a slight variation of decibel may send them into a panic. This sensitivity to noise in those with autism is vividly explained by Temple Grandin, PhD, an individual with autism. She states:

> When I was little, loud noises were also a problem, often feeling like a dentist's drill hitting a nerve. They actually caused

pain. I was scared to death of balloons popping, because the sound was like an explosion in my ear. Minor noises that most people can tune out drove me to distraction. When I was in college, my roommate's hair dryer sounded like a jet plane taking off. Some of the sounds that are most disturbing to autistic children are the high-pitched, shrill noises made by electrical drills, blenders, saws, and vacuum cleaners. Echoes in school gymnasiums and bathrooms are difficult for people with autism to tolerate. The kinds of sounds that are most disturbing vary from person to person. A sound that caused me pain may be pleasurable to another child.[9]

Addressing this sensitivity to sound is necessary when creating environments that individuals with autism will utilize.

Environmental Noise

In order to design for auditory sensitivity, a brief explanation of key terms is needed. Pitch, loudness, reverberation, and signal to noise ratio (SNR) must be addressed during design. Pitch is "the subjective impression of how high or low a sound is" and is measured in Hertz (Hz). Generally, young people hear sound frequencies from approximately 20 to 20,000 Hz. In order to understand speech, one must be able to hear a range from approximately 500 to 6,000 Hz.[10]

Loudness may be defined as "the subjective impression of the intensity of a sound" and is measured in decibels (dB).[11] Reports of hearing loss with high noise levels are well-documented. However, a study by Lercher, Evans, and Meis determined that the cognitive development of young children may be delayed due to modest noise levels.[12] The study took place in typical North American neighborhoods. Table 6.2 compares the loudness of some everyday sounds.

Reverberation is important to understanding speech. Reverberation is defined as the "amount of time a sound lingers in a space before it diminishes to an imperceptible level."[13] Reverberation within a space can be caused by too many sound-reflecting surfaces.

Additionally, an understanding of signal to noise ratio (SNR) is necessary for proper acoustical design. SNR is "the difference between the decibel level of a speaker's voice minus the level of the background noise."[14] Children need higher SNRs than

Table 6.2 Comparison of Decibel Levels.

NOISE	DECIBEL LEVEL (dB)
Normal conversation	60–65dB
City traffic (inside car)	85dB
Possible hearing loss with sustained exposure	90–96dB
Jet engine at 100	140dB
Possible permanent hearing damage with short-term exposure	140dB

adults to develop speech and language. For example, the SNR in a classroom should be greater than +15.[15] Understanding and acquiring speech in an environment with background noise may be difficult for young children.

Additionally, a study by Nober and Nober determined that students diagnosed with learning disabilities were more adversely affected by background noise than children without this diagnosis.[16] Children with learning disabilities made more auditory discrimination errors. However, both groups made more auditory discrimination errors in noise than in quiet.

Designing for Auditory Hyper-Sensitivity

An individual may have a hyper-sensitive auditory system if they are distracted easily by background sounds, overreact or demonstrate unpredictable reactions to sounds, try to physically block noise from entering their ears by covering them, respond physically to sound, or show no response to any kind of sound.[17] These individuals are typically light sleepers, dislike loud noises, and do not enjoy tasks such as having their hair cut.[18, 19] Most individuals on the spectrum who are hyper-sensitive to sound are easily distracted by even the softest noise, have difficulty functioning with background noise, and find some noises painful.

Children with hyper-sensitivity can be easily overwhelmed by incoming sensory information. The environment can be terrifying at times because loud or sudden noises feel physically painful to hyper-sensitive individuals.[20] Some experts believe that this kind of sensory overload is experienced more among individuals with Asperger's syndrome than other individuals on the spectrum.[21]

When sensory integration spaces are incorporated, a stereo should be provided for individuals on the spectrum to listen to music and other sounds. A method known as "auditory integration," which involves listening to digitally modified music through headphones, has been shown to help auditory hyper-sensitive children grow accustomed to the frequencies that they overreact to the most.[22]

Individuals with ASD who are hyper sensitive to sound will be distracted by soft noises and may experience pain with some noises. Instead of striving to eliminate all noise, the goal should be to help build tolerance to noise to enable individuals on the spectrum to gain independence.

Designing for Auditory Hypo-sensitivity

An individual may have a hypo-sensitive auditory system if they do not respond to their name, seem oblivious to sounds in their environment, create constant sounds, or show no reaction to sounds that indicate danger. These individuals may seek sound or create it to stimulate their hearing and may be prone to bang doors, tap items, and tear or crumple paper.[23] Hypo-sensitivity is displayed by a child who fails to respond even when the background is quiet. They do not seem to be aware of matters going on around them.

Auditory hypo-sensitivity in children often appears to be a hearing impairment because the child does not always respond when his or her name is called.[24] This is sometimes referred to as "auditory filtering."[25] A child with auditory hypo-sensitivity may enjoy hearing and making loud, excessive noises.[26] If a soft environment is in place, soft materials will absorb sound instead of reflecting it, as hard surfaces do. Many children on the spectrum with auditory sensitivities have difficulty functioning if there is background noise in the area.[27] Ensuring that the individual has a quiet space for sleeping, doing homework, etc. will help the individual stay focused.

Controlling Noise

Noise control should be addressed early during the planning phase of construction. In this way, noise from mechanical systems and silencers may be implemented in construction. Materials are an aspect of the overall design that can realize vast improvements in sound absorption. Hard surfaces should be avoided on walls, floors, and ceilings to reduce noise and reverberation.[28] These hard surfaces are significant contributors to the reverberation time (RT) within a space. Sound-absorbing panels can be installed over drywall or suspended from the ceiling in order to reduce the amount of hard surfaces within a space. Additionally, fluorescent lighting may create noise levels of 50 dB.[29] Trying to avoid areas with fluorescent lighting and utilizing natural light are ways to address this issue.

Selecting sound-absorbing materials during construction or renovation are other ways to reduce noise levels. Using carpet instead of vinyl composite tile or other hard flooring materials can also aid in decreasing reverberation. Wood products also tend to have more absorptive properties than many laminates. Curtains and wall-mounted cork boards are simple ways to aid in noise reduction in existing spaces. Figure 6.1 (overleaf) illustrates the use of tennis balls on chair legs as a way to reduce noise in the classroom.

Gaines and Sancibrian identified soft background music as a way to reduce the impact of excessive auditory stimulus.[30] Classical, instrumental, familiar music, and nature sounds were identified by teachers as recommendations for students with ASD. Mozart and Vivaldi are thought to be beneficial for learning, so playing classical music in the background may prove to be therapeutic in classrooms.[31] Additionally, music exposure affects spatial-temporal reasoning that is the foundation for math, engineering, and chess skills.[32] By utilizing headphones, excess noise may be blocked out, and the individual with autism can listen to their preferred music without disturbing others.

Optimally, designing for noise reduction prior to construction will benefit all users of a space, including those with ASD. However, modifications may be made to existing environments to improve the auditory environment. Even simple modifications, such as the use of headphones, may help individuals with ASD adapt to interior and exterior spaces.

6.1 (facing page)
Chairs with tennis balls attached to the legs
reduce noise. Rio Grande High School,
Albuquerque, NM

6.2 (top right) Poorly Insulated Wall

6.3 (bottom right) Well Insulated Wall

Practical Applications for Design

Noise may be addressed in a variety of ways during the construction of a building. The structure of walls around an environment can greatly affect the sound qualities within the space. Walls are often constructed of thin, lightweight materials in order to keep a project economical.[33] These walls are made up of a single row of studs sandwiched between two thin pieces of drywall (Figure 6.2). In order to increase the amount of sound insulation, walls can be alternatively constructed with two layers of staggered studs, one layer housing sound-absorbing insulation and the other becoming an airspace, and two sheets of drywall outside each stud. This greatly dampens sound's ability to travel through walls. Additional insulation can be achieved by staggering drywall seams so that they don't line up between the two layers. Two seams in the same location will allow sound to travel through them. Placing the second layer of drywall to cover the first layer's seams is also an effective way to reduce the travel of noise between spaces (Figure 6.3).

Reverberation is a common problem found within typical learning environments. The main way to decrease Reverberation Time (RT) within a classroom is through finish selections. However, this can also be addressed in the initial construction of a space. Reverberation often prevents sound from traveling from the front of a classroom to the back because of all of the reflective and absorptive features in-between. In order to diffuse this issue, a hard plaster surface in the middle of the ceiling can help to reflect sound to the back of a classroom. A sloped ceiling reflector at the front of the room (Figure 6.4 overleaf) can also aid in helping sound travel from the front of a classroom to the back.

Materials

Providing a variety of surfaces with sound-absorbing qualities is a unique solution to negating poor RT values.[34] Determining the specific amount of sound-absorbing materials is actually quite simple: "The area of sound absorbing materials should be approximately equal in area to the floor area of the room."[35] Using acoustical ceiling tiles in appropriate areas or applying acoustical tiles to the walls could accomplish this. In classrooms, acoustical wall tiles could also serve as tack boards where instructors could hang student work or class instructions.

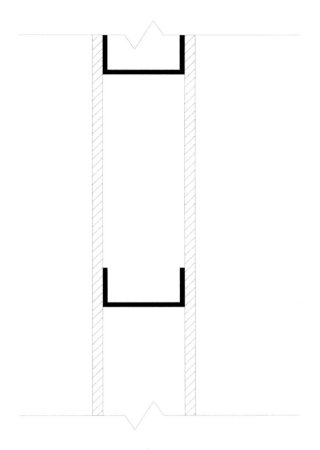

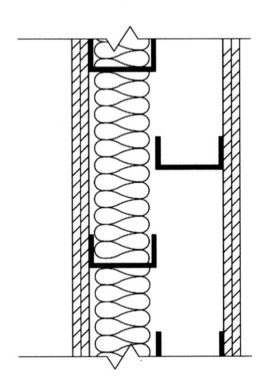

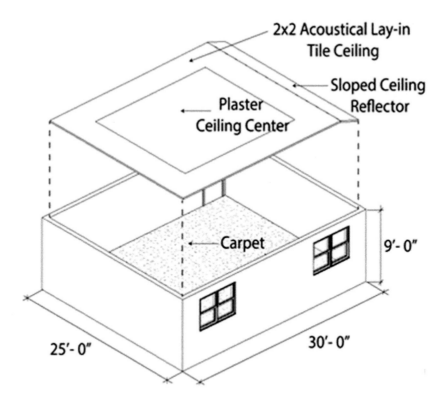

6.4 Ceiling Design to Reduce Reverberation

Equipment

Heating, ventilation, and air conditioning (HVAC) equipment is one of the most common contributors to unwanted sound within the built environment and can be especially problematic in classrooms. Not only do these systems produce mechanical noise, but noise can also travel through ductwork from room to room if not designed properly.[36] Ducts located directly above classrooms that connect one classroom to the next as shown in Figure 6.5 are an example of poorly designed ductwork. Instead, by designing the ductwork to lead from inside a classroom to the hallway as shown in Figure 6.6, sound is less likely to be transferred to adjacent spaces. Sound can travel directly from the classroom into the hallway, where it can diffuse.

Many additional solutions can help address noise from HVAC systems within the classroom. Selecting larger ductwork can help to alleviate noise by reducing the velocity of air traveling through the ducts.[37] Additionally, the shape of the ductwork may affect how easily noise enters and escapes the ducts. Terzigni, of the Sheet Metal and Air Conditioning Contractors' National Association (SMACNA), recommends round ductwork over rectangular.[38] He also points out that heavier gauge ductwork or thick duct liners can effectively insulate mechanical noise. Finally, locating air-handling units further away from areas that may be sensitive to noise is beneficial for reducing noise from mechanical systems.[39]

Layout/Plan

The layout or footprint of spaces can also contribute to noise levels within learning environments. Any direct passageways or connections between classrooms can provide a path for sound to travel. Doors that line up across corridors or that are located directly adjacent to one another should be avoided. This provides a direct route of travel for noise from one room to another. Instead, staggering doorways down a hallway and spacing doors an appropriate distance from one another can aid in eliminating these direct routes for noise. In this solution, the hallway provides a buffer space for sound between rooms instead of a direct passageway.

An important consideration is zoning different areas of a layout by distinguishing the level of sound they produce and the desired sound levels for the tasks within a space. For example, a noisy gymnasium where loud activities typically take place is not ideally located adjacent to classrooms where students and instructors must remain focused in order to complete tasks.[40] A better location for the gymnasium may be adjacent to a music room or cafeteria. Exterior noise should also be considered. Classrooms located next to playgrounds where students can see and hear the activities outside would be detrimental to students' focus within the classroom.

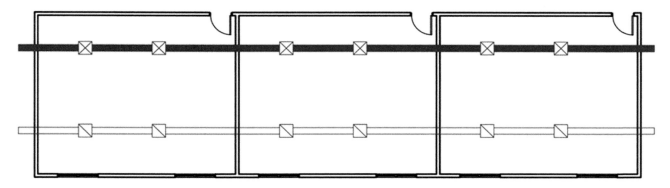

6.5 Poor HVAC Duct Arrangement

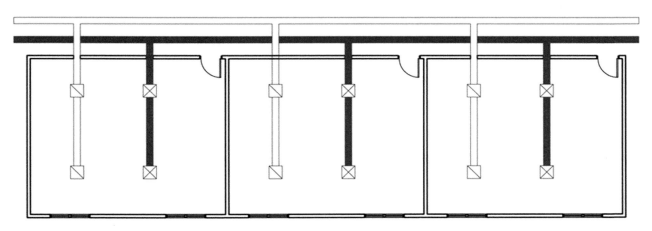

6.6 Better HVAC Duct Arrangement

Architectural Features

Architectural features within a building can have a profound effect on the noise levels within learning environments. Spacious classrooms with large volumes of space may seem necessary for accommodating a larger number of students and supplies comfortably, but these large volumes are actually detrimental and cause excess reverberation.[41] Ceiling heights from nine feet to twelve feet tend to create the most ideal acoustical conditions.[42]

Windows are another architectural feature of buildings with the probability to allow sound transmission between spaces. Windows should be located appropriately in order to reduce the amount of sound transmission from exterior and adjacent spaces. Windows near busy play areas or highways may be detrimental to a student's focus. Selecting windows with an acceptable sound transmission class (STC) rating can help to alleviate this issue.[43]

Notes

1. Grandin, Temple. *Thinking in pictures: My life with autism* (expanded edition). New York: Vintage, 2006.
2. Shabha, Ghasson, and Kristi Gaines. "A comparative analysis of transatlantic design interventions for therapeutically enhanced learning environments—Texas vs West Midlands." *Facilities* 31, no. 13/14 (2013): 634–658.
3. Ashburner, Jill, Jenny Ziviani, and Sylvia Rodger. "Sensory processing and classroom emotional, behavioral, and educational outcomes in children with autism spectrum disorder." *American journal of occupational therapy* 62, no. 5 (2008): 564–573.
4. Tomchek, Scott D., and Winnie Dunn. "Sensory processing in children with and without autism: A comparative study using the short sensory profile." *American journal of occupational therapy* 61, no. 2 (2007): 190–200.
5. Quill, Kathleen Ann. *Teaching children with autism: Strategies to enhance communication and socialization.* Cengage Learning, 1995.
6. Talay-Ongan, Ayshe, and Kara Wood. "Unusual sensory sensitivities in autism: A possible crossroads." *International journal of disability, development and education* 47, no. 2 (2000): 201–212.

7. Grandin, Temple. *Thinking in pictures: My life with autism* (expanded edition). New York: Vintage, 2006.

8. Hall, Kenneth B., and Gerald A. Porterfield. *Community by design: New urbanism for suburbs and small communities*. McGraw Hill Professional, 2001.

9. Grandin, Temple. *Thinking in pictures: My life with autism* (expanded edition). New York: Vintage, 2006. p. 67.

10. Manlove, Elizabeth E., Tom Frank, and Lynne Vernon-Feagans. "Why should we care about noise in classrooms and child care settings?" In *Child and youth care forum* (vol. 30, no. 1, pp. 55–64). Kluwer Academic Publishers-Plenum Publishers, 2001.

11. Manlove, Elizabeth E., Tom Frank, and Lynne Vernon-Feagans. "Why should we care about noise in classrooms and child care settings?" In *Child and youth care forum* (vol. 30, no. 1, pp. 55–64). Kluwer Academic Publishers-Plenum Publishers, 2001.

12. Lercher, Peter, Gary W. Evans, and Markus Meis. "Ambient noise and cognitive processes among primary schoolchildren." *Environment and behavior* 35, no. 6 (2003): 725–735.

13. Clark, Greg. "The ears have it." *American school & university* 76, no. 3 (2003): 298–301.

14. Manlove, Elizabeth E., Tom Frank, and Lynne Vernon-Feagans. "Why should we care about noise in classrooms and child care settings?" In *Child and youth care forum* (vol. 30, no. 1, pp. 55–64). Kluwer Academic Publishers-Plenum Publishers, 2001. p. 58.

15. Manlove, Elizabeth E., Tom Frank, and Lynne Vernon-Feagans. "Why should we care about noise in classrooms and child care settings?" In *Child and youth care forum* (vol. 30, no. 1, pp. 55–64). Kluwer Academic Publishers-Plenum Publishers, 2001.

16. Nober, Linda W., and E. Harris Nober. "Auditory discrimination of learning disabled children in quiet and classroom noise." *Journal of learning disabilities* 8, no. 10 (1975): 656–659.

17. Ministry of Education. Special Programs Branch. "Teaching students with autism: A resource guide for schools." 2000.

18. Bogdashina, Olga. *Sensory perceptual issues in autism and Asperger Syndrome: Different sensory experiences, different perceptual worlds*. Jessica Kingsley Publishers, 2003.

19. Williams, Emma. "Who really needs a 'theory' of mind? An interpretative phenomenological analysis of the autobiographical writings of ten high-functioning individuals with an autism spectrum disorder." *Theory & psychology* 14, no. 5 (2004): 704–724.

20. Jones, Robert, Ciara Quigney, and Jaci Huws. "First-hand accounts of sensory perceptual experiences in autism: A qualitative analysis." *Journal of intellectual and developmental disability* 28, no. 2 (2003): 112–121.

21. Myles, Brenda Smith, Winnie Dunn, Louann Rinner, Taku Hagiwara, Matthew Reese, Abby Huggins, and Stephanie Becker. "Sensory issues in children with Asperger syndrome and autism." *Education and training in developmental disabilities* 39, no. 4 (2004): 283–290.

22. Dawson, Geraldine, and Renee Watling. "Interventions to facilitate auditory, visual, and motor integration in autism: A review of the evidence." *Journal of autism and developmental disorders* 30, no. 5 (2000): 415–421.

23. Bogdashina, Olga. *Theory of mind and the triad of perspectives on autism and Asperger syndrome: A view from the bridge*. Jessica Kingsley Publishers, 2006.

24. Alcántara, José I., Emma J.L. Weisblatt, Brian C. J. Moore, and Patrick F. Bolton. "Speech-in-noise perception in high-functioning individuals with autism or Asperger's syndrome." *Journal of child psychology and psychiatry* 45, no. 6 (2004): 1107–1114.

25. Ashburner, Jill, Jenny Ziviani, and Sylvia Rodger. "Sensory processing and classroom emotional, behavioral, and educational outcomes in children with autism spectrum disorder." *American journal of occupational therapy* 62, no. 5 (2008): 564–573.

26. Tomchek, Scott D., and Winnie Dunn. "Sensory processing in children with and without autism: A comparative study using the short sensory profile." *American journal of occupational therapy* 61, no. 2 (2007): 190–200.

27. Ashburner, Jill, Jenny Ziviani, and Sylvia Rodger. "Sensory processing and classroom emotional, behavioral, and educational outcomes in children with autism spectrum disorder." *American journal of occupational therapy* 62, no. 5 (2008): 564–573.

28. Manlove, Elizabeth E., Tom Frank, and Lynne Vernon-Feagans. "Why should we care about noise in classrooms and child care settings?" In *Child and youth care forum* (vol. 30, no. 1, pp. 55–64). Kluwer Academic Publishers-Plenum Publishers, 2001.

29. Manlove, Elizabeth E., Tom Frank, and Lynne Vernon–Feagans. "Why should we care about noise in classrooms and child care settings?" In *Child and youth care forum* (vol. 30, no. 1, pp. 55–64). Kluwer Academic Publishers-Plenum Publishers, 2001.

30. Gaines, Kristi, and S. Sancibrian. "The effects of environmental noise on the behavior of children with ASD." *The international journal of architectonic, spatial, and environmental design* 7, no. 2 (2014): 51–64.

31. Koomar, Jane, Carol Stock Kranowitz, Stacey Szklut, Lynn Balzer-Martin, Elizabeth Haber, and Deanna Iris Sava. *Answers to questions teachers*

ask about sensory integration: Forms, checklists, and practical tools for teachers and parents. Future Horizons, 2001.

32. Freed, Jeffrey, and Laurie Parsons. *Right-brained children in a left-brained world: Unlocking the potential of your ADD child.* Simon and Schuster, 1998.

33. Seep, Benjamin, Robin Glosemeyer, Emily Hulce, Matt Linn, and Pamela Aytar. "Classroom acoustics: A resource for creating environments with desirable listening conditions." *Acoustical society of America.* (2000).

34. Siebein, Gary W., Martin A. Gold, Glenn W. Siebein, and Michael G. Ermann. "Ten ways to provide a high-quality acoustical environment in schools." *Language, speech, and hearing services in schools* 31, no. 4 (2000): 376–384.

35. Siebein, Gary W., Martin A. Gold, Glenn W. Siebein, and Michael G. Ermann. "Ten ways to provide a high-quality acoustical environment in schools." *Language, speech, and hearing services in schools* 31, no. 4 (2000): 376–384.

36. Seep, Benjamin, Robin Glosemeyer, Emily Hulce, Matt Linn, and Pamela Aytar. "Classroom acoustics: A resource for creating environments with desirable listening conditions." *Acoustical society of America.* (2000).

37. Terzigni, Mark. "HVAC-System Acoustics-Methods of reducing unwanted sound associated with mechanical systems in commercial buildings." *Heating/Piping/Air Conditioning engineering: HPAC* 80, no. 8 (2008): 18.

38. Terzigni, Mark. "HVAC-System Acoustics-Methods of reducing unwanted sound associated with mechanical systems in commercial buildings." *Heating/Piping/Air Conditioning engineering: HPAC* 80, no. 8 (2008): 18.

39. Terzigni, Mark. "HVAC-System Acoustics-Methods of reducing unwanted sound associated with mechanical systems in commercial buildings." *Heating/Piping/Air Conditioning engineering: HPAC* 80, no. 8 (2008): 18.

40. Seep, Benjamin, Robin Glosemeyer, Emily Hulce, Matt Linn, and Pamela Aytar. "Classroom acoustics: A resource for creating environments with desirable listening conditions." *Acoustical society of America.* (2000).

41. Siebein, Gary W., Martin A. Gold, Glenn W. Siebein, and Michael G. Ermann. "Ten ways to provide a high-quality acoustical environment in schools." *Language, speech, and hearing services in schools* 31, no. 4 (2000): 376–384.

42. Bradley, John S. "Speech intelligibility studies in classrooms." *The journal of the acoustical society of America* 80, no. 3 (1986): 846–854.

43. Siebein, Gary W., Martin A. Gold, Glenn W. Siebein, and Michael G. Ermann. "Ten ways to provide a high-quality acoustical environment in schools." *Language, speech, and hearing services in schools* 31, no. 4 (2000): 376–384.

Touch/Tactile

CHAPTER

7

After accentuated hearing (Chapter 6), hyper-sensitive touch is the most prevalent sensory characteristic observed by children with sensory dysfunction.[1] Nerves under the skin's surface send tactile information to the brain. Light touch, pain, temperature, and pressure are all perceived through the sense of touch. The tactile sense tells a person what an object feels like. For people with ASD, engagement of the tactile sense is especially important, as they learn by engaging physically with materials. Table 7.1 outlines the common difficulties observed through the tactile system.

Table 7.1 Common Difficulties with Sensory Systems: Observable Behaviors.

HYPER-REACTIVE BEHAVIOR INDICATORS	HYPO-REACTIVE BEHAVIOR INDICATORS
TACTILE SYSTEM	
• touch defensive—does not like to be touched	• does not seem to grasp concept of personal space
• avoids tasks with strong tactile element (clay, water play, paint, food preparation)	• does not seem to notice touch of others
• complains about discomfort of clothing	• frequently puts things into mouth
• refuses to wear certain items—tugs at clothes	• does not adjust clothing that would seem to be an irritant
• responds negatively to textures in foods, toys, furniture	• high pain threshold, unaware of danger because of low response to pain

Tactile experiences are evaluated simultaneously with other sensory encounters (Konkle, Wang, Hayward, and Moore, 2009).[2] Konkle et al. explored how the senses of touch and sight influence each other. They determined that the way something feels is influenced by how it looks, and vice versa. Every significant experience of architecture is multi-sensory.[3] The senses are specializations of the skin, and all sensory experiences are related to tactility. Ashley Montagu's (author and professor) view, based on medical evidence, confirms the primacy of the tactile realm: "[The skin] is the oldest and the most sensitive of our organs, our first medium of communication, and our most efficient protector [...]. Even the transparent cornea of the eye is overlain by a layer of modified skin [...]. Touch is the parent of our eyes, ears, nose, and mouth. It is the sense which became differentiated into the others, a fact that seems to be recognized in the age-old evaluation of touch as 'the mother of the senses.'"[4]

7.1 Hands-on craft-like activities stimulate the senses and engage the residents in productive work

According to Jan Cline, coordinator of training at Bittersweet Farms Inc. in Ohio, when people with ASD interact "hands on" with materials in an art class, for example, they connect with what they are creating and develop communication skills through their works of art. The intimate connection with materials such as clay, paint, paper, and textiles enables them to engage their sense of touch and develop deeper meaning of what's happening in the environment around them. Engaging in physical work such as farming, planting and tending to gardens, caring for animals, and cleaning also provides tactile connections that provide people with ASD positive sensory feedback. Administrators from workplace and training companies such as Brookwood community in Texas and Camphill Copake in New York State believe that "hands on" jobs are best for this group.

Tactile Defensiveness

Tactile defensiveness is a condition in which the tactile system is immature or working improperly. Individuals may resist being touched or hugged, wearing certain types of clothing, and complain about having their hair or face washed.[5] This may cause the brain to be overly stimulated and lead to excessive brain activity, making it difficult to concentrate or organize behavior, leading to developmental delays, learning problems, and other sensory problems.[6, 7] Exercise and deep pressure stimulation may help reduce behavior problems.[8] Figure 7.1 illustrates an example of a craft space at the Brookwood Community in Texas.

According to Temple Grandin,[9] individuals with autism often seek deep pressure sensations. Deep pressure is defined as "the type of surface pressure that is exerted in most type of firm touching, holding, stroking, petting of animals or swaddling."[10] The use of "squeeze machines" in sensory integration (SI) therapy have

7.2 (top) Weighted blankets may be used to apply deep pressure

7.3 (bottom) Many individuals with autism enjoy surrounding themselves with soft textures

shown beneficial results when used with children with ASD. Firm massages, weighted vests, and weighted blankets (Figure 7.2) are other ways to apply deep pressure.[11]

Sensitivity to scratchy clothing or textiles may create additional tactile issues for individuals on the spectrum. Shin and Gaines[12] determined that organic bamboo and organic cotton were the two most preferred textiles by individuals with autism. The soft touch and moisture wicking properties were found to be the most positive features. Although this study looked at textiles for apparel, the same principles are relevant for designing interior spaces.

Designing for Tactile Sensitivities

Tactile preferences of people with ASD are as varied as they are for NT people. Observations of young adult residents in research conducted by Dr. Angela Bourne[13] revealed that this group either prefers their personal space such as their bedroom to be heavily adorned with stuffed animals, pillows, and blankets or, in contrast, minimally decorated with tailored bedding. Whatever their preference, evidence suggests that preferences are important to these individuals and that they covet their belongings in unique ways that bring meaning through the tactile sense.

For the most part, the majority of people in Bourne's research collected numerous soft, furry, stuffed animal toys and surrounded themselves with clothing and bedding that was soft. This supports Childers and Peck,[14] who revealed soft textures/surfaces are generally seen as more pleasant and preferred to hard ones. Figure 7.3 illustrates the importance of soft collections and textures for an individual with ASD.

Zuo, Hope, Jones, and Castle[15] studied human responses to metal surfaces: "Smooth metallic surfaces evoke positive emotional responses such as lively/cheerful, modern, elegant, and comfortable. In contrast, rough metallic surfaces evoke negative emotional responses such as dull/depressing, traditional, ugly, and uncomfortable." Results were obtained after blindfolded touching. In Bourne's[16] interviews with adults with ASD, several of the men commented on liking images of residential interiors that had smooth, shiny surfaces. Comments were made about how they liked the shiny floors, counter tops, and lighting in the images they were

7.4 Personalization of bedding soft textures

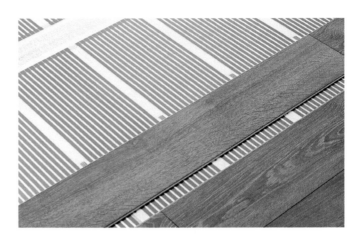

7.5 Heated floor systems. Carbon film floor heating

shown. These individuals further explained that the shiny features looked "rich" and clean.

Juhani Pallasmaa stated, "Vision reveals what the touch already knows."[17] People almost always know how something will feel just by seeing it, and this is followed by the feelings that accompany that sensory experience. For example, when one sees a large duvet covering on a bed, they know from past experience that the material the item is made from is soft, and this knowledge evokes a feeling of comfort, warmth, and safety. Conversely, if a person sees a bed of nails, they will most likely identify the hard material and its sharpness with discomfort and as cold and uninviting. Therefore, a variety of textures and patterns that reflect a hand-crafted quality and are seamlessly integrated in the interior and exterior spaces allow the person with ASD to touch and feel and gain knowledge from their surroundings and become more self-reliant.

The concept of personal space is associated with the sense of touch. People diagnosed with ASD may resist being close to other people or having other people close to them. Quite frequently they choose to stand or sit in locations where they can hug the wall and/or are translucent as an act to attain privacy. Doing this sets them apart from conversations, and their acquisition of information is restricted. Standing back in the comfort of a wall to lean on also means the person with ASD is not positioned where a lot of conversation takes place. In order to help a person with ASD to feel more comfortable in public spaces, a variety of design interventions need to be implemented. Providing opportunities for a person with ASD to ease into a space and acclimatize to their surroundings is one way. A variety of small group seating arranged at right angles, which include high backs and upholstered seats, provide a cocooning affect. Cocooning makes the vulnerable person feel more protected, hence more likely to feel less stress in crowded situations.

Private bedrooms are beneficial for many individuals with ASD. Figure 7.4 illustrates individual preferences of textures and layers

observed in bedding by individuals at intentional communities. Some individuals with ASD prefer to keep the thermostat low and wrap themselves in layers of blankets. As previously mentioned, this provides deep touch pressure that calms the nervous system.[18, 19]

Finding a balance in temperature may be challenging for individuals with ASD, and quick temperature changes can be alarming.[20] Heated floor systems help to regulate flooring temperature to eliminate this issue. Figure 7.5 illustrates a heated floor system. Heat and humidity might also direct the tactile defensive person to feel the need to cool off by separating themselves from others. Heat may also increase unpleasant bodily odors that create an unpleasant environment for those who have sensory sensitivities.

As with the other senses, a wide range of preferences may be displayed in designing spaces for tactile sensitivity. The use of sensory integration spaces and indoor playgrounds (Figures 7.6 and 7.7) illustrate how indoor playgrounds can be designed with consideration for tactile sensitivity and deep pressure. Indoor playgrounds are further discussed in Chapter 14.

Design interventions may be implemented to support the principles of sensory integration therapy. Several environmental features can be manipulated to support the comfort of individuals with ASD. Some of these elements include allowing for private spaces and providing adequate room to transition through the environment without touching other people. The regulation of temperature should be addressed for maximum comfort through materials such as heated floors and individual temperature controls when appropriate. Soft textiles and other soft textures should also be considered. Implementing therapy rooms, craft rooms, and places for playgrounds (indoor and outdoor) into the design will also address these needs. The design solution is not "one size fits all." Personal needs and preferences are important considerations when designing for tactile and other sensory features of the built environment.

7.6 (top) Soft textures in play spaces address tactile hyposensitivity

7.7 (bottom) Ball pits address the sense of touch

Notes

1   Freed, Jeffrey, and Laurie Parsons. *Right-brained children in a left-brained world: Unlocking the potential of your ADD child.* Simon and Schuster, 1998.

2   Konkle, Talia, Qi Wang, Vincent Hayward, and Christopher I. Moore. "Motion aftereffects transfer between touch and vision." *Current biology* 19, no. 9 (2009): 745–750.

3   Montagu, Ashley. *Touching: The human significance of the skin.* Harper & Row, 1971.

4   Pallasmaa, Juhani. *The eyes of the skin: Architecture and the senses.* Chichester, UK: John Wiley & Sons, 2005.

5   Hatch-Rasmussen, Cindy. "Sensory integration." Center for the Study of Autism at www.autism.org/si.html. 1995.

6   *The Tactile Defensive Child.* (n.d.). Retrieved June 3, 2003, from http.//babyparentingabout.com.

7   Hatch-Rasmussen, Cindy. "Sensory integration." Center for the Study of Autism at www. autism.org/si.html. 1995.

8   Grandin, Temple. *Thinking in pictures: My life with autism* (expanded edition). New York: Vintage, 2006.

9   Grandin, Temple. "Calming effects of deep touch pressure in patients with autistic disorder, college students, and animals." *Journal of child and adolescent psychopharmacology* 2, no. 1 (1992): 63–72.

10 Grandin, Temple. "Calming effects of deep touch pressure in patients with autistic disorder, college students, and animals." *Journal of child and adolescent psychopharmacology* 2, no. 1 (1992): 63–72.

11 Grandin, T. *The autistic brain: Helping different kinds of minds succeed.* New York: Houghtin Mifflin Harcourt Publishing, 2013.

12 Shin, Su, and Kristi Gaines. "Team of Texas Tech researchers create sensory clothing." *Lubbock avalanche journal (TX)*, May 26, 2015. http://lubbockonline.com/local-news/2015-05-25/team-texas-tech-researchers-create-sensory-clothing.

13 Bourne, Angela. "Neuro-considerate environments for adults with intellectual developmental diversities: An integrated design approach to support wellbeing." PhD diss., Texas Tech University, 2013.

14 Childers, T. L., and J. Peck. "Informational and affective influences of haptics on product evaluation: Is what I say how I feel?" In *Sensory marketing: Research on the sensuality of products* (pp. 63–72). New York: Routledge/Taylor & Francis Group, 2010.

15 Zuo, H., T. Hope, M. Jones, and P. Castle. "Sensory interaction with materials." In *Design and emotion* (pp. 223–227). CRC Press, 2004.

16 Bourne, Angela. "Neuro-considerate environments for adults with intellectual developmental diversities: An integrated design approach to support wellbeing." PhD diss., Texas Tech University, 2013.

17 Pallasmaa, Juhani. *The eyes of the skin: Architecture and the senses.* Chichester, UK: John Wiley & Sons, 2005.

18 Grandin, Temple. "Calming effects of deep touch pressure in patients with autistic disorder, college students, and animals." *Journal of child and adolescent psychopharmacology* 2, no. 1 (1992): 63–72.

19 Heller, Tamar, Alison B. Miller, and Kelly Hsieh. "Eight-year follow-up of the impact of environmental characteristics on well-being of adults with developmental disabilities." *Mental retardation* 40, no. 5 (2002): 366–378.

20 Heller, Tamar, Alison B. Miller, and Kelly Hsieh. "Eight-year follow-up of the impact of environmental characteristics on well-being of adults with developmental disabilities." *Mental retardation* 40, no. 5 (2002): 366–378.

Proprioceptive and Vestibular Senses

The vestibular and proprioceptive senses are often referred to as the hidden or inner senses. The vestibular sense "helps with movement, posture, vision, balance, and coordination of both sides of the body" (p.28).[1] Balance and the sense of spatial orientation rely on the vestibular apparatus. Proprioception informs a person as to where his or her body parts are in space and the appropriate amount of force needed to perform an activity such as picking up a glass of milk. Bogdashina explains how the vestibular system and the proprioceptive system affect visual and spatial perception.[2] As with the other senses, hyper- and hypo-sensitive responses to these inner senses cause challenges for people with ASD.

Spatial cognition/perception is developed through the proprioceptive system. The proprioceptive sense is regulated by one's muscles, joints, ligaments, tendons, and connective tissues. Kranowitz and Miller refer to it as one of the "deep senses" and as the "position sense."[3] Without a well-developed proprioceptive system, the ability to touch, see, and hear can be distorted. One may not know where he or she is in space or have a sense of time. The distortion may be so distracting that an individual with ASD cannot perceive their world like NT people. Common signs of dysfunction are clumsiness, a tendency to fall, difficulty manipulating small objects such as buttons, and resistance to new motor movement activities.[4] Proprioception is necessary to organize all the senses.[5]

Characteristics that contribute to a ND person's ability to maneuver through space include "distorted body postures such as toe walking, arching of the back, and hyperextension of the neck" (p. 233).[6] Proprioceptive, vestibular, and the visual systems contribute to balance.[7] These disturbances in motion and gait influence their visual perception and consequently their balance and spatial orientation. This visual dysfunction prevents a person with ASD from experiencing an integrated visual perception of events and objects in their environment. Some people with ASD lose track of their own position in space, compromising their posture, self-esteem, and comfort level with participating in social settings. Others may perceive these individuals as clumsy and awkward. Research has speculated that the cause for this distortion is partially due to a deficit in their ambient vision. From a design standpoint, ensuring the forms and shapes are well delineated, using contrasting materials and finishes, and creating dominance by varying the portion and scale of a space can help them manage this deficit. This is especially important for the person who, for example, kicks the wall as he or she walks down a corridor or from room to room.

Observers may think the individual who is kicking the wall is angry and acting out physically. However, people who have proprioception challenges may strike the wall to register where they are in space, as the horizontal and vertical planes are no more than objects on the move to them.[8] According to Bogdashina, kicking the wall helps them orient themselves and allows them to confidently make their way through a space.[9]

Weak vestibular and proprioceptive systems also hinder the ability of a person with ASD to remember landmarks and make connections to where they have been and what they have seen. As a result, this may negatively affect their ability to navigate a space with confidence. A field of environmental behavior known as wayfinding is devoted to accommodating this deficit.

A study by Bourne noted that individuals with ASD were affected most when they transitioned from space to space and when the number of people in a space changed.[10] This was observed in clinging to the wall and walking rigidly along the perimeter of the room to avoid touching and getting close to people. They appeared to avoid areas where there were groups of people actively talking. The participants with ASD also appeared to need more personal space, as they frequently demonstrated a variety of kinetic actions such as walking on the tips of their toes/shoes, rocking, twirling, and pacing. Energetic movements were especially evident in the younger adults observed and interviewed in the study. The older, frailer individuals had difficulty maintaining their balance and coordinating their body. Most had health problems in addition to their developmental diversity, and a few had been diagnosed with Parkinson's disease. Most of the elders wore glasses; several had hearing aids and wore orthotics shoes. In Bourne's study, she observed that a few used assistive devices to manage their vestibular challenges such as walkers, but most people were ambulatory (able to walk).

Designing for Proprioceptive and Vestibular Sensitivity

Social inhibitions can occur when individuals with ASD are uncomfortable approaching and maneuvering through a space. This challenge is primarily due to a weak vestibular and proprioceptive system. Compromised vestibular and proprioceptive systems need to be addressed in the design of the physical space. Accommodating proprioception deficits can be achieved by the careful planning of spaces and the application of materials, patterns, and textures that permit differentiated engagement of the senses. For example, Bourne observed that permitting one to touch and feel textures and forms in a space helps them register where they connect their thoughts and feelings to where they are in time and space. As a result, this tempers their anxiety levels and allows them to perceive their environment with less frustration and reduced confusion. A weak sense of proprioception has been associated with the "clumsiness,"[11] and therefore requires special attention to durability and maintenance of spaces. Common observed behaviors in individuals with ASD relating to the vestibular system are outlined in Table 8.1.

Interiors that are made up of defined forms and shapes that profile the perimeter of a space can help a person overcome these challenges. Archway transoms located at entrances to hallways and at the entrance to rooms, and moldings outlining the perimeter of the space at the floor level and ceiling provide clarity (Figure 8.1).

Table 8.1 Common Difficulties with Sensory Systems: Observable Behaviors.

HYPER-REACTIVE BEHAVIOR INDICATORS	HYPO-REACTIVE BEHAVIOR INDICATORS
VESTIBULAR SYSTEM	
• overreacts to movement activities	• seems to need constant movement
• has difficulties navigating on different surfaces (carpets, grass, etc.)	• rocks, travels in circles
• walks close to wall, clings to supports such as banisters	• seems to tire easily when engaged in movement activities
• seems to be fearful when movement is expected, muscles seem tense	• generally slow to move, lethargic in movement
• rigid about positioning of body, keeps head in same rigid angle	• takes long time to respond to directions to move
• seems to become physically disoriented easily	

8.1   Defined forms and shapes and contrasted molding in
interiors help with orientation in space

Contrasting floor materials such as carpet or wood, finishes, and colors also aid in wayfinding.

Additionally, spaces that accommodate opportunities for kinesthetic enrichment such as performing jobs and activities can help alleviate these challenges (Figure 8.2). People with ASD, especially the sensory seekers (those with vestibular hypo-sensitivity who are under-responsive to movement) need constant motion. They frequently wiggle their legs, tap their feet, flap their hands, and need to keep moving so their brain knows where their body is. They love to jump, run, bounce, spin around in circles, and to wrap themselves tightly in blankets.[12, 13, 14] Therefore, providing supports

in the built and surrounding environments that accommodate their vestibular and spatial needs are important. Figures 8.3 and 8.4 illustrate how hammocks and swings help manage the need to rock and swing. Spacious pools allow for energetic movement common in people with ASD who have hypo-vestibular sensory needs (Figure 8.5). Spacious walkways allow for release of physical energy manifested in spinning, arm flapping, and overall body movements that require more space.

Placing the bedrooms in pods of two also aids in privacy, as the residents only have two bedroom doors to remember and choose from (cognitive privacy) rather than several doors along

8.2 (top) Indoor playground with soft textures

8.3 (bottom) Swings provide a simple intervention
for vestibular sensory input

8.4 (top) Adults also benefit from swings for vestibular needs

8.5 (bottom) Supervised pools may be beneficial for sensory seekers

a corridor, which is often the case in group living situations. The short corridors also provide spatial privacy for residents who may have proprioception deficits, as they do not have to maneuver long distance to get to their bedroom. Short hallways reinforce a more home-like atmosphere. Additionally, wider staircases with handrails on both sides provide safer passage for individuals with ASD. Accentuated stair risers, applying molding outlining steps, and edge strips will aid in secure footings.

The vestibular and proprioception senses must be considered when designing spaces for individuals on the spectrum. This may be partially achieved by providing transition spaces that use some of the principles discussed in this chapter. Practical means of implementing wayfinding techniques for this population should also be incorporated. Several examples are further explained and illustrated in other chapters of this book. Additionally, providing spaces such as therapy rooms and play spaces will help address these needs. Designers may have fewer ways to address vestibular and proprioceptive needs than some of the other senses. Although limited in scope, these interventions can provide a significant impact for individuals with ASD.

Notes

1. Myles, Brenda Smith. *Asperger syndrome and sensory issues: Practical solutions for making sense of the world.* AAPC Publishing, 2000. p. 28.

2. Bogdashina, Olga. *Sensory perceptual issues in autism and Asperger Syndrome: Different sensory experiences, different perceptual worlds.* Jessica Kingsley Publishers, 2003.

3. Kranowitz, Carol, and Lucy Miller. *The out-of-sync child: Recognizing and coping with Sensory Processing Disorder.* Skylight Press, 2005.

4. Hatch-Rasmussen, Cindy. "Sensory integration." Center for the Study of Autism at www.autism.org/si.html. 1995.

5. Koomar, Jane, Carol Stock Kranowitz, Stacey Szklut, Lynn Balzer-Martin, Elizabeth Haber, and Deanna Iris Sava. *Answers to questions teachers ask about sensory integration: Forms, checklists, and practical tools for teachers and parents.* Future Horizons, 2001.

6. Carmody, Dennis P., Melvin Kaplan, and Alexa M. Gaydos. "Spatial orientation adjustments in children with autism in Hong Kong." *Child psychiatry and human development* 31, no. 3 (2001): 233–247.

7. Weimer, Amy K., Amy M. Schatz, Alan Lincoln, Angela O. Ballantyne, and Doris A. Trauner. "'Motor' impairment in Asperger syndrome: Evidence for a deficit in proprioception." *Journal of developmental & behavioral pediatrics* 22, no. 2 (2001): 92–101.

8. Bogdashina, Olga. *Autism and the edges of the known world: Sensitivities, language, and constructed reality.* Jessica Kingsley Publishers, 2010.

9. Bogdashina, Olga. *Autism and the edges of the known world: Sensitivities, language, and constructed reality.* Jessica Kingsley Publishers, 2010.

10. Bourne, A. "Neuro-considerate environments for adults with intellectual developmental diversities: An integrated design approach to support wellbeing." PhD diss., Texas Tech University, 2013.

11. Weimer, Amy K. *Motor impairment in Asperger Syndrome: Evidence for a deficit in proprioception.* No publisher information, 1999.

12. Bogdashina, Olga. *Sensory perceptual issues in autism and Asperger Syndrome: Different sensory experiences, different perceptual worlds.* Jessica Kingsley Publishers, 2003.

13. Hall, Edward T. *The silent language.* Garden City, NY: Doubleday, 1959.

14. Williams, Emma, Alan Costall, and Vasudevi Reddy. "Children with autism experience problems with both objects and people." *Journal of autism and developmental disorders* 29, no. 5 (1999): 367–378.

PART 3

Designing Realistic Environments

Design Considerations for ASD

The fundamental purpose of the built environment is to support people and the activities they engage in while using a space. To design compatible environments for people with ASD, designers need to understand the behavioral characteristics of this population. Individuals with ASD have differentiated sensory sensitivities and cognitive awareness. The challenges they experience in processing sensory information frequently results in non-productive behaviors that can be alleviated through design. However, the environment needs to be flexible to accommodate other users unless the space is used solely for individuals with ASD. For example, neurotypical (NT) students may share classrooms with students with ASD, therefore the psychological and physical well-being of users without neurological diversities must be accounted for through design whenever possible.

Evidence shows that people with ASD experience buildings and spaces that surround them differently than NT people.[1] Chapters 5, 6, 7, and 8 outline the different sensory issues found in individuals with ASD and provide context for the recommendations suggested in this chapter. The design recommendations outlined in this chapter are evidence-based and draw on theories of environmental/ interior design and architecture, theories of ASD, and from research conducted by the authors. Each suggestion promotes well-being for the adult sector of this population and emphasizes an environmental fit that fosters independence, autonomy, and a sense of self-worth. The recommendations are holistic and embrace a non-pharmaceutical approach to well-being and the achievement of an optimal Quality Of Life (QOL).

Quality Of Life

The quality of life and well-being of people with ASD is an ongoing concern for families, caregivers, and society at large. With the rapid growth of this population and the magnitude of potential health-related issues they may experience, the cost to society over the next few decades is astounding. Generally, well-being is associated with the term *health*, but it is extremely difficult to establish clear boundaries for what a health outcome is. The World Health Organization defines health as a "state of complete physical, mental, and social well-being and not merely the absence of disease or infirmity" (p.42).[2] Well-being and health are often associated with QOL.

For people with ASD, their QOL is often challenged due to their inability to fit into environments they use like NT people. The way people with ASD come to know and make sense of their environment is influenced by their sensory sensitivities and the neurodiverse (ND) manner in which they process information. Frequently, they are agitated when trying to cope with a variety of physical attributes in their environment and, as a result, their stress is manifested in adverse behaviors. Architects, designers, environmental psychologists, and researchers recognize the effect that the setting can have on the perception, behavior, and cognitive processing of people. Numerous empirical studies have confirmed the impact the environment (built and natural settings) has on QOL. Areas of study include: home-like environments versus institutional environments' ability to enhance adaptive behaviors[3]; personalization, distinctiveness, and stimulation[4]; independence[5]; enhanced resident functioning, activity level, and social contact; learning environments[6, 7, 8, 9]; therapeutic environments[10, 11]; healing gardens[12]; and biophilia design/neurological nourishment.[13] Collectively, this research provides stimulus for the development of spaces in order to provide an optimum environmental fit for individuals with ASD.

Currently there are limited guidelines available to designers, architects, and facility managers to help create spaces that accommodate and ameliorate the challenges and conditions faced by adults with ASD. Given the neuro-sensitivities individuals on the spectrum experience in processing the environments with which they interact, a more informed and systemic approach to the design of these spaces is required. Although the Americans with Disabilities Act (ADA) has done much to make buildings accessible for people with physical impairments, it has had minimal impact on environmental accessibility issues for those with intellectual disabilities.[14, 15] Providing equitable building access for the disabled is a complex and ongoing global issue, especially since controlling legislation and building standards vary according to each country's understanding and/or acceptance of the issue.

The majority of design information available to designers who work with this population focuses on the physical needs of people with disabilities and the needs of a typical aging population. Although research on learning environments for this population and housing for aging and dementia-related diseases has advanced, there are few studies that examine housing and living environments for adults with autism. Additionally, although housing for the aged who are cognitively challenged can help provide direction for the design of environments for people with ASD, they do not take into account the "ableness" of this population and celebrate the many talents and abilities they have the potential to share. They also do not typically acknowledge the necessity of providing opportunities for residents to be contributing members of the household with their own economic stability.

Designing to Promote Routine

Individuals with ASD tend to thrive in environments that are laid out in orderly, predictable ways. Spaces should be straightforward and easy to navigate.[16] This is because individuals with autism have difficulty forming mental maps of spaces they travel through.[17] Mostafa recommends compartmentalization of spaces because dedicated spaces for specific activities help people with autism maintain daily routines.[18] Compartmentalization is particularly desirable when activities are consistently completed in the same manner. Spaces that are compartmentalized can limit the sensory inputs that a person needs to process, and encourages concentration on a task. For example, an individual with ASD may get ready for their day in the same location each morning to streamline the dressing and personal hygiene process.

People who care for and support people with ASD put a substantial amount of time into helping individuals build skills to care for themselves. Having the environment they use planned to facilitate learning is important. Reinforcing routines may be accomplished through incorporating appropriate adjacencies (Figure 9.1) and configuring spaces to communicate the sequencing of activities. These activities include taking care of morning and nighttime routines. Morning routines may include a) performing personal hygiene upon waking, b) getting ready for work, and c) tidying room. Nighttime routines may involve a) bathroom routines such as bathing, brushing teeth, using toilet, b) choosing and laying clothing out for the next day, and c) going to bed. The organization and order in the closet shown below (Figure 9.2) can also aid a person with ASD in developing a routine to get dressed on their own.

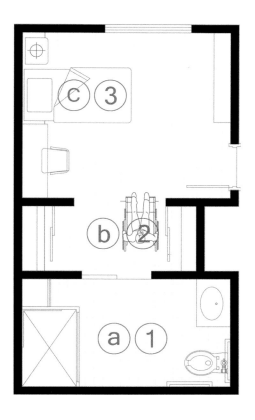

9.1 (top) Designing for Routine

9.2 (bottom) Designing for Routine: Organized storage of personal items helps establish and reinforce routines

Designing for Predictability

One of the keys to providing empowerment to people with ASD is to help them gain independence. Improving an individual's ability to navigate throughout spaces is especially important for empowerment and independence. Clear sight lines, definable architectural forms and surfaces, and purposeful, meaningful spaces serve as modeling devices that help the occupant learn independently. Careful configuration and application of the forms within a space—including ceilings, floors, walls, and architectural features and fixtures including doors, windows, cabinetry, and furnishings—all contribute to empowerment and predictability.

Building materials, finishes, textures, patterns, and colors provide meaning within a space and serve as a learning tool that can empower an individual with ASD to be more independent. Providing transparency throughout spaces can allow individuals to predict what is around them. This transparency can be accomplished with areas that allow one to see beyond the immediate setting, or in more subtle applications like screens and frosted or textured glass. Opportunities to overlook, sit to the side and view a space from a distance, as afforded in an open concept, allows someone with ASD to adjust to an environment and make a decision about how and when they would personally like to be engaged with a space. The opportunity to preview a space before entering also permits them to observe, ponder, digest, and learn what appropriate behavior is and to develop an understanding of what activities take place in a room.

Buildings, interiors, and surroundings that include order help people with ASD adjust to NT environments. Designers can bring order to spaces by:

- clearly defining individual parts and groupings
- identifying intersections of spaces
- clarifiying the intent of visability
- creating sequencing of spaces
- creating hierarchal arrangement of spaces

9.3 Designing for Predictability: Views from a distance provide insights into the purpose and activities of a particular space

Communication of Purpose

Providing spaces that communicate their purpose and the expected behaviors within the setting is important to help a person with ASD fit into an environment and contribute in a productive and meaningful way. Careful manipulation and configuration of built forms like furnishings, finishes, and equipment allows an individual with ASD to experience and maneuver through a space with cognitive clarity. For example, spaces, such as kitchens, that demonstrate food preparation, storage, and clean up areas help individuals

on the spectrum understand the meaning and purpose of each space. The visual representation of fixtures, equipment, appliances, and cabinetry helps put a space into context. The positioning of work centers in the kitchen helps one see the steps in a process, satisfying their need for predictability and routine. In the following image (Figure 9.4), an individual can see different stations within this kitchen area. There is an area for hand washing and dishes (A), an area for food prep (B), and an area for cooking at the stove (C). Sequencing these stations in a way that follows the natural order of cooking would promote routine for an individual on the spectrum.

9.4 Communication of Purpose: Careful spatial arrangements of plumbing and cooking fixtures help indicate the function of a space and the sequence of events

9.5 Sequence of Events: Unobstructed sightlines reinforce the function of a space

Locating spaces such as dining areas adjacent to kitchens and family rooms also helps people with ASD to see the sequence of activities. The visual connection between spaces (Figure 9.5) allows them to forecast what's next and learn the appropriate behaviors and activities associated with each space. For example, in the above figure (Figure 9.5), the eating area is very close to a lounge area. This may give an individual on the spectrum clues as to what is going to come next, or indicate the natural sequence of events.

Selecting a layout, furniture, finishes, and accessories that convey important information to the user allow individuals with ASD to develop behaviors that are expected by NT populations. Placing dining table settings, placemats, and chairs to identify personal space, and setting the table to reflect cultural norms of eating as a group helps an individual develop an appreciation of the meal-making process. This also encourages them to have proper manners and eating techniques to help with their tendency to eat quickly and potentially choke.[19]

Wayfinding

Clearly defined access, entries, and exits enable one to approach a social setting, engage in conversation, and leave if he or she is overwhelmed. Predictable, permanent landmarks also help individuals with ASD orient themselves in a given space. Carefully

9.6 Designing for Wayfinding: Clearly defined architectural forms and finishes help those with ASD find their way

laid out landmarks such as columns, archways, and views to a garden leave a lasting impression on people. These landmarks can also help people remember where they have been and where they want to go. Identifiable, permanent features also enable individuals to see and make connections with the space around them. These types of features may also trigger memories that help people recognize appropriate behaviors in settings. All of these triggers are important in communicating how an individual on the spectrum should act in different settings. Various applications of the elements and principles of design such as pattern, texture, light, and color in the environment can help one adjust to social settings, because people on the spectrum rely on the sense of touch to make their way through a space.[20]

The organization of a space helps one understand a space and empowers them to be an informed user. Thoughtful places, forms, shapes, colors, and textures can help people create mental maps, which is challenging for individuals with ASD.[21] The spatial characteristics within a given setting are defined by destination places, boundaries, circulation systems, and furnishings.

The physical environment can be confusing for all people and difficult to read and understand regardless of one's abilities. The multitude of information (in most cases) can be identifiable by engagement of the senses. Some places are intended for movements and exchanges and others are intended for withdrawal and isolation. Both directions suggest one take action or pause. According to Lynch, destination places are frequently categorized as districts or domains where people go to perform duties or participate in activities.[22] In large settings such as shopping centers, hospitals, and campuses, destination places are usually prominent points on a pathway that a person takes to get from one area to another. Circulation systems determine the way one moves around within a facility. Attributes within a circulation system can form lasting memories and enable people to make connections. In Figure 9.6, architectural delineation and curvilinear walls create memorable spaces that aid in wayfinding. These shapes work with human body forms and provide direction for means of travel.

Usually, circulation systems are made up of arrival spaces, pathways, and nodes. Arrival spaces serve to make an initial overall impression on the visitor and serve as a departure point. Arrival spaces represent a transition between the inside and outside. Depending on the occupancy load of the facility, most public spaces work well if their volume is increased by width, depth, and height. Additionally, if the circulation space is adorned with interesting architectural features, there is a better chance it will leave a lasting impact on an individual and help them remember where they started. Similarly, spaces that branch off the arrival area need to be clearly defined. Flooring, in particular, needs to be considered, as people with ASD frequently look at the floor to become grounded and establish their footing. Flooring that delineates transitions from space to space is essential. However, this delineation should not include complex patterns that someone on the spectrum may fixate on and become distracted by. Changes in ceiling heights, wall colors and textures, and variation in light can also help this group determine changes in spatial levels, i.e. from public to private. In design, these pathways are often referred to as primary, secondary, and tertiary pathways.

Clearly defined transitions should include nodes of transition. Nodes frequently include special places along a pathway that invite social connections and communication. In urban planning, this is where the coffee shop, bakery, or convenience store is located. Often, these are considered in-between places and are used as a place of rest or conversation. For individuals with ASD, nodes can be helpful for them to pause, gather their thoughts, and make decisions about which way to go. Sometimes nodes denote an intersection where pathways lead off to narrow areas of privacy or more open areas that are very public.

Within pathways, boundaries serve as a means of communicating information. They may be used to inform a person about where a setting or activity stops and starts. Boundaries can be opaque and signify an end or a turning point. They can also be transparent or semi-transparent with the use of glass, frosted glass, or diffused glass.

Designing for Social Interaction

The development of social competencies as a child is imperative to being accepted as an adult. People with ASD are at risk for failure in social competence because social skills may be lacking.[23, 24] Frequently, they misinterpret social information and act on these errors in their social relationships. Hobson reported a series of studies demonstrating that children with autism cannot discriminate emotional and social cues nearly as well as their typically developing peers of comparable mental age.[25] Specifically, deficits were noted in interpersonal relationships, use of play and leisure time, and coping skills relative to typically developing people. Others, too, have found pervasive impairments in social development.[26, 27] This suggests that no one particular facet of socialization distinguishes autism from other developmental disorders.

Designing spaces that respect the social inhibitions common in people with ASD means creating environments that help them overcome their "mind-blindness," the lack of ability to understand the way others think and behave, read body language, facial expressions, etc.[28, 29] Providing opportunities for one to look and see what is going on in a space is one way to help them overcome their mind-blindness. This can be achieved in several ways such as creating positive versus negative space, providing homelike settings, and providing opportunities for prospect and refuge. The open-concept family, kitchen, and dining room shown in Figure 9.7 opposite illustrates this design intervention for encouraging social interaction. In this example, the adjacencies of positive and negative spaces provide interventions for social interaction.

Positive spaces are generally preferred by people for lingering and social interaction. "Negative spaces tend to promote movement rather than dwelling space" (p.6).[30] Positive spaces can be created by providing residential furnishings, warm colors, and the implementation of focal points such as a fireplace in a great room. The warm color[31, 32] draws them into the storytelling environment around the fire, which is known to be the inviting heart of the home.[33]

Spaces that provide for prospect and refuge also encourage social interaction. Refuge is a place free from predators and harsh weather. Large areas should be divided into smaller areas. Areas with lower ceilings that permit looking out to more open spaces are positive, as they provide refuge and the opportunity to look for prospect.[34, 35] Social inhibitions can also occur when individuals with ASD are uncomfortable approaching and maneuvering through a space. This challenge is primarily due to a weak vestibular and proprioceptive system. Research has concluded that it is due to diversities in neurological processing and vision in people with ASD.[36] The vestibular system relates to the positioning of the head in relation to the body. The proprioceptive system relates to the position and movement of the body in relation to space and objects. The placement of architectural features, furniture, fitments, and finishes can help a person with ASD interact more

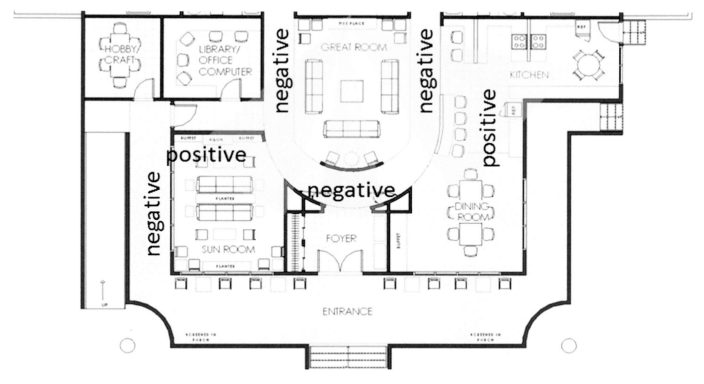

9.7 The adjacencies of positive and negative spaces in the plan provide interventions for social interaction

socially by defining clear pathways and delineating where spaces start, branch off, and finish.

Engagement

Several design interventions are recommended to help a person with ASD fit into the environments they use. One of the key suggestions in this chapter is the implementation of the elements and principles of design that support concepts inherent of Appleton's prospect-refuge theory.[37] Providing a sheltered space where individuals can look onto other settings can create areas for prospect. Incorporating both open and closed spaces into the building configuration and using floor-to-ceiling windows like those found in a sunroom also enable individuals to gain control over their environment and feel more engaged. These types of spaces allow individuals with ASD to "visually test the waters" and observe their surroundings without being noticed. This is important for these individuals' well-being, as they are often intimidated by large group settings and are unsure of what is expected of them in certain social settings.

Spatial engagement can be directed or encouraged by designing walls strategically to communicate purpose. Accent walls that emphasize variety in scale, proportion, texture, pattern, and color help people understand what activities take place in an area and often dictate formal or informal behaviors. A wall heavily adorned with detailed moldings and fresco work can signify fomality, whereas a painted concrete wall can communicate rough play. Walls that are divided, transparent, or permeable allow for sensory differentiation.

One of the biggest challenges people with ASD experience is how they perceive the environments they interact with. Contrary to the manner in which NT people perceive space, most people with ASD perceive their surroundings in pieces rather than as a whole.[38] Because of this challenge, it is important to organize or group objects, fixtures, and equipment in such a manner that they make up a whole. Patterning the space in such a manner that it is not boring, but rather is an organized complexity, is advocated by Salingaros in his biophilia design approach.[39]

Pattern helps code a space to communicate with the complex mind, breaking it down into parts that make up a whole. The parts act as a communication tool to construct the whole and thereby foster communication to the level of NT population expectations. One way to achieve this is to arrange seating in groups that are demarcated by floor finishes. The following image (Figure 9.8) illustrates a setting/grouping that is defined by floor finishes and the architectural detailing on the ceiling. The area rug denotes a sitting area, and the ceiling delineates a large open plan.

9.8 Defining areas with area rugs and ceiling structures help contain a space within an open-concept plan and help the occupant feel grounded

Another is to provide fixed furnishings such as built-in cabinetry. The consistency of the layout helps build understanding and relates to the individual's need for predictability, as they feel more assured knowing the furnishings and surrounding materials belong together as a unit, and they do not have to work as hard mentally to think about creating a recognizable composition. The format also reassures them that the setting is less likely to change when there is a defined configuration.

Neurologically engaging design can also be achieved by integrating symmetrical elements—forms, shapes, textures, patterns, and color—in the built space or reinforcing the sense of unity and harmony through careful application and juxtaposition of forms, patterns, textures, and colors to create a harmonious

space. Communication can also be enhanced when people with ASD spend time in spaces they can predict. Forms and shapes that are symmetrical, similar in proportion and scale, and are finished with materials that absorb sound provide the consistency they need and reduce the distraction of loud sounds. Repetition of color, texture, and pattern can further enhance a sense of belonging,[40] and memorabilia in a space that one can relate to are also important to encourage one to feel comfortable with joining in a conversation and/or activity. For example, the following plan and perspective (Figure 9.9) illustrate how symmetry can be integrated into design. This increases predictability and can put individuals on the spectrum at ease.

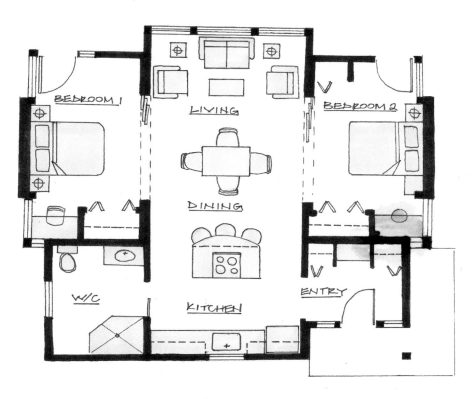

9.9 (top) Symmetrical floor plans provide predictability and fulfill the desire for sameness; (bottom) Symmetrical furniture arrangements provide predictability and fulfill the desire for sameness

9.10 Too much pattern is disturbing for people with ASD, as it is overstimulating and requires one to separate items into too many parts

Enhancing Communication Skills to Aid Social Interaction

Articulating needs and participating actively in conversation is difficult for many adults with ASD. Often the environment did not encourage them, although they may have completed several years of speech development and exposure to a variety of situations where they could practice communicating. Design interventions that are strategically implemented into the built environment may help people with ASD develop their ability to speak and act appropriately. Rooms with an open-concept layout and versatile seating layouts allow one to sit with another person, in a group, or alone in a room and permit viewing from a variety of angles. Ensuring these spaces have minimum vertical obstructions, such as columns, can encourage social interaction. Ensuring there is natural light in every room also promotes social interaction.[41] Additionally, having an organized, clutter-free environment with a neutral color palette helps individuals concentrate on the conversation or activity taking place. A space with too many objects or patterns, as illustrated in

Figure 9.10, may cause individuals on the spectrum to become distracted.

Spaces should be designed to reflect their intended use. For example, spaces for individual reflective thought, solitude, and intimacy should include smaller volumes of space, closed or semi-closed layouts, lower ceiling heights, subdued lighting, and soft finishes. Figure 9.11 shows the contrast of more intimate areas like the dining room and kitchen with lower ceilings to more social areas like the living room with higher ceilings. Spaces that serve as more social areas may feature larger volumes of space, open layouts, taller ceiling heights, brighter lighting, and hard finishes. It may also be helpful for spaces to include nostalgic or themed décor to help people with ASD temper their emotions and be more open to communicate.

Many of the interventions recommended in the communication theme are tensile and can fit within this dimension of engagement as well as communication. For example, the communication of activities and routines can help a person with ASD get involved in activities that they might not readily do on their own. Engagement

9.11 Variation in ceiling heights provides options for the
occupants. Lower ceiling heights provide for intimate, quiet
engagement, whereas higher ceiling levels encourage more
extraverted engagement

can also be encouraged through the careful design of spaces, furnishings, and finishes that connect and stimulate the senses. Given the behavioral characteristics of this population, it is important to engage the visual, kinesthetic, and tactile senses. Varying the composition of the volume of spaces can enable a person with ASD to have a choice and experience an environment at their own pace. The contrast of large, open areas with ample sunlight and high ceilings next to small spaces with low ceilings, subtle lighting, and connecting spaces can create this element of choice for an individual. Developing this choice and creating a comfortable environment for individuals on the spectrum builds confidence and nurtures self-esteem.

Designing for Motivation

Architects and designers know the value of creating buildings and interiors that enrich the lives of those who inhabit them. Well-known architects like Le Corbusier write passages like "My house is practical. I thank you, as I might thank the railway engineers and the telephone service. You have touched my heart." His work expresses the idea that one of the key functions of good design is to enrich the user's experience and, subsequently, their lives. Enriching the lives of people with ASD can take many forms. In the TERI, Campus of Life design, which was conceptualized and developed by Cheryl Gillmor, engagement is an integral part of their operational philosophy. Careful consideration is given to integrating activities and providing opportunities for individuals with ASD to have experiences that expand their mind, enrich them personally, and allow them to see in ways that require looking beyond the obvious.

Throughout this book, we have advocated for the design of environments that are orderly, uncomplicated, safe, satisfying, and provide stability. However, there are times when experiencing spaces that are different than those commonly experienced need to be explored. Spaces that offer a change provide the occupants with opportunities to grow, learn, and feel invigorated. Designing the environment to invigorate includes opportunities for the users to engage independently in areas that interest them. Access to spaces that are not usually experienced in everyday work or life create curiosity. Additionally, spaces that include interesting objects

have a tendency to attract people. These spaces may be theaters, auditoriums, concert halls, spiritual centers, galleries, museums, aquariums, or gardens. Linking buildings for daily use to places for special occasions creates a sense of curiosity. These special occasion spaces are often inspiring to those on the spectrum because they are decorated differently and include festive adornments.

Incorporating different spatial features such as textures, patterns, colors, and different spatial volumes can create elements of surprise. Building entrances, waiting areas, circulation spaces, and destination spaces can be conformed and accented in such a manner that they enrich the occupant's experience. Textures that can be seen and felt can trigger positive sensory resonation and allow individuals with ASD to engage and meet their sensory needs, as they desire.

Providing opportunities for self-directed spatial management of furnishings can also provide enrichment. Many readers can most likely recall their childhood memories of building forts out of cushions or boxes. The ability to manipulate items at a scale similar to one's body size and create different forms and shapes is empowering. Therefore, opportunities for this group to move furnishings (in a safe manner) such as sofas, chairs, pillows, and other objects, and stack them, align them, or arrange them in groupings to determine their own traffic flow can develop their spatial awareness and social interaction skills.

Designing in order to enrich spaces includes incorporating variety and complexity. Variety can be achieved at macro and micro levels. In the building assembly, it could include varying ceiling heights and forms, wall characteristics, and the types of windows and doors. At a more detailed level, variety may be achieved through the lighting, color schemes, patterns, and textures. Varying the proportions and scale to make a statement can provide stimulation and a break from the monotony of regular spaces that may be used on a more frequent basis. Larger spaces that contain unusual forms, surfaces, and artifacts provide a unique experience for people with ASD and can help increase memory function. Special event spaces, for example, attached to a school should be different in scale, proportion, and theme to excite people. Another strategy for creating enrichment in an environment is to embed contrast into the overall setting. This can be provided with the integration of sensory rooms. Enriching spaces can also be achieved through personalization. Adorning spaces that tell a story through themes and images creates feelings of nostalgia and, in some cases, connectedness that establishes the development of friendship and community amongst people.

Encourage

Spaces can be encouraging to individuals when personalization or memorabilia of sentimental value is incorporated. The goal of the design of spaces to encourage is to build self-esteem, motivate, inspire, develop, and grow individuals so they succeed in developing skills to function independently in daily life. Allowing people to have a choice in spaces is also important. It may be possible for residential settings to provide job opportunities for an individual on the spectrum. This opportunity would encourage and empower them.

Flexible furnishings that can adjust as needed to accommodate standing, fidgeting, swinging, or pacing can provide a sense of control over their environment. Including recognizable forms with symmetry and shapes that are rhythmic and orderly assures people with ASD that they are heading the right way and will not get lost. This active involvement sets up a momentum, whereby an individual is motivated to explore each area and develop an understanding of forms, spaces, and actions and therefore feel more comfortable joining in social settings.

Meyers-Levy and Zhu's study on volume of space found that ceiling heights could encourage and discourage social interaction and willingness to participate in activities.[42] They reported that higher ceilings promoted more social interaction and lower ceilings reduced social interaction. Other researchers, such as Rodiek and Schwarz and Kaplan and Herbert, report on "inspiring" design for mental clarity and encouragement.[43,44] Their philosophies reinforce the benefits of integrating nature and nature-like forms in a setting to encourage exploration beyond the obvious. Similarly, Scott used environmental preference theory in interior settings to study the validity of complexity and mystery as predictors of interior preferences and sought to identify design attributes associated with their perception in an indoor setting.[45] The results showed that complexity and mystery, as well as preference, were positively related to each other. Characteristics of interior features associated with complexity included the quantity and variety of architectural and interior components in a scene, the scene's spatial geometry, and the overall composition of the setting. Perceptions of mystery included physical accessibility to the promised information in the scene, distance of view to the nearest point of interest, spatial definition, screening of the promised information, and lighting that offered dramatic contrasts in brightness.[46] In their study they noted homes with higher ceilings induce clarity and improve thinking,

as do a variety of open and closed rooms. Large open-concept areas with high ceilings permit more active conversation with groups, and smaller closed-in rooms with lower ceilings encourage communication on a one-on-one basis or with a couple of people. Being able to see into a room before making a commitment to enter it can satisfy this need for control. Regnier and Denton label this as "previewing." The concept of previewing can be accomplished by sidelights, windows in doors, and subdividing spaces so one has a view from a distance.[47] Previewing methods also help to make entrances and exits more visible once inside a space. This can be helpful for individuals, particularly children, who feel the need to escape from a stressful social situation. Exits that are made more visible by a sidelight or window will help inhabitants to clearly identify an escape route.

All of these recommendations are useful for creating spaces that make individuals with ASD feel more comfortable. It is important that each unique characteristic of individuals on the spectrum is considered when designing spaces that they will frequent. Creating spaces that promote routine can be accomplished by designing environments that are organized based on the sequence of activities that take place in a space. Spaces must also be predictable to individuals on the spectrum in order to foster independence. Environments that are designed to communicate purpose allow individuals to understand how to behave appropriately. Social interaction and engagement should also be promoted whenever possible in order to encourage people on the spectrum to interact with friends, colleagues, and caretakers. While none of these interventions will eliminate the symptoms of ASD, anything to improve an individual's ability to interact with the environment and others should be promoted.

Notes

1. Shabha, Ghasson, and Kristi Gaines. "A comparative analysis of transatlantic design interventions for therapeutically enhanced learning environments—Texas vs West Midlands." *Facilities* 31, no. 13/14 (2013): 634–658.

2. World Health Organization. "Preamble to the Constitution of the World Health Organization as adopted by the International Health Conference." [Official Records of the World Health Organization, no. 2, p. 100]. New York, 1946. pp. 19–22.

3. Heller, Tamar, Alison B. Miller, and Kelly Hsieh. "Eight-year follow-up of the impact of environmental characteristics on well-being of adults with developmental disabilities." *Mental retardation* 40, no. 5 (2002): 366–378.

4. Thompson, Travis, Julia Robinson, Mary Dietrich, Marilyn Farris, and Valerie Sinclair. "Architectural features and perceptions of community residences for people with mental retardation." *American journal of mental retardation: AJMR* 101, no. 3 (1996): 292–314.

5. Moos, Rudolf H., and Sonne Lemke. "Assessing the physical and architectural features of sheltered care settings." *Journal of gerontology* 35, no. 4 (1980): 571–583.

6. Parmelee, Patricia A., and M. Powell Lawton. "The design of special environments for the aged." In *Handbook of the psychology of aging* (pp. 464–488). Academic Press, 2013.

7. Regnier, Victor, and Jon Pynoos. *Housing the aged: Design directives and policy considerations.* Elsevier Publishing Company, 1987.

8. Ulrich, Roger. "View through a window may influence recovery." *Science* 224, no. 4647 (1984): 224–225.

9. Zeisel, John. *Inquiry by Design: Environment/behavior/neuroscience in architecture, interiors, landscape and planning.* New York: WW Norton & Company, 2006.

10. Kaplan, Rachel, and Stephen Kaplan. *The experience of nature: A psychological perspective.* CUP Archive, 1989.

11. Kellert, S. R., J. Heerwagen, and Martin Mador. *Biophilic design: The theory, science, and practice of bringing buildings to life.* Chichester, UK: John Wiley & Sons Ltd., 2008.

12. Zeisel, John, and Martha Tyson. "Alzheimer's treatment gardens." In *Healing gardens: Therapeutic benefits and design recommendations* (pp. 437–504). New York: John Wiley & Sons, 1999.

13. Kellert, S. R., J. Heerwagen, and Martin Mador. *Biophilic design: The theory, science, and practice of bringing buildings to life.* Chichester, UK: John Wiley & Sons Ltd., 2008.

14. Americans with Disabilities Act of 1990 (ADA)—42 U.S. Code Chapter 126, 1990.

15. Castell, Lindsay. "Building access for the intellectually disabled." *Facilities* 26, no. 3/4 (2008): 117–130.

16. Pellicano, Elizabeth, Alastair D. Smith, Filipe Cristino, Bruce M. Hood, Josie Briscoe, and Iain D. Gilchrist. "Children with autism are neither systematic nor optimal foragers." *Proceedings of the National Academy of Sciences* 108, no. 1 (2011): 421–426.

17. Lind, Sophie E., David M. Williams, Jacob Raber, Anna Peel, and Dermot M. Bowler. "Spatial navigation impairments among intellectually high-functioning adults with autism spectrum disorder: Exploring relations with theory of mind, episodic memory, and episodic future thinking." *Journal of abnormal psychology* 122, no. 4 (2013): 1189.

18. Mostafa, Mohamed M. "A hierarchical analysis of the green consciousness of the Egyptian consumer." *Psychology & marketing* 24, no. 5 (2007): 445–473.

19. Brookwood Community Interviews and Observations: Brookwood Community, Brookshire, Texas, June 2013.

20. Bogdashina, Olga. *Autism and the edges of the known world: Sensitivities, language, and constructed reality.* Jessica Kingsley Publishers, 2010.

21. Lind, Sophie E., David M. Williams, Jacob Raber, Anna Peel, and Dermot M. Bowler. "Spatial navigation impairments among intellectually high-functioning adults with autism spectrum disorder: Exploring relations with theory of mind, episodic memory, and episodic future thinking." *Journal of abnormal psychology* 122, no. 4 (2013): 1189.

22. Lynch, Kevin. *The image of the city.* Vol. 11. MIT press, 1960.

23. Gresham, Frank M. "Assessment of children's social skills." *Journal of school psychology* 19, no. 2 (1981): 120–133.

24. Odom, Samuel L., and Scott R. McConnell. *Social competence of young children with disabilities: Issues and strategies for intervention.* Paul H Brookes Pub Co, 1992.

25. Hobson, R. Peter. "The autistic child's appraisal of expressions of emotion." *Journal of child psychology and psychiatry* 27, no. 3 (1986): 321–342.

26. Ungerer, Judy A., and Marian Sigman. "Symbolic play and language comprehension in autistic children." *Journal of the American Academy of Child Psychiatry* 20, no. 2 (1981): 318–337.

27. Volkmar, Fred R., Rhea Paul, Ami Klin, and Donald J. Cohen, eds. *Handbook of autism and pervasive developmental disorders, diagnosis, development, neurobiology, and behavior.* Vol. 1. John Wiley & Sons, 2005.

28. Belmonte, Matthew. "What's the story behind 'theory of mind' and autism?" *Journal of consciousness studies* 16, no. 6–8 (2009): 118–139.

29. Frith, Uta. "Mind blindness and the brain in autism." *Neuron* 32, no. 6 (2001): 969–979.

30. Frederick, Matthew. *101 things I learned in architecture school.* Cambridge: MIT Press, 2007.

31. Bellizzi, Joseph A., Ayn E. Crowley, and Ronald W. Hasty. "The effects of color in store design." *Journal of retailing* 59, no. 1 (1983): 21–45.

32. Augustin, Sally. *Place advantage: Applied psychology for interior architecture.* John Wiley & Sons, 2009.

33. Alexander, Christopher, Sara Ishikawa, and Murray Silverstein. *A pattern language: Towns, buildings, construction.* Vol. 2. Oxford University Press, 1977.

34. Hildebrand, Grant. *Origins of architectural pleasure.* University of California Press, 1999.

35. Regnier, Victor, Jennifer Hamilton, and Suzie Yatabe. *Assisted living for the aged and frail: Innovations in design, management, and financing.* Columbia University Press, 1995.

36. Weimer, Amy K., Amy M. Schatz, Alan Lincoln, Angela O. Ballantyne, and Doris A. Trauner. "'Motor' impairment in Asperger syndrome: Evidence for a deficit in proprioception." *Journal of developmental & behavioral pediatrics* 22, no. 2 (2001): 92–101.

37. Appleton, Jay. *The Experience of landscape.* New York: John Wiley & Sons, 1975.

38. Köhler, W. *Gestalt psychology.* New York: H. Liveright, 1929.

39. Salingaros, Nikos A., and Michael W. Mehaffy. *A theory of architecture.* UMBAU-VERLAG Harald Püschel, 2006.

40. Reed, Ron. *Color+design: Transforming interior space.* Fairchild Books, 2010.

41. Alexander, Christopher, Sara Ishikawa, and Murray Silverstein. *A pattern language: Towns, buildings, construction.* Vol. 2. Oxford University Press, 1977.

42. Meyers-Levy, Joan, and Rui Juliet Zhu. "The influence of ceiling height: The effect of priming on the type of processing that people use." *Journal of consumer research* 34, no. 2 (2007): 174–186.

43. Rodiek, Susan, and Benyamin Schwarz. "Perceptions of physical environment features that influence outdoor usage at assisted living facilities." In *The role of the outdoors in residential environments for aging* (pp. 95–107). Binghamton, NY: Haworth Press, 2005.

44. Kaplan, Rachel, and Eugene J. Herbert. "Cultural and sub-cultural comparisons in preferences for natural settings." *Landscape and urban planning* 14 (1987): 281–293.

45. Scott, Suzanne C. "Visual attributes related to preference in interior environments." *Journal of interior design* 18, no. 1–2 (1993): 7–16.

46. Meyers-Levy, Joan, and Rui Juliet Zhu. "The influence of ceiling height: The effect of priming on the type of processing that people use." *Journal of consumer research* 34, no. 2 (2007): 174–186.

47. Regnier, Victor, and Alexis Denton. "Ten new and emerging trends in residential group living environments." *Neurorehabilitation* 25, no. 3 (2008): 169–188.

Learning Environments

A serious problem among individuals with ASD, particularly children, may be a lack of interest and motivation in academics and learning. Academic tasks may be too challenging or simply boring for students on the spectrum. Students with ASD may exhibit disruptive behavior as a way to avoid or escape an academic task.[1] Inattentiveness is often caused by sensory overload. Children on the spectrum become easily distracted from too much incoming information from the environment. Another prominent challenge involved in designing spaces for children with ASD is that no two cases are alike. Symptoms vary from mild to severe, and some children on the spectrum have intellectual disabilities or impaired speech, while others do not.[2]

The education of students with ASD may be compromised in many cases by their inability to process sensory information typically.[3] Teachers and students alike are dissatisfied with their current learning environments.[4] Poorly designed schools that are too loud, bright, and unstructured will be confusing to a child with ASD, and they will receive little benefit from attending school.[5] Modifying the design of a classroom for students has been shown to improve learning performance, reduce negative behaviors, and increase attention span.[6] Some environmental factors that cause distraction and lead to sensory triggers are background noise, glare, open storage systems, clutter, and large numbers of students and teachers.[7] Creating environments with limited or well-controlled sensory stimuli will help students learn and stay focused. Depending on their level of function, students on the spectrum go to school to learn skills that will help them live independently in the future. Quite possibly, a disruptive and confusing learning environment might prevent individuals with ASD from learning these skills and achieving future independence.

Federal law in the United States requires that students with disabilities, including ASD, be educated in the general education classroom to the fullest extent possible. While this may not be the ideal placement for all students on the spectrum, for many, learning within an inclusive environment with other typically developing students can be very beneficial. In reality, much of the built environment is actually inhibiting a student's ability to learn the necessary skills to become successful, inclusive members of society.[8] For these reasons, every learning space, from full inclusion to self-contained, should be designed to foster a positive learning environment for students with ASD.

Table 10.1 Categories, Issues, and Findings Related to Advantages or
Disadvantages in Inclusion of Students in the General Education Classroom.

CATEGORY	ISSUES AND FINDINGS	RELATED ARTICLES
Advantages	1. Growth in social outcomes	Baker et al., 1994–1995
	2. Improvement in self-concept	Peck, Carlson & Helmstetter, 1992
	3. Cost effectiveness	Banerji & Dailey, 1995
	4. Improved academic performance	Affleck et al., 1988
	5. Improved motivation	Baker et al., 1994–1995
	6. Fewer behavioral infractions	Benerji & Dailey, 1995
		Rea et al., 2002
		Waldron & McLeskey, 1998
		Benerji & Dailey, 1995
		Rea et al., 2002
Disadvantages	1. Served better in special education classrooms	Holloway, 2001
	2. No benefit/difference	McDonnell et al., 2003
	3. Effective for some/not all	Affleck et al., 1988
		Fore et al., 2008
		Manset & Semmel, 1997

Inclusion versus Special Education

Inclusion is a controversial concept in education. Inclusion strives to educate each student to the fullest extent possible in a general education classroom. The support services may be brought to the child instead of moving the child for services. Proponents of inclusion believe that the student should begin in a general education classroom and should only be removed if the necessary interventions cannot be provided in a regular classroom.

The Individuals with Disabilities Education Act (IDEA) addresses the legal rights of students with disabilities.[9] The IDEA enables millions of children with disabilities to receive special services designed to meet their unique needs, and requires that students with disabilities be provided with supplementary aids and services as needed to help them succeed. These may include teacher assistance, additional services, equipment or accommodation, modification of lessons, computer–assisted devices, and preferential seating. The IDEA also states that a child may only be removed from general education when "the nature and severity of the disability" does not allow the child to be satisfactorily educated in general education classes, even with the use of supplementary aids and services.

A continuum of placements should be made available from full inclusion to self-contained special education classrooms. Full inclusion is not required by law and is not beneficial for all students with learning differences. An Individual Education Program (IEP) is developed for a child with disabilities. An IEP team composed of educators, administrators, parents, and therapists determines the proper placement for each individual. The educational benefits, non-academic benefits, the effect the child has on the teacher and other students in the general education classroom, and costs are considered in placement.

A review of literature revealed varied outcomes for students with disabilities in inclusive classroom settings. However, the majority of studies contend that academic and behavioral performance for students with disabilities is improved in inclusive classrooms.[10, 11, 12, 13, 14] Other benefits of inclusion include growth in social outcomes and improved self-concept. Additionally, inclusive education is more cost-effective.[15]

A number of studies suggest that students with disabilities prefer and do better in special education classrooms.[16, 17, 18] Other studies show no academic benefit to general education settings compared to special education classrooms.[19, 20, 21, 22] These studies contend that students' needs are better served in self-contained classrooms or that inclusion is beneficial for some students but not all. Table 10.1 outlines the categories, issues, and findings related to advantages and disadvantages of inclusion. An important step in providing a therapeutic learning environment for students with ASD will be to determine the proper educational placement for each individual student.

The TEACCH Approach to Autism Spectrum Disorders

The principles of the therapeutic environment may be seen through the TEACCH (Treatment and Education of Autistic and related Communication-handicapped Children) approach. This method strives to provide the optimal learning environment geared for students with ASD by taking into account the sensory and psychological differences. TEACCH was developed in the 1970s by Eric Schopler. The emphasis is placed on individualized assessment. The skills of each student are used to determine whether a student should be educated in regular educational programs or spend part or all of a day in special classrooms where the physical environment and curriculum can be organized based on individual needs.

An important priority is cultivating the strengths of individuals with ASD, such as visual skills, recognizing details, and memory. Another focus of TEACCH is an individual's interest and talents. Incorporating strengths and interests encourages positive interactions and makes students with ASD easier to teach.

The TEACCH method is also called Structured Teaching and includes elements such as:

- Organization of the physical environment
- A predictable sequence of activities
- Visual schedules
- Routines with flexibility
- Work/activity systems
- Visually structured activities

Visual and physical organization are extremely important in the classroom. The first step is developing an appropriate physical layout. The furniture must be placed to "decrease stimulation, limit distractions, reduce anxiety, and promote independence and more consistent and effective work."[23] The students need visual cues and physical boundaries to know which activity takes place in various parts of the classroom.

The various ages of students require differences in physical organization. Younger children need areas for play, snacks, and individual and group activities. Older students need to be able to develop vocational skills, have places for individual and group work, and pursue leisure interests. No matter the age, all academic materials should be clearly marked and located in close proximity to where they will be used in order to promote independence.

A study by Panerai, Ferrante, and Zinagle compared a TEACCH program and an integration program for individuals with disabilities.[24] The TEAACH program was applied to eight students in the control group, while eight other subjects were integrated in regular schools with a support teacher. All students were diagnosed with autism according to DSM-IV criteria. The results did not show a statistically significant difference in communication and interpersonal skills between the two groups. Significant decreases in stereotypic behaviors were not noted in either setting. However, PsychoEducation Profile—Revised scores showed a statistically significant difference in all aspects except fine motor skills in the control group. The other categories showing improvement were imitation, perception, gross motor skills, hand-eye coordination, cognitive performance, and developmental age.

The TEACCH model has also been shown to decrease behavioral difficulties in adults with autism with severe disabilities.[25] The participants were recruited from the Carolina Living and Learning Center, and 85 percent had moderate to severe mental disabilities. They received an increase in structure and individualized programming in communication, independence, socialization, developmental planning, and positive behavior management.

Higher-functioning students with ASD may be educated in regular classrooms or divide up the day between TEACCH and general education settings. In a regular classroom, students with ASD may need an area to work where there are minimal distractions. A quiet area (such as a break-out space) should be provided where the student can go at times if noise and visual stimulation become difficult to handle. According to Division TEACCH, the following are some questions for teachers to consider when arranging their classroom:

- Is there space provided for individual and group work?
- Are work areas located in the least distractible settings?
- Are work areas marked so that a student can find his or her own way?
- Are there consistent work areas for those students who need them?
- Does the teacher have easy visual access to all work areas?
- Are there places for students to put finished work?
- Are work materials in a centralized area and close to work areas?

- Are a student's materials easily accessible and clearly marked for him or her?
- Are play or leisure areas as large as possible? Are they away from exits?
- Are they away from areas and materials that students should not have access to during free time?
- Are boundaries of the areas clear?
- Can the teacher observe the area from all other areas of the room?
- Are the shelves in the play or leisure area cluttered with toys and games that are broken or no one ever uses?

Physical/Visual Location of Student

Mesibov and Howley found that pupils with ASD that are educated in general education classrooms frequently have difficulty with independent work.[26] They must have clear understanding of an independent work space. Many times, the students will perform better when seated near or facing the teacher at the end of a row of desks or at the corner of a table. For some students, a work space in a quiet part of the classroom is beneficial. Visual barriers are necessary for some students.[27]

Additionally, they found that students who change classrooms may benefit from having the same place to sit in each classroom. The needs and strengths of individuals with ASD vary; however, a seat close to the door will allow a student to easily leave the room if feeling anxious. This placement would not be appropriate for all students, but might work for a secondary student with Asperger's, for example.

Another benefit delineated by Mesibov and Howley is that independent work areas also benefit many students with ASD.[28] A systematic approach is a strategy that includes the tasks that need to be completed within a lesson. This approach will build independence and generalization of skills outside of the setting. If more than one student needs such a work space, a schedule may be established so that only one student works in the space at a time. This work space should be designed to reduce distraction and clarify the purpose of the area. Students need to learn to focus on the assigned tasks, sustain attention, and learn to work independently.[29]

All students need to develop work and organization skills. Many students with ASD display poor organizational or sequencing skills.[30]

They may not understand what assignment they are to do, where to place the finished assignment, or what to do after they complete a task. This may lead to challenging behavior. Different students will benefit from different work systems. Mesibov and Howley state that teachers can enable students to participate by considering:

- The learning environment
- Organization and sequencing
- Motivation and concentration
- Communication[31]

Students need to understand what to do when they are finished with an assignment. A simple arrangement is the left-to-right work system. The student's work is placed on the left in trays or baskets. When finished, the assignment is placed in a space on the right. The student places finished work in a clearly marked box. The finished box helps the student transition to other activities. This type of system prevents students from becoming overwhelmed by too many choices. The same type of system can be set up for multiple tasks, with separate boxes to place each individual task in. Giving students a visual reminder of what they may do once each task is complete may motivate them to finish tasks. These objects should be placed in the student's field of vision, but contained in a clear bag or box of some kind.[32]

A one-size-fits-all approach to classroom placement does not work for students with ASD. Many students benefit from full inclusion, while others require all or a portion of the day in a self-contained or TEACCH classroom. Since every classroom is potentially inclusive, the design of all classrooms should abide by the guidelines of a therapeutic environment to promote learning for every student.

Environmental Considerations

Visual Learning

Students on the spectrum may lack motivation in school because information is not always presented in the ideal way to convey a message to someone with ASD. Many individuals on the spectrum are highly visual thinkers, so much so that they have difficulty learning words other than nouns for which a mental image cannot be created.[33] Some children prefer information in a musical form, for example, as opposed to a verbal or visual format.[34] Others prefer to communicate in writing rather than verbally.[35] Teachers need to learn how students with ASD prefer to communicate and be open to presenting information in unconventional, creative ways.

Spatial Organization

Visual supports through spatial organization should be considered in any environment where the child interacts. Clear and visual boundaries should be apparent to help minimize visual and auditory distractions. Large, wide-open areas should be avoided since some individuals with ASD may not segment their environments.[36] The increase in structure will improve the concentration of all students in a classroom.[37]

Research has shown that children with autism have a tendency to organize their surroundings through their senses rather than relating to spaces according to their function.[38, 39] Therefore, spaces that cater to the differentiated ways of understanding of this group are essential. One way to accommodate these differences is to design spaces in zones. Zoning a space requires a match to the expected activity that will take place in it. For example, spaces that include activities that are highly physical, such as gymnasiums, and high acoustical levels, such as music rooms, need to be grouped together, and less physically active, quieter areas need to be put together. This zoning intervention can help students relate to spaces and understand appropriate behaviors associated with a space. Spaces that are intentionally zoned for order, sequencing, and routine are essential to the needs of children with autism. Purposeful zoning of school facilities and classrooms also relates to Grandin's perspective that people with autism think in pictures and learn to make sense of their environments through pattern associations and color.[40] In her well-known book *Thinking in Pictures*, she illustrates the importance of providing spatial queuing through patterns and colors conscientiously applied to space to develop comprehension. Rupal Engineer of Design Plus in Albuquerque, New Mexico and Christopher Beaver of GA Architects in the United Kingdom recognize these differences and have designed spaces that support these principles.

Zoning

A lack of physical structure can result in a student with ASD wandering around a classroom.[41] Each area of the environment should be clearly defined through furniture placement and use of boundary markers such as carpet squares, colored floor tape, or screens.[42, 43] A beneficial classroom structure would provide for independent work, group work, and leisure. An adjacent quiet or break-out room slightly to the side will help ease some of the sensory distractions of a larger room. Pictures, color-coding, numbers, and symbols can be used to teach the children to keep the physical environment organized.[44] Specific learning stations should provide order, and organized bins should help students to get their own materials. Visual distractions should be limited, and unnecessary equipment should be stored in another area. Alcoves and table groupings within a classroom help facilitate social learning and stimulate the social brain.[45] Figure 10.1 (overleaf) provides a prototype classroom.

Spatial relations also need to be designed to complement the differentiated rhythm of movement (proprioception and vestibular senses) children with ASD often express. As noted earlier in this book, many children with autism display physical bodily movements that require greater personal space, areas to expel energy, and other times to comfort themselves. Meeting all of these needs in a shared public environment such as a school can be a challenge. Purposeful zoning is one approach to accommodate the differentiated kinetic being and sensory differences. GA Architects recognize the need for purposefully designed spaces and reinvent corridors into decompression zones to enable students to collect their thoughts and emotions and manage their behavior. Their approach eliminates corridors and configures them into spaces that invite social interaction and places to pause. These spaces often include fixed bench seating and areas with views to nature (Figure 10.2). The alcoves allow for impromptu conversations and encourage one-on-one communication while slowing the pace in the corridors. The strategically laid out architectural forms noted in the change of planes and finishes help students transition from space to space. The architectural forms, colors, and signage remind them where they have come from and where they are going. Space alcoves and furniture in hallways discourage high-speed traffic and create places of pause. GA Architects recognize these principles in designing for individuals with ASD as illustrated in Figure 10.2 (overleaf). This image shows ways to incorporate places to pause into circulation spaces.

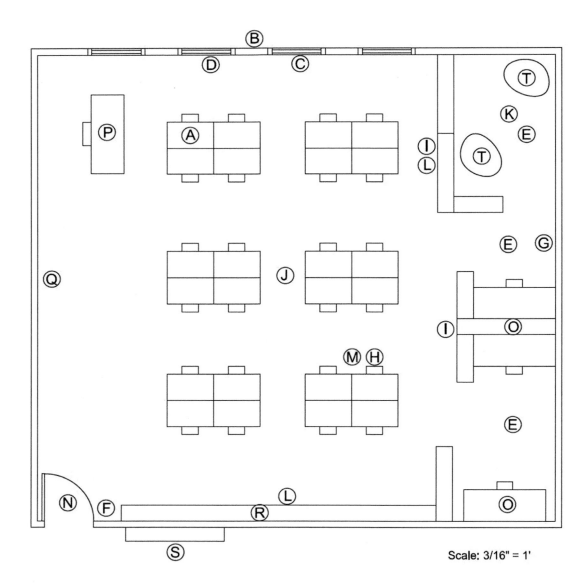

Scale: 3/16" = 1'

A A student with ASD should sit near the teacher's desk.

B Daylighting or full-spectrum lighting is preferred.

C Cover the bottom part of windows with an item such as a bulletin board to reduce distractions yet allow natural light.

D Provide window blinds to control light.

E Use incandescent table or floor lamps as primary or supplementary sources of light.

F Flexible switching should be available for overhead lighting.

G Use natural colors such as blue and green.

H Discover the student's favorite color and use it in the environment for instruction.

I Use boundary markers such as screens, tape, and furniture arrangement.

J Provide an informal seating arrangement.

K Provide a break-out space or attached auxiliary space.

L Keep items hidden that are a source of distraction (e.g. toys).

M Provide study carrels.

N Close classroom door during passing periods.

O Provide independent work stations.

P Teacher's desk.

Q White board/chalk board.

R Lockers.

S Display area for student work.

T Provide some soft furnishings such as beanbag chairs.

10.1 (facing page) Classroom Arrangement for Students with ASD

10.2 (above) Places of pause in circulation spaces

Other Learning Spaces

Quiet Spaces

A majority of learning spaces will likely feel overwhelming to a student on the spectrum. Because the majority of children with ASD have hyper-sensitivities with heightened senses, they will need a space to retreat and regroup away from the rest of the class.[46, 47, 48] A quiet area (such as a break-out space) should be provided where the student can go at times if noise and visual stimulation become difficult to handle. A tent or teepee may be included in the corner of a room to create this quiet space. An adjacent quiet or break-out room slightly to the side of the room can also help to ease some of the sensory distractions of a larger room.

Play Space

A structured play space may be incorporated into classrooms. The area should have a low-level divider to set it apart from the rest of the room. Two tables arranged alongside one another will help a child with ASD learn to work and play next to another student.[49]

A therapeutic environment should also provide for external access. Learning should take place in a school's external environment as well as the interior. Outdoor spaces should be provided for recreation and physical education, social development, and academic learning. Pathways, gardens, seating, ball fields, covered porches, and playgrounds contribute to optimal learning. Urban schools should incorporate interior courtyards or play areas above parking lots or lunch rooms.

Furniture

Providing comfortable and appropriate furniture for all students is an important consideration in the classroom. Students in the same grade often experience size differences, creating ergonomic problems when using one-size-fits-all furniture. For example, third and fourth graders remain seated for two thirds of the school day. A seated position places 75 percent of the total body weight on only four square inches of a person's body.[50] The use of the legs, feet, and back in contact with other surfaces is necessary for equilibrium. Without properly proportioned furniture, sitting requires more control and use of muscles to maintain stability and equilibrium. The result can be fidgeting, poor posture, and back or neck pain.[51]

10.3 Node chair with tripod base, cup holder, work surface, and media stand

A furniture intervention that researchers at Steelcase Education recommend for classrooms supporting an individual's active learning, thereby fostering support for special needs, is the Node™ chair. Their research observations showed that students bring a lot of "stuff" to class, including backpacks full of books, electronic devices, notebooks, etc. If the teacher asks students to move around the space, then these items are often left behind as tripping spots. Additionally, if a student needs an item, it is not convenient for retrieval. Thus, the Node chair's design was born out of understanding a new problem to solve (Figure 10.3). The following aspects of the design are worth noting: (1) the Node is a self-contained learning "pod," (2) a swivel seat allows for fluid pedagogical modal switch, (3) a work surface means when the student turns to engage in a different direction, the work surface goes with him or her, (4) a storage compartment under the seat holds backpacks, as does the curved arm for vertical access, (5) castors allow the teacher to have students move into different groups without major disruption, (6) ergonomic fit and flex supporting micro movements, and (7) this chair may become one's personal space.

Schools that specialize in educating students with autism such as Newmark, have implemented Node chairs into most of their classrooms. According to Dr. Regina Peter, Executive Director

10.4 (top) Node chairs are arranged with desks in clusters to accommodate small groups of students

10.5 (middle) The flexible seating arrangement in this classroom provides opportunities for students to collaborate at a digital board or view presentations from a variety of angles

10.6 (bottom) Newmark School. Steelcase, Inc.

at Newmark Education, they allow children with autism to wiggle and fidget without interrupting their classmates and allow them secure ownership of their personal space and belongings, a main concern of most children with autism. According to education researcher and designer Lennie Scott-Webber, PhD, former founding Director of Education Environments at Steelcase Education, now Owner :: Principal of INSYNC: Education Research + Design, the ability to have a new "tool" in the classroom, the Node chair, allows designers to plan differently and thereby be more attentive to their client's individual needs such as flexibility.

Another discovery through research by Steelcase, Inc. is that choice and control may be accomplished by designing different settings within one space. A "Palette of Place, and of Posture" has been written about for some time, and the idea was introduced to Newmark (Figures 10.4, 10.5, and 10.6) on a visit to the Steelcase University and Global Headquarters in Grand Rapids, Michigan. The idea for a classroom situation is through design:

- give permission to act differently—freedom to move
- set up different "stations" within the same classroom supporting different types of activities
- provide multiple setting types supporting different posture situations and different senses of place
- provide a more personal place for each individual through the addition of the Node chair

Learning environments today need to focus on active learning and student engagement. Therefore, the design of the classroom has to welcome, in fact embrace, a new way of thinking about this formal setting. "Dr. Lennie" emphasizes that students have to be able to open the door and realize that "learning will be different" here. Intentionally designing to support these behaviors is necessary.

Practical Applications for Design

Case Study 1: Flexible Classroom

Rio Grande High School, Intensive Support Program (ISP) & School Based Health Clinic (SBHC). Design Plus, Architects, Albuquerque, NM.

These versatile classrooms are equipped with moveable furniture that can be regrouped according to the learning activity taking place in the space.

Consideration of the Senses

PROPRIOCEPTION AND VESTIBULAR

The exposed truss work in the ceiling and the clerestory windows create a sense of openness, thereby increasing the feeling of volume of space, which accommodates some of the proprioception and vestibular challenges experienced by people with ASD.

SIGHT: LIGHTING

Suspended horizontal lights have been equipped with light-emitting diode (LED) lamps to provide full-spectrum light quality. The fixtures are positioned to direct the light up to the ceiling, thereby allowing light to reflect and be diffused with natural light, which eliminates shadows and glare.

ACOUSTICAL

Sound absorbent wall baffles, carpet tiles, sheet vinyl flooring as well as upholstered furniture help absorb sound in the space and make it more comfortable for the students.

SAFETY

Most of the materials have antimicrobial properties and low VOC (volatile organic compounds) emittance ratings. The corridor outside the Sensory Room (Figure 10.9) at Rio Grande High School is generously lit with natural light and helps students temper their emotions as they travel from classroom to classroom. The concrete block wall is burnished smooth for tactile engagement and allows the students to run their fingers along a surface that can remind

10.7 (facing page) Flexible Classroom. Furnishings. Rio Grande High School, Intensive Support Program (ISP) and School Based Health Clinic (SBHC), Albuquerque, NM

10.8 (top) Small size classes. Classroom, Rio Grande High School, Intensive Support Program (ISP) and School Based Health Clinic (SBHC), Albuquerque, NM

10.9 (bottom) Corridor outside the Sensory Room, Rio Grande High School, Intensive Support Program (ISP) and School Based Health Clinic (SBHC), Albuquerque, NM

them where they are in the school. The lightly polished concrete floor absorbs light to diminish reflections and shadows. Decorative sound baffles serve as interesting decoration and help direct the students' attention upward so they can practice body language skills that promote self-confidence and build their social interaction skills. The wide corridors allow several students to pass one another without touching each other. A neutral color scheme is used in the space to ensure that the students' sensory sensitivities are respected.

Case Study 2: Sensory Approach

Design Plus, Architects, Albuquerque, NM

Design Plus, Architects have established a sensory aproach to the design of several schools that have been built and several others that are in the planning stages. Their conscientous approach takes into account eight factors noted in this legend. Floor plan 10.11 is for Rio Grande High School and the floor plan below is for the Albuquerque Public Schools ISP Prototype (Design Plus is the Specialized Design Consultant, Vigil & Assoc. is the Architect of Record). The legend in Figure 10.10 is applied to Figures 10.11 and 10.12.

10.10 (below) Sensory Approach to Design

10.11 (facing page, top) Annotated Sensory Floor Plan. Rio Grande High School, Albuquerque, NM

10.12 (facing page, bottom) Sensory Floor Plan. Intensive Support Hub, Albuquerque Public Schools Prototype, Albuquerque, NM

 Making Transitions

 Focus and Attention Difficulties

 Time Management, Organization, Task Sequence, Completion

 Communication and Verbal Limitations

 Auditory Processing Impairments

 Sensory Processing Impairments

 Physical Impairments

 Calm Down / Re-Boot

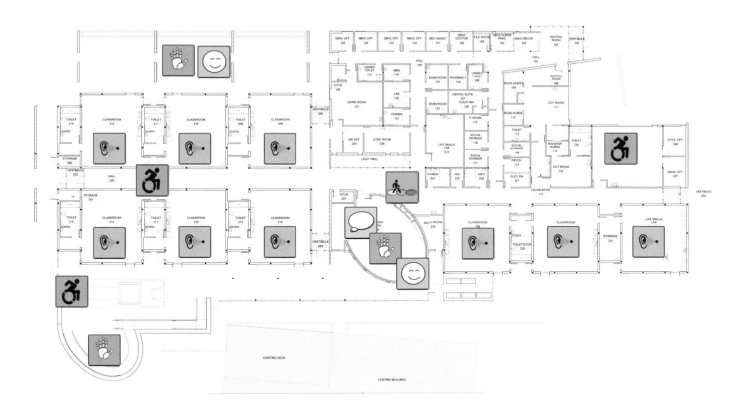

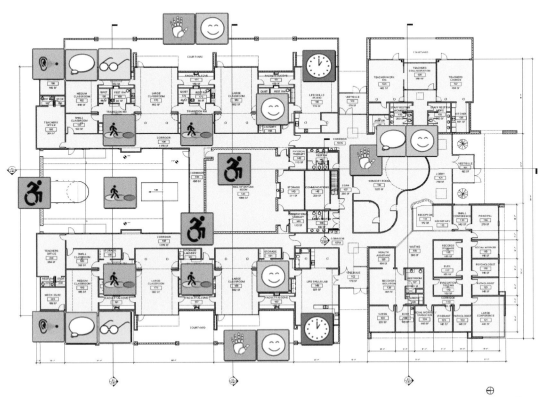

FLOOR PLAN 30,600 HEATED SQ. FT.

INTENSIVE SUPPORT HUB (PROTOTYPE)
ALBUQUERQUE PUBLIC SCHOOLS
03/04/15

VIGIL & ASSOCIATES
ARCHITECTURAL GROUP, P.C.

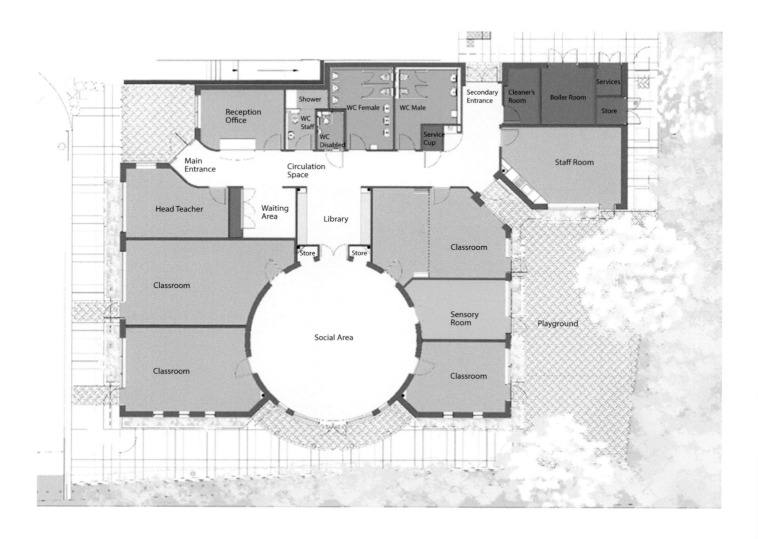

Case Study 3: Whitton School, Kingston Upon Thames

GA Architects, London, UK

The existing mainstream school required a specialist teaching unit for fifteen to twenty children with autism. A new stand-alone building was designed and built (Figure 10.13). The school comprises three classrooms and sensory and therapy rooms grouped around a central social area. A short corridor connects these rooms to support facilities. Circulation space is generous. Several windows were built into the curvature of the social area wall, creating an atrium feel for the entrance. Curved walls lead the children naturally from classroom to classroom, avoiding sharp angles, obstructive corners, and hidden doorways. Other features of the project include the acoustical treatment of the double-height social space, which also incorporates passive ventilation to ensure the movement of fresh air and the secure external space, which provides the opportunity for "outside learning."

10.13 Floor plan, Whitton School, Kingston Upon Thames

Case Study 4: Acland Burghley School

GA Architects, London, UK

This mainstream school had pressing need for a Resource Base to be used for the specialist teaching of children with autism. The facility was to be housed within an unused part of the existing school and designed for twenty children. Features of the project are:

- Ceiling heating due to an existing concrete floor, which limited the option to put in underfloor heating. However, the ceiling heating offered the opportunity to locate recessed LED lighting in the heating panels.
- Lighting generally came from an indirect source to minimize disturbance to children.
- New fixed windows due to noise from the playground right outside the Resource Base. This resulted in the need for mechanical ventilation so that the windows could be kept closed.
- Double glazing to all new windows with Venetian blinds between the two glass layers to deal with distraction due to other children in the playground. This also dealt with glare, as the blinds could be operated remotely. Damage to blinds as a result of challenging behavior was reduced to virtually nil.
- The colors of walls were selected based on color research by GA Architects in collaboration with Kingston University and after consultations with the children. The children were very clear about how they wanted to attract other pupils into their space by the use of bright colors in the entrance space, but they wanted soft muted colors in the classrooms.
- The principal feature of the social space and LSA (Learning Support Assistance) classroom was that staff in the office had visual command of the whole area due to the design of the walls and doors. This meant that a number of children could be discreetly observed by a single member of staff.

Notes

1. Koegel, Lynn Kern, Anjileen K. Singh, and Robert L. Koegel. "Improving motivation for academics in children with autism." *Journal of autism and developmental disorders* 40, no. 9 (2010): 1057–1066.
2. Landrigan, Philip J. "What causes autism? Exploring the environmental contribution." *Current opinion in pediatrics* 22, no. 2 (2010): 219–225.
3. Ashburner, Jill, Jenny Ziviani, and Sylvia Rodger. "Sensory processing and classroom emotional, behavioral, and educational outcomes in children with autism spectrum disorder." *American journal of occupational therapy* 62, no. 5 (2008): 564–573.
4. Benedyk, R., A. Woodcock, and A. Woolner. "Applying the hexagon-spindle model for educational ergonomics to the design of school environments for children with autistic spectrum disorders." *Work journal* 32 (2009): 249–259.
5. Benedyk, R., A. Woodcock, and A. Woolner. "Applying the hexagon-spindle model for educational ergonomics to the design of school environments for children with autistic spectrum disorders." *Work journal* 32 (2009): 249–259.
6. Khare, Rachna, and Abir Mullick. "Incorporating the behavioral dimension in designing inclusive learning environment for autism." *ArchNet-IJAR* 3, no. 3 (2009): 45–64.
7. Shabha, Ghasson, and Kristi Gaines. "A comparative analysis of transatlantic design interventions for therapeutically enhanced learning environments—Texas vs West Midlands." *Facilities* 31, no. 13/14 (2013): 634–658.
8. McAllister, Keith, and Barry Maguire. "A design model: The autism spectrum disorder classroom design kit." *British journal of special education* 39, no. 4 (2012): 201–208.
9. U.S. Department of Education, Office of Special Education Programs. "Individuals with Disabilities Education Act (IDEA) data." Retrieved March 21, 2008, from https://www.ideadata.org/index.html.
10. Baker, Edward T. "The effects of inclusion on learning." *Educational leadership* 52, no. 4 (1995): 33–35.
11. Banerji, Madhabi, and Ronald A. Dailey. "A study of the effects of an inclusion model on students with specific learning disabilities." *Journal of learning disabilities* 28, no. 8 (1995): 511–522.
12. Rea, P. J., McLaughlin, V. L., and Walther-Thomas, C. "Outcomes for students with learning disabilities in inclusive and pullout programs." *Council for exceptional children* 68, no. 2 (2002): 203–223.
13. Baker, Edward T. "The effects of inclusion on learning." *Educational leadership* 52, no. 4 (1995): 33–35.

14. Roweton, William E., and Murray-Seegert, C. *Nasty girls, thugs, and humans like us: Social relations between severely disabled and nondisabled students in high school*. Baltimore: Brookes, 1989.

15. Affleck, James Q., Sally Madge, Abby Adams, and Sheila Lowenbraun. "Integrated classroom versus resource model: Academic viability and effectiveness." *Council for exceptional children* 54, no. 4 (1988): 339–348.

16. Holloway, John H. "Inclusion and students with learning disabilities." *Educational leadership* 58, no. 6 (2001): 86–88.

17. Van Hover, Stephanie D., and Elizabeth A. Yeager. "'Making' students better people?" A case study of a beginning history teacher." In *International social studies forum* (vol. 3, pp. 219–232). Information Age Publishing Inc., 2003.

18. Weiss, Margaret P., and John Lloyd. "Conditions for co-teaching: Lessons from a case study." *Teacher education and special education: The journal of the teacher education division of the council for exceptional children* 26, no. 1 (2003): 27–41.

19. Affleck, James Q., Sally Madge, Abby Adams, and Sheila Lowenbraun. "Integrated classroom versus resource model: Academic viability and effectiveness." *Council for exceptional children* 54, no. 4 (1988): 339–348.

20. Manset, Genevieve, and Melvyn I. Semmel. "Are inclusive programs for students with mild disabilities effective? A comparative review of model programs." *The journal of special education* 31, no. 2 (1997): 155–180.

21. Fore III, Cecil, Shanna Hagan-Burke, Mack D. Burke, Richard T. Boon, and Steve Smith. "Academic achievement and class placement in high school: Do students with learning disabilities achieve more in one class placement than another?" *Education and treatment of children* 31, no. 1 (2008): 55–72.

22. McDonnell, John, Nadine Thorson, Stephanie Disher, Connie Mathot-Buckner, Jerri Mendel, and Lavinia Ray. "The achievement of students with developmental disabilities and their peers without disabilities in inclusive settings: An exploratory study." *Education and treatment of children* 26, no. 3 (2003): 224–236.

23. Mesibov, Gary B., Victoria Shea, and Eric Schopler. *The TEACCH approach to autism spectrum disorders*. Springer Science & Business Media, 2004.

24. Panerai, Simonetta, L. Ferrante, and M. Zingale. "Benefits of the Treatment and Education of Autistic and Communication Handicapped Children (TEACCH) programme as compared with a non-specific approach." *Journal of intellectual disability research* 46, no. 4 (2002): 318–327.

25. Van Bourgondien, Mary E., Nancy C. Reichle, and Eric Schopler. "Effects of a model treatment approach on adults with autism." *Journal of autism and developmental disorders* 33, no. 2 (2003): 131–140.

26. Mesibov, Gary B., and Marie Howley. *Accessing the curriculum for pupils with autistic spectrum disorders: Using the TEACCH programme to help inclusion*. David Fulton Publishers, 2003.

27. Mesibov, Gary B., and Marie Howley. *Accessing the curriculum for pupils with autistic spectrum disorders: Using the TEACCH programme to help inclusion*. David Fulton Publishers, 2003.

28. Mesibov, Gary B., and Marie Howley. *Accessing the curriculum for pupils with autistic spectrum disorders: Using the TEACCH programme to help inclusion*. David Fulton Publishers, 2003.

29. Mesibov, Gary B., and Marie Howley. *Accessing the curriculum for pupils with autistic spectrum disorders: Using the TEACCH programme to help inclusion*. David Fulton Publishers, 2003.

30. Mesibov, Gary B., and Marie Howley. *Accessing the curriculum for pupils with autistic spectrum disorders: Using the TEACCH programme to help inclusion*. David Fulton Publishers, 2003.

31. Mesibov, Gary B., and Marie Howley. *Accessing the curriculum for pupils with autistic spectrum disorders: Using the TEACCH programme to help inclusion*. David Fulton Publishers, 2003.

32. Mesibov, Gary B., and Marie Howley. *Accessing the curriculum for pupils with autistic spectrum disorders: Using the TEACCH programme to help inclusion*. David Fulton Publishers, 2003.

33. Grandin, Temple. *Thinking in pictures: My life with autism* (expanded edition). New York: Vintage, 2006.

34. Heaton, Pamela, Beate Hermelin, and Linda Pring. "Autism and pitch processing: A precursor for savant musical ability?" *Music perception* 15, no. 3 (1998): 291–305.

35. Jones, Robert, Ciara Quigney, and Jaci Huws. "First-hand accounts of sensory perceptual experiences in autism: A qualitative analysis." *Journal of intellectual and developmental disability* 28, no. 2 (2003): 112–121.

36. Stokes, S. "Structured teaching: Strategies for supporting students with autism." *USA: CESA* 7 (2001).

37. Mesibov, Gary B., and Marie Howley. *Accessing the curriculum for pupils with autistic spectrum disorders: Using the TEACCH programme to help inclusion*. David Fulton Publishers, 2003.

38. Bogdashina, Olga. *Sensory perceptual issues in autism and Asperger Syndrome: Different sensory experiences, different perceptual worlds*. Jessica Kingsley Publishers, 2003.

39. Grandin, Temple. *Thinking in pictures: My life with autism* (expanded edition). New York: Vintage, 2006.

40. Grandin, Temple. *Thinking in pictures: My life with autism* (expanded edition). New York: Vintage, 2006.

41. Mesibov, Gary B., and Marie Howley. *Accessing the curriculum for pupils with autistic spectrum disorders: Using the TEACCH programme to help inclusion.* David Fulton Publishers, 2003.

42. Mesibov, Gary B., and Marie Howley. *Accessing the curriculum for pupils with autistic spectrum disorders: Using the TEACCH programme to help inclusion.* David Fulton Publishers, 2003.

43. Stokes, S. "Structured teaching: Strategies for supporting students with autism." *USA: CESA* 7 (2001).

44. Stokes, S. "Structured teaching: Strategies for supporting students with autism." *USA: CESA* 7 (2001).

45. Lackney, Jay. "School building design principles for an assessment program," (1998) in *School building assessment methods*, ed. Henry Sanoff. Washington, DC: National Clearing House for Educational Facilities, 2001.

46. Freed, Jeffrey, and Laurie Parsons. *Right-brained children in a left-brained world: Unlocking the potential of your ADD child.* Simon and Schuster, 1998.

47. Grandin, Temple. *Thinking in pictures: My life with autism* (expanded edition). New York: Vintage, 2006.

48. Hatch-Rasmussen, Cindy. "Sensory integration." Center for the Study of Autism at www.autism.org/si.html. 1995.

49. Mesibov, Gary B., and Marie Howley. *Accessing the curriculum for pupils with autistic spectrum disorders: Using the TEACCH programme to help inclusion.* David Fulton Publishers, 2003.

50. Jacobs, Karen, and Nancy A. Baker. "The association between children's computer use and musculoskeletal discomfort." *Work* 18, no. 3 (2002): 221–226.

51. Parcells, Claudia, Manfred Stommel, and Robert P. Hubbard. "Mismatch of classroom furniture and student body dimensions: Empirical findings and health implications." *Journal of adolescent health* 24, no. 4 (1999): 265–273.

Home Environments

CHAPTER

11

Research has shown that an educational environment can have a significant effect on students, especially those with Autism Spectrum Disorders (ASD).[1] Unquestionably, learning environments are important for children, but the home environment is equally, if not more, vital to growth and learning. However, there is little information on how to design residential spaces to support the needs of children or adults with ASD.

Ideally, home environments would be individually designed for each user on the spectrum, as no two cases of ASD are alike.[2] The ideal home environments would be designed to both accommodate each unique symptom and help individuals with ASD build a tolerance to environmental stimulus. McCallister states that environments for individuals on the spectrum should not just cater to symptoms, but in contrast prepare them for the challenges and problems they will face in everyday life: "Cocooning the ASD pupil from all external factors will not necessarily help them reach their full potential in life."[3] In other words, the home environments of those with ASD should not create unrealistic environments that will leave them unprepared to face other environments.

Children and Adolescents

Because the majority of the existing research for children with ASD is related to classroom environments, many of the design methods used in classrooms can be modified for a residential setting. Families that have a child with ASD in the home often face many of the same difficulties as teachers in the classroom. Most children on the spectrum struggle with communication and social interaction, changes in their environment or routine, and sensory processing.[4, 5, 6] A number of design solutions can be integrated into the home to help minimize the kinds of challenges children with ASD often face.

Parents or caregivers should realize that having an autistic child in the home doesn't necessarily mean one must spend a fortune on custom furniture. Often, some of these expensive solutions are not appropriate and give the home an institutional feel. This is a serious problem because a house that looks like a home and not a hospital is a better environment for a child with any disability. A home that is warm, inviting, and comfortable will benefit every

11.1 (facing page, top) Floor plan for hyper-sensitivities

11.2 (facing page, bottom) Designing with transition and buffer zones

member of the family. Many appropriate furniture choices can be found in popular home stores.

Residential Design for the Hyper-Sensitive

As previously mentioned, a child that is hyper-sensitive is often prone to sensory overload, and each case of ASD comes with its own opportunities and challenges. Therefore, some design recommendations may prove to be a great success for one child and have no effect on another. The following floor plan (Figure 11.1) was developed to meet the needs and symptoms that are commonly associated with hyper-sensitivities with the intention of providing suggestions for parents and caregivers to integrate into their own home.

Space Planning

Figure 11.1, designed for an individual with hyper-sensitivities, does not follow the current trend of large, multi-purpose, "great" rooms. These kinds of spaces could be overwhelming for a child on the spectrum because of difficulty deciphering and understanding the purpose of each space. Instead, the entire home is made up of several, more closed-off rooms by employing spatial sequencing or zoning. Having walls or visual partitions minimizes distractions and helps keep the child focused on the activity that is typical in that particular area.[7] For example, in the bedroom there are no toys, television, or games; only items that are associated with sleeping or dressing are located in the bedroom. Without other distractions in the bedroom, making the transition to sleep is much less stressful.

Designing for Auditory Hyper-Sensitivity

Most individuals on the spectrum who are hyper-sensitive to sound are easily distracted by even the softest noise, have difficulty functioning with background noise, and find some noises painful. Because of this sensitivity, many might think it would be most appropriate to soundproof every room, but the goal of this design is not to cater to every symptom and build an unrealistic, unnatural environment, but to help build tolerance and learn independence. However, separating the "loud" spaces and "quiet" spaces within the home is a good idea; this will be beneficial to every member

of the family. Spaces like the kitchen, TV room, and dining room that typically create a lot of noise are located on one side of the home, while bedrooms are on the other side. An escape space is located on the "quiet" side of the house to reduce the amount of auditory stimuli, in particular, that will reach the space. Similarly, the play room and sensory integration space are located on the noisier side of the home. Between the "loud" and "quiet" spaces are "transition" or "buffer" zones to keep noise from traveling from the loud spaces to the quiet spaces (Figure 11.2).

Designing for Visual Hyper-Sensitivity

Individuals with visual hyper-sensitivity are typically unable to ignore small visual details and as a result prefer a perfectly clean environment. Many children on the spectrum might find bright lights or colors physically painful. Colors should be kept light and neutral, and complicated patterns and textures should be excluded. Specifically, colors found in nature are the most calming and relaxing without being garish or too bright. Finishes that might create glare or harsh reflections should be carefully considered. For example, matte paint finishes, fabric wall coverings, wallpapers, carpet, or flooring options that do not require a glossy, reflective wax finish help create calming environments.

Providing ample amounts of storage is very important for children with visual hyper-sensitivities that have a tendency to focus on extraneous details and become distressed by clutter in the environment. Closed storage systems that can hide clutter will help organize a room. Storage options should be provided in every room and should be kid-friendly. For example, baskets and trunks are storage compartments that are low to the ground and can be easily used by a child. Furniture pieces that have storage compartments will maximize space and keep rooms clutter free.

Lighting is very important for individuals with visual hyper-sensitivities. In the home, lighting should be flexible with dimmers, ceiling mounted choices, lamps, and controllable natural light. The child should be able to control lights that are painfully bright by either dimming a lamp or arranging blinds or curtains without the help or supervision of an adult. Ordinary slat blinds can create a bright, pattern glare during the day time that can be distracting or painful.[8] Rolling shades offer uninterrupted shade without creating bright patches of light, and most are designed to absorb heat and block UV rays to better control temperature in a space. Fluorescents

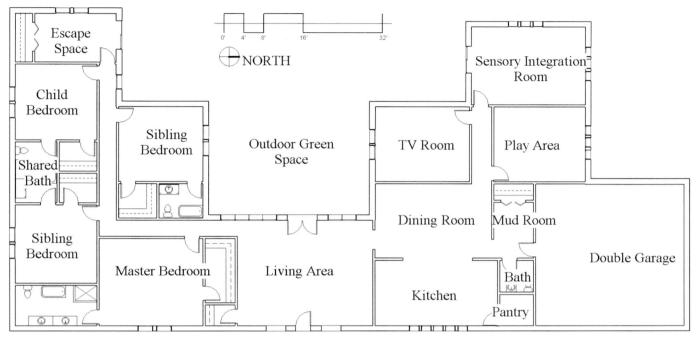

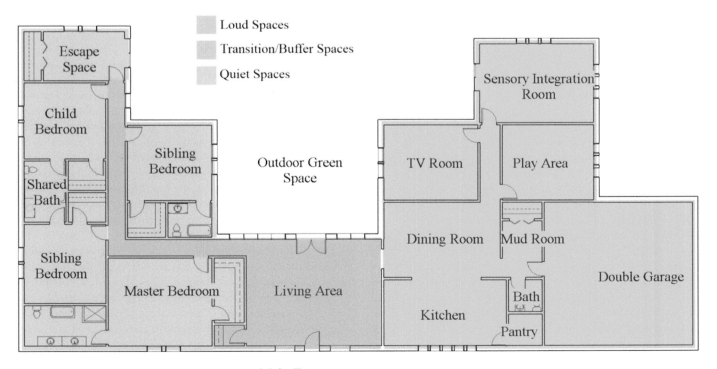

11.3 Residential Escape Space Sketch

should be avoided, as they flicker and can be distracting. This flickering may be imperceptible to most, but for a child on the spectrum with sensitive vision, this flickering can be frustrating and disruptive.[9, 10]

Retreat spaces or escape spaces were created specifically for children prone to sensory overload. Children with hyper-sensitive symptoms can be easily overwhelmed when too much stimulation is present in the environment or simply because they are tired or in a bad mood. Escape spaces in the classroom have been very successful and are especially helpful to children that tend to be hyper-sensitive, as the environment is particularly stressful for them. Attention span, learning performance, and focus improved while negative behaviors decreased.[11] An escape space in the home can have equal benefits for a child on the spectrum. The design is simple: A few bean bag chairs or other seating components and, if necessary (Figure 11.3), a few outside items for sensory integration can be brought in like a stereo or an item with a pleasing texture. The escape space is meant to be an area of solitude where the child can retreat to relax, and regain control.

The escape space (Figure 11.3) featured in Figure 11.1 is located on the quiet side of the house. This room has access to natural light that can be dimmed with roller shades and artificial light that can also be controlled. The space also has an exit to the outside should the child need to seek an escape while playing outside or if they might feel like venturing outdoors to help them stay calm. A study by Mostafa implemented an escape space in a classroom and observed that over time the space was used less frequently and the children spent decreasingly less time inside.[12] The escape space can also be a quiet reading room as long as any books and other materials can be stored in a way they are completely hidden from view. In homes where space is not a luxury, an escape space can be a spare closet that has been emptied of its contents or a screened-off corner of a quiet room.

A carefully designed sensory integration space will also be helpful for children with ASD that show frequent signs of sensory overload. A sensory integration space should incorporate the child's individual interests and needs. The space shouldn't feel like therapy or school but be intriguing and engaging. For example, a "tactile wall" is an excellent way to engage a child with tactile sensitivities. A tactile wall also provides visual stimulation. The tactile wall is made up of a variety of items with different tactile sensations, textures, and materials. Parents can create their own

11.4 Exits and Escapes

tactile wall using old toys, materials from a hardware store, old stuffed animals, fabric, etc.

Other methods that can be used in the sensory integration space are as simple as providing a stereo for listening to music and other sounds. A method known as "auditory integration," which involves listening to digitally modified music through headphones, has been shown to help auditory hyper-sensitive children grow accustomed to the frequencies that they find most disturbing.[13] A hanging chair or hammock will provide experiences related to motion and balance. Using a projector to illuminate the room with lights and colors is a simpler way to achieve the same concept seen in some of the featured sensory integration spaces. Methods for sensory integration should not be limited to one area of the home. Installing lambskin rugs, textured throw pillows, or woven textiles are all ways to occupy the senses without being overwhelming. Activities for the sensory integration space should be selected based entirely off of an individual child's symptoms and interests.

Designing for Tactile Hyper-Sensitivity

Individuals that are sensitive to touch may be particular about certain textures and fabrics, avoid using their hands in play, have an abnormally low threshold for pain, and find human touch uncomfortable.[14] A child on the spectrum may have very specific needs about clothing and bedding and should be able to choose what they are most comfortable with. A soft environment is of particular importance to this population and will protect them from injury and promote a feeling of security.

A soft environment serves a variety of spectrum symptoms, including symptoms that result in weak mobility and balance, and helps to reduce injuries from "stimming." Creating a soft environment would be a safe choice for a child with hyper-sensitive tactile tendencies, who often appear to have a very low pain threshold. A soft environment would also benefit children with ASD who have proprioceptive and vestibular problems, as they will often misperceive distances and have trouble with balance. A softer environment with upholstered furniture, carpet, rounded edges, etc. would make the home more comfortable and help protect

the child from injury. In addition, soft materials will absorb sound, benefitting those with sensitive hearing.

Areas like the bedroom and the escape space should have fewer textures and materials that the child dislikes. Again, these are different for each child. In areas of the house that other members of the family will frequent, a little more stimulation can be provided. Some stimulation is appropriate in order to teach tolerance and control. Items that provide minimal sensory integration are throw blankets, throw pillows, lambskin rugs, and other decorative items that are not breakable.

Designing for Individuals Prone to Sensory Overload

Because of sensory processing difficulties, crowds and small spaces may be distressing for children on the spectrum.[15] Feelings of claustrophobia are common among individuals with auditory hyper-sensitivity when in a crowd because of higher levels of noise that are both unfamiliar and unpredictable. Children may also be fearful of coming in physical contact with others because of tactile hyper-sensitivity. Every room of the house is spacious, with plenty of room to fit the entire family at the same time. Corridors are also a little wider than usual in order to protect personal space. Exits and escape routes from each room should be made clearly visible in case the child feels the need to flee a stressful situation. Doors can be painted a different color than the wall, or wall openings can form an arch for more emphasis. Incorporating a crown molding in a room that is in a contrasting color to the wall will also make doorways more identifiable (Figure 11.4).

Residential Design for the Hypo-Sensitive

As mentioned, a child that is considered to be hypo-sensitive is considered sensory seeking, meaning he or she seeks to create sensory experiences, which can be harmful to him- or herself and to others.[16] Similar to the previous, the following floor plan utilizes design solutions meant to target the symptoms of ASD. All of the featured design solutions are meant to serve as suggestions for

11.5 (facing page, top)
Designing for Parental Observation

11.6 (facing page, bottom)
Designing Active and Inactive Spaces

parents and designers. Because every case of ASD is different, not all of the design methods will work for every child. Furthermore, these design solutions will aim to make day-to-day life a little easier for individuals with ASD and their families. These design solutions should not be thought of as treatments that will completely erase all spectrum symptoms.

Space Planning

Sensory seeking behaviors often put children at risk for injury, so a home environment should allow easy supervision by a parent. The plan in this prototype is much more open than the hyper-sensitive floor plan. A parent should be able to easily observe children at play in most areas of the house. For example, while a parent is preparing dinner, he or she can easily observe the child in the backyard, active living area, and the screened-in porch or sensory integration space (see Figure 11.5).

Even though this plan is much more open, spatial sequencing is still employed by dividing the spaces between active and inactive spaces (see Figure 11.6). In the active areas, the child is free to play and explore, but in the inactive spaces, the child should be sleeping, doing homework, or other "inactive" activities. Providing active spaces or spaces where a child is free to interact and engage in the environment are important, especially for an active, sensory-seeking child, because discouraging behavior that feels natural to them is likely to result in the child engaging in these behaviors somewhere inappropriate. The inactive spaces include the bedrooms, bathrooms, and a "quiet" living area that can also serve as a guest room. The active spaces consist of a larger living area, kitchen, dining room, backyard, and screened-in porch, which serves as a sensory integration space. Instead of multiple closed-off rooms, an open plan also encourages social interaction with the family, which will help the child develop and practice social skills to use outside the home.

Designing for Visual Hypo-Sensitivity

A child with visual hypo-sensitivity frequently can only see the outlines of objects, cannot visually perceive the texture or weight of objects, and often loves bright colors, reflections, and harsh sunlight. Visual hypo-sensitivity is similar in a lot of ways to a visual impairment. For a child with hypo-sensitive vision, contrasting colors

should be used to increase visibility. For example, if the walls and floors in a space are light and neutral, the furniture should be dark and bold to contrast. This will help make furniture more identifiable and will help the child notice them in the space. Similarly, painting walls different colors will help distinguish corners, which usually blend into the wall for visually hypo-sensitive individuals, becoming unnoticeable. Painting the borders around a door or painting the doors a different color than the wall helps to distinguish doorways. Children with visual hypo-sensitivity often enjoy bright colors, and using them in the home will allow a child to feel comfortable and derive pleasure from their surroundings.

Designing for Sensory-Seeking Behaviors

Often, children prone to sensory-seeking behaviors enjoy rough play or lean on objects in an attempt to find stability in their environment.[17] Therefore, all furniture should be durable. Bean bag chairs, for example, are inexpensive, durable, and easy to replace. Additionally, they provide stimulating sensory input. Sensory integration spaces are also important for sensory-seeking children, because they serve as a safe place for sensory engagement where exploration and play are welcome. In the floor plan shown above, the sensory integration space is located in a screened-in porch off of the active living area and leads outside. A drain could be installed in the middle of the floor, and the space could also serve as a craft room. Children can engage in messy play inside the room and also in the backyard with relatively simple clean-up. Lastly, soft environments are essential for sensory-seeking children. Carefully selected finishes and furniture will protect them from injury, whether this occurs by accident or as a result of sensory-seeking behaviors.

Designing for Auditory Hypo-Sensitivity

Auditory hypo-sensitivity in children often appears to be a hearing impairment because the child does not always respond when his or her name is called.[18] This is sometimes referred to as "auditory filtering."[19] A child with auditory hypo-sensitivity may enjoy hearing and making loud, excessive noises.[20] Firstly, if a soft environment is in place, soft materials will absorb sound instead of reflecting it, as hard surfaces do. Many children on the spectrum with auditory sensitivities have difficulty functioning if there is background noise

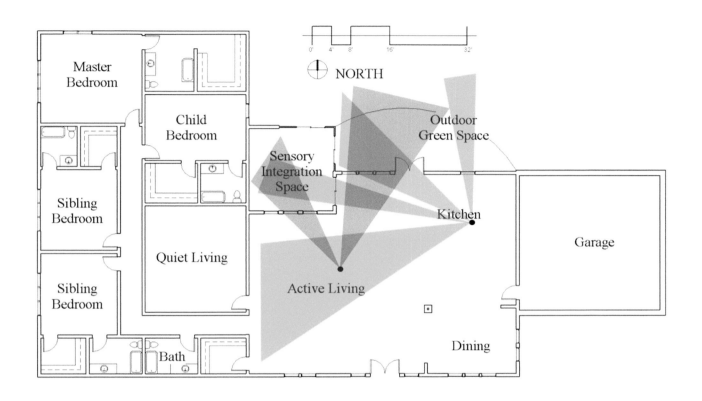

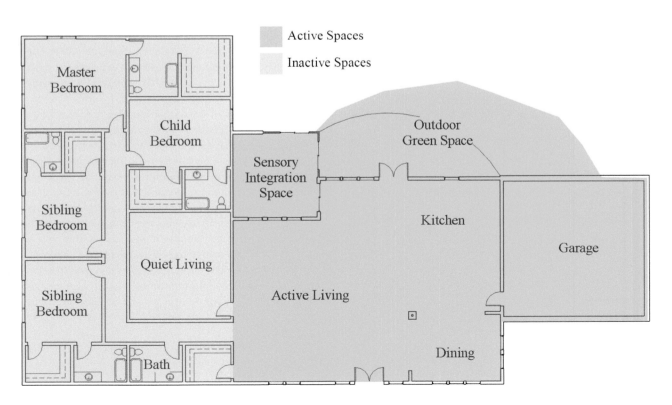

in the area.[21] Ensuring that the child has a quiet space for sleeping, doing homework, etc. will help the child stay focused.

Designing for Tactile Hypo-Sensitivity

Children with tactile hypo-sensitivity sometimes enjoy rough and messy play and often are not bothered by physical injury.[22] For these reasons, they need adequate supervision at all times. Open floor plans make supervision by a parent, teacher, or guardian much easier. As described above, even open spaces can be organized and incorporate spatial sequencing by using furniture arrangements and finishes. Children that are under-responsive to touch may also feel objects and people unnecessarily in order to create a tactile experience. Therefore, all furniture should be durable, and any breakable, valuable objects should be kept out of reach. Again, providing spaces where the child is free to feel objects and play roughly is highly encouraged. Trying to entirely eliminate sensory-seeking behaviors in a child with ASD will likely only result in the child employing sensory-seeking behaviors elsewhere.[23] Appropriate sensory integration activities for tactile hypo-sensitivity include a tactile wall with varying textures, clay, skin brushing, a sandbox, etc. The sensory integration space in the floor plan designed for hypo-sensitivity (Figure 11.5) is located in a screened-in porch with easy access to outdoor areas and a drain in the floor so the child can safely engage in messy play during all types of weather.

Designing for Proprioceptive Hypo-Sensitivity

Proprioceptive hypo-sensitivity in ASD often appears to others like clumsiness. Children have little awareness of their body position or body location in space.[24] They may lean on objects to help navigate a space and frequently miscalculate depths and distances. Along with proprioceptive and vestibular senses, vision and hearing play a major role in the body's ability to balance. A soft environment to protect from injury as a result of bumping into furniture is beneficial for individuals with proprioceptive sensitivities, but how the space looks will also be helpful. As described above, making furnishings, objects, and doors more visible can be done by using contrasting colors. For example, a cream-colored furniture arrangement will be easier to see when placed on a dark colored rug. Again, providing a soft environment will help absorb noise and potentially improve balance due to fewer distracting stimuli in the space.

Other Design Solutions for Children with ASD

Perhaps because of a lack of executive functions, individuals with ASD prefer sameness both in their physical environment and in their routines.[25] Children may become upset with change, even of the smallest magnitude, such as when an item is moved on a bookshelf. Making sure adequate storage is available in every room of the home is one way to ease stress over these kinds of changes. Closed storage systems like wardrobes with drawers and cabinets instead of open bookshelves will hide clutter and distracting visual stimuli from view. Open bookshelves can still be used, but instead, items should be organized into bins, baskets, or boxes and placed on shelves. Trunks, booths, or chairs with hollow seats and bed frames with storage drawers are some other options for hiding clutter.

Employing spatial sequencing often helps preserve routines and ease transitions for children on the spectrum. Spatial sequencing is most successful when each space has only one or two designated activities. This helps to organize the space and teach the child what he or she is expected to do in that room. For instance, if the only activities allowed in the dining room are eating and family discussions, then over time, the child will associate the dining room with eating or family discussions. This may also help keep children from eating in other areas of the house.

Narrow, obsessive interests are another common trait found in individuals with ASD and might also be due to a lack of executive functions.[26] Though these can be a distraction, designers and parents should incorporate them into some aspects of the design of their home. If a child has a love of baseball, a baseball tee can be set up in the backyard. Under supervision, this creates a proprioceptive, vestibular, visual, and tactile experience, not to mention provides the child with physical exercise and time spent in nature. Make sure items associated with these interests—in this case baseball cards, equipment, or images of baseball players—should be kept out of spaces like the bedroom, where they could distract from sleeping or getting ready for school.

Aging Adults

By 2020, there will be 4 million people with autism in the United States. Within the same time frame, 500,000 children with ASD are expected to reach adulthood.[27] Furthermore, hundreds of thousands of people across the United States with ASD live with caregivers, who are aging themselves. This, coupled with the fact that more and more children are being diagnosed with ASD every day, is creating an elevated need for housing as individuals transition to adulthood and their parents' age.

As previously mentioned, the number of children diagnosed with ASD has been steadily increasing over time. As the diagnosed children transition into adulthood, there is concern there will not be adequate support services for education, employment, and residential establishments. According to Laura Klinger, PhD, of the University of North Carolina, Director of the TEACCH Autism Program

> … little is known about the long-term outcome and needs of aging and older adults with ASD. We simply don't know whether the quality of life improves, declines, or plateaus for individuals with ASD who are past the transition to adulthood years. Additionally, little is known about how symptoms change from childhood to mid-adulthood and what factors predict adult outcome. This is a relatively unchartered research field.[28]

Designing for Adults with ASD

An environment for an adult with ASD will, in many ways, echo the needs and design features he or she needed as a child. In other words, as adults individuals will often experience many of the same sensitivities and find relief in many of the same design features. Again, each environment should be designed or developed in a case-by-case scenario and aim to meet the needs of the individual user. The following are some generalized guidelines to help determine what design elements may help or hinder an individual with ASD.

Recently, the research of Regnier and Denton[29] and Ahrentzen and Steele[30] focused on adult populations with ASD. Their research advocates for small clusters, non-institutional in appearance (homelike), visual and physical access to outdoors, daily living life skills enrichment, privacy, involvement of friends/family, apartment for life, and attention to the individual environmental sensitivities of individuals with cognitive challenges.

The aesthetic attributes of a room have been shown to influence the perception of viewers. For example, researchers found that individuals associate positive attributes to individuals in a photograph when they appear to be in an aesthetically pleasing room.[31] This suggests that architectural elements, when combined to make a building appear more or less homelike, may influence how inhabitants are viewed and treated by direct care staff members. For example, people living in a homelike setting may be more likely to or expected to make their own choices, to socialize with others in a broader society, and to be entitled to privacy.

An environment is perceived as being homelike when it has qualities linked with family living rather than characteristics linked with environments that are not usually associated with a home such as a hospital, bank, or office building. Thompson, Robinson, Dietrich, Farris, and Sinclair conducted research on home-likeness for this population with three fundamental aims in mind: (1) to determine whether home-likeness could be reliably evaluated; (2) to identify architectural features associated with perceived home-likeness; and (3) to examine the effects of residential home-likeness on behavior of the residents.[32] The researchers identified the following architectural features as being associated with perception of home-likeness:

1. ground floor entrance/exits
2. room dimensions; size, proportion
3. corridors to be more like hallways
4. minimal number of doorways
5. wall, floor, and ceiling materials
6. number and type of light fixtures
7. number, style, and size of furniture pieces; disability-specific adaptations
8. miscellaneous personal items.

For many adults with autism, specifically in group living, their primary territory is often their bedroom. Individuals should be allowed to personalize or make the space their own. The need to personalize is usually a result of a need for territorial control and/or connected to ownership. The bedroom is a perfect space for personalization because it is usually only occupied by one resident and permits a resident to fill his or her space with their items of

11.7 (facing page)
Building exterior of Sunfield Center for Autism,
ADHD, and Behavioral Health

sentimental value. The ability to personalize provides a sense of control and caters to some of the behavioral needs of people with ASD such as keeping things orderly, predictable, and organized. The personalization can be done through simple additions such as having their favorite items distributed around the space, their name on the entrance door, friends and family pictures on the wall, a themed bedspread, etc.

Although the majority of research has focused on visually based perceptions of home-likeness and the correlations with physical properties of the residence, the study of other architectural interventions such as acoustics, spatial arrangements, lighting, ceiling heights, and technology are also important. A study by Day, Carreon, and Stump revealed that homes having unusual acoustical properties can inhibit normal conversation, promote undesirable vocalization, or create an aversive ambient environment.[33] Loud sound levels from radios and televisions (from 61–73 decibels) during mealtime in a group home for people with ASD significantly decreased social interactions among the residents. In addition, individuals with autism may be hyper-sensitive or hypo-sensitive to temperature and therefore will need opportunities to adjust their thermostats and/or have the ability to close off or let in outside air.

Research on architectural elements—such as building and room size and heights, arrangement of furniture, proximities, territory, privacy, and physical activity—on the behavior of individuals with ASD have also begun to be more prevalent in environmental design and include studies that delve into volume of space, such as a study on ceiling heights by Meyers-Levy and Zhu.[34] In their study, they found that ceiling heights could encourage and discourage social interaction and willingness to participate in activities, and they reported that higher ceilings promote more social interaction and lower ceilings reduce social interaction.

Studies of residents for vulnerable populations also indicate the importance of lighting on one's well-being. Sloane et al. discovered that facilities with low light levels were linked to higher agitation levels in the residents.[35] Research examined the relationship between environmental lighting interventions (full-spectrum lighting, micro-slatted glazed windows, and electronic controls to maintain a constant level of light intensity) and agitation levels among residents with Alzheimer's disease.[36] The study showed a significant drop in disruptive behaviors when residents were in the experimental setting (constant light levels) rather than the control setting (varying light levels).

Independent Living

Independent living could be defined as a multi-unit housing development that may provide supportive services such as meals, housekeeping, social activities, and transportation to its residents.[37] According to Kozma, Mansell, and Beadle-Brown, individuals who live in these settings have more chances to acquire new skills, develop or maintain existing skills, and are more satisfied with their living arrangements.[38] The national health organization, care specialists, and parents of young adults with ASD realize the need to create Supportive Independent Living (SIL) environments, as they are preferred by residents. Researchers in the social sciences and in environmental design professions have also provided evidence to show SIL facilities facilitate independence and are more homelike than large institutional spaces. They believe "the environment can help to maintain or increase independence and provide the highest quality of life" (p. 169) for this population.[39]

Purposeful Built Homes for Adults

To date there are a limited number of self-sustained purposeful living and learning communities that address the crisis of a growing and aging population with ASD in the United States. Albeit few, there are excellent models such as Brookwood Community and Marbridge Place in Texas, Camphill Communities in various states, and specific communities that focus on ASD such as Bittersweet Farms in Ohio and the Training, Education and Research Institute (TERI, Inc.) in California. These communities provide educational and residential support in large, physical, campus-like settings (often in urban areas).

Living and learning communities create tailor-made programs of activities that reflect the residents' interests and needs. The carefully structured and balanced learning and leisure opportunities are developed to promote overall well-being in the ASD population and provide opportunities for each individual to develop their own independence. This person-centered approach practiced in most communities is facilitated in a variety of types of buildings and spaces. The facilities include classrooms, group resident spaces, enterprise facilities, and community centers that include spiritual, recreational, and health-related services. The properties are usually spread out over large geographical areas in campus-like formats and surrounded by natural spaces (sensory gardens, water features, and hiking trails and animals) that encourage individual enrichment.

In most cases, the campuses evolved over time, often through donations from church groups, teachers, or caring families who provided land/farms. The farm-like settings were often chosen for the site of purposeful housing. The farm-like settings are a natural fit given they enable a person with an intellectual disability to contribute to their well-being by performing duties around the farm that they could manage, as the work is often predictable and repetitive in nature. The fact that the settings are surrounded by nature and include a variety of natural elements such as plants and animals is enriching given current research supports the presence of nature in spaces as having therapeutic benefits.

Research has also confirmed that people living in these types of arrangements have a better objective quality of life than do people in large, congregate settings.[40] These types of environments provide opportunities for more choice-making opportunities, immediate access to social networks, access to more mainstream facilities, and better access to community life.

The majority of adults with autism living outside of their parental homes live in shared residences with other people who have intellectual disabilities and are supervised by paid care providers. Although group homes remain the largest residential model nationally, the trend is moving toward an array of supported living arrangements[41] that offer options for the development of self-actualization. In these settings, which often are set up as communities, the individual has an opportunity to work in close proximity to their home and create social connections in a campus-like environment. Recent studies on behavioral outcomes of deinstitutionalization for people with intellectual disabilities, such as ASD, confirm that these individuals develop greater adaptive behavior skills in the community, specifically in the areas of academics, community living, communication, motor, domestic, social, and vocational skills.

Practical Applications for Design

Housing Options for Children

Children with autism live in a variety of places, including their own homes with their families, care homes, or in group living situations. An individual's intellectual challenges, abilities, and healthcare needs may be contributing factors to where he or she can live. Some existing residential options are connected to or near schools designed for ASD and all individuals participate in short-term stays.

Sunfield

Sunfield, located in the United Kingdom, is a twenty-four hour residential school for children with severe learning disabilities and autism (Figure 11.7). The estate includes a school with a number of residential buildings. The residential buildings were built and added to over time to meet the demand of an increasing population of individuals with ASD. Approximately one hundred children live at the school.

On the Sunfield estate, GA Architects was commissioned to design and build a residential facility for twelve children with profound autism. The building immediately became recognized as a state-of-the-art project and has since been visited by a number of organizations and individuals from across the UK. This particular structure at Sunfield has been widely studied and illustrated. Recently, research by Teresa Whitehurst, published in Good Autism Practice (May 2006 Issue 1), found that the behavior of the inhabitants had improved significantly after moving into the new facility.

11.8 (top) Seating and quiet activity area in the corridor, Sunfield Center for Autism, ADHD, and Behavioral Health

11.9 (bottom) Corridor, Sunfield Center for Autism, ADHD, and Behavioral Health

The symmetrical layout of the floor plan is anchored around a courtyard. The layout includes six bedrooms, two bathrooms (each shared by three residents), laundry areas, a game room, sensory studio, covered play area and staff room, dining rooms, living rooms, and a kitchen on each side of the building. The building was designed to design out corridors and replace them with *circulation spaces*. The generous circulation spaces are equipped with flexible seating and items to play with, and afford the children an opportunity to interact with their environment in a manner that resonates with their way of being. Designing spaces in this manner provides for autism-friendly personal space (appropriate proxemics) and allows children to "invent" uses for this space (Figure 11.8). This flexible space is frequently used for reading stories at bedtime and for play. By creating additional locations for socialization, the living room is often used for a quiet room, watching television, and playing board games

The circulation spaces were designed with acoustic ceilings and carpet on the floor to absorb sound. The ceilings feature timber boarding with ten-millimeter gaps between each board. Behind the boarding is an acoustic blanket that helps absorb sound (Figure 11.9). The result of the acoustic installations is a calm space, even when a number of children are playing.

The bedrooms are designed as private spaces with windows overlooking a nature-filled view. The windows are placed on an angled wall and provide visual privacy for the occupant. There are also windows surrounding the courtyard area. The caregivers and staff particularly like the fact that children playing in the courtyard can be observed from the living rooms without their awareness. Playing without fear of being watched encourages a sense of freedom in the children.

Little City Foundation

Little City Foundation is a proposed residential building for eight children with autism spectrum disorder (ASD) in Chicago. The building was designed by Christopher Beaver, a partner at GA Architects in London, UK (Figure 11.10). During the design of the facility, the architect introduced a number of key design features, including:

- one shower room and one bathroom shared between four children

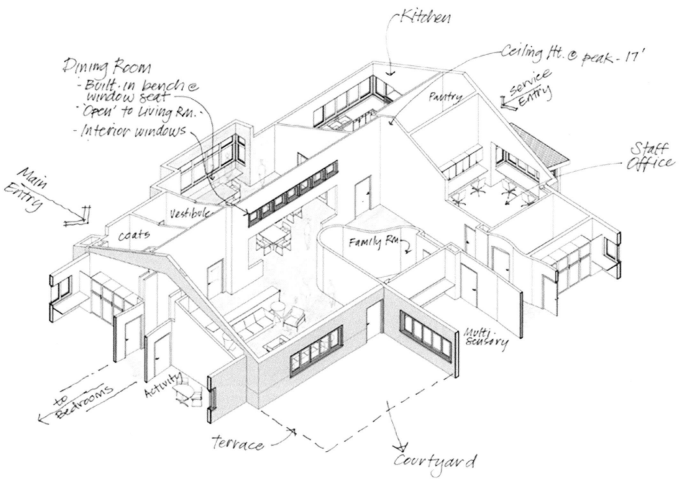

11.10 Little City Foundation in Chicago, Illinois

- curved walls on the interior
- reduced length of corridors
- creation of circulation spaces with seating
- no air-conditioning extract or intake grills within reach of children
- landscaping to incorporate sensory features
- a canopy at front entrance to provide shelter
- a large entrance space with separate space for coats and boots
- kitchens and communal rooms designed based on interviews
- materials selection for environments for children with challenging behavior based on interviews.

Housing Options for Adults

Adults with autism often live in a variety of places. Depending on their challenges and abilities, an adult with autism may live on their own, with their parents, or in group living with support

services. As mentioned above, group living can take on a variety of forms including a campus-like setting or an integration into existing neighborhoods. Often young adults will spend time in respite homes to help them adjust to communal living. The following is an example of a respite home located in the United Kingdom.

NORSACA Respite
Nottingham Regional Society for Adults and Children with Autism (NORSACA) is a facility located in Langley Mill, Nottingham, United Kingdom, and is designed by GA Architects. The structure (Figure 11.11) is designed for six adults with autism and serves as a "home away from home." The goal of the facility is to help the visitors develop socialization skills and participate in a number of engaging activities. The facility features some key design elements, including:

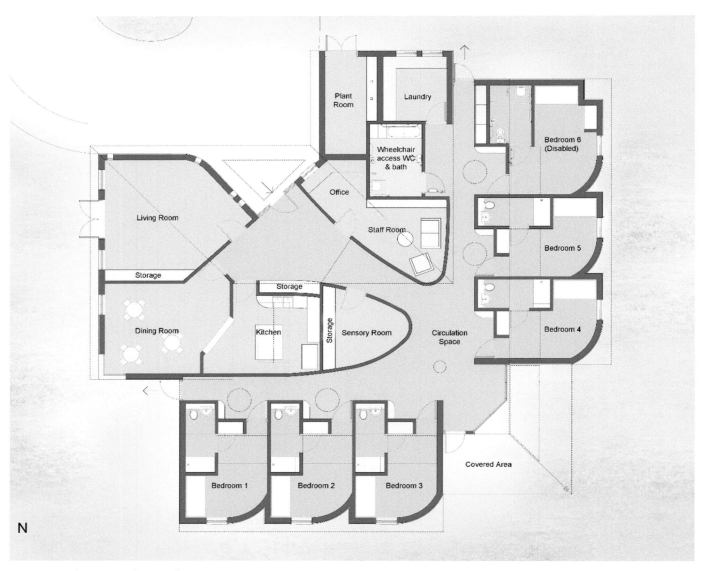

11.11 Nottingham Regional Society for Autistic Children and Adults, Nottingham, UK

- circulation spaces replacing corridors
- curved walls
- rooms with a clear identity and purpose
- small seating spaces throughout to provide observation points to different locations
- windows installed at a high level to provide cross ventilation
- and private restrooms for each resident.

Group Home Case Study

The following floor plans represent a typical group home layout for adults with Autism and other intellectual developmental disabilities. Depending on the geographical setting and local culture, the homes vary in architectural style and decoration. Daily running of the homes is usually monitored by staff that work shifts and/or live in separate quarters within the home. Residents are encouraged to manage their own daily routines. Each of the facilities have variation in style, size, and composition. However, there are a number of similar design features that have been integrated to support the users. For example, most communities have house parents or managers who live onsite to monitor the care and work schedules of the residents. Typically, residents take care of their own daily needs and are responsible for getting to on-site work or training. The houses sizes that were evaluated ranged from 3500 square feet for four residents to 8000 square feet for twelve residents.

As illustrated in Figure 11.12 and Figure 11.13 the homes include several rooms and spaces, each with their own purpose.

11.12 (top) Communal Living Example: First-Floor Plan of Group Living Home

11.13 (bottom) Communal Living Example: Second-Floor Plan of Group Living Home

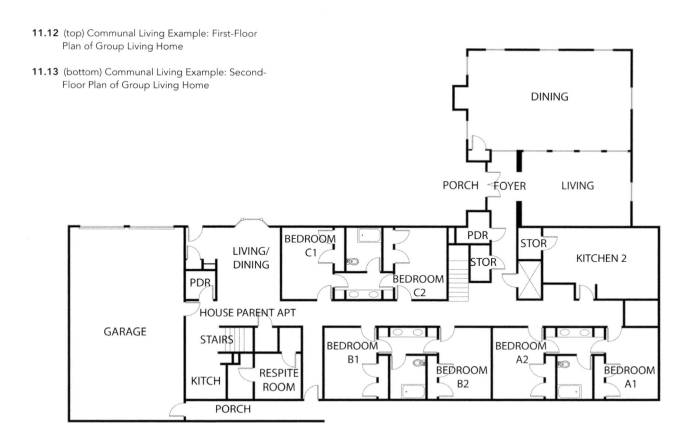

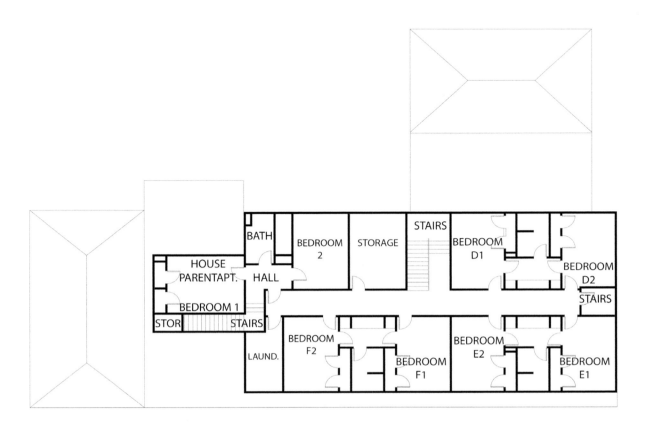

11.14 Communal Living Example: Kitchen, open concept to dining and staff area example

Typically the homes have large kitchens (Figure 11.14), family-style dining areas, and open-concept family rooms. Large laundry rooms, nursing offices, and storage are all in close proximity to the kitchen and dining areas. In order to accommodate the number of people living in the homes, large storage spaces and pantries are provided. Some homes have unique features such as quiet rooms and exercise spaces.

Bedrooms are either private or shared with one other person. In addition, residents are allowed and encouraged to personalize their bedrooms. Personalized decoration can include childhood treasures, medals, trophies, stuffed animals, window treatments, and bedding. By comparison, the male residents' rooms are much less adorned with decoration than the females'. Most of the residents share a bathroom with at least one other person (Figures 11.15 and 11.16). Some bathrooms have bathtubs, some have showers, and some provide both. The newer homes typically have bathrooms with roll-in showers, but no bathtubs.

Notes

1. Khare, Rachna, and Abir Mullick. "Incorporating the behavioral dimension in designing inclusive learning environment for autism." *ArchNet-IJAR* 3, no. 3 (2009): 45–64.

2. National Institutes of Health. "Autism spectrum disorders (ASDs)." Eunice Kennedy Shriver: National Institute of Child Health and Human Development, November 15, 2011. http://www.nichd.nih.gov/health/topics/asd.cfm.

3. McAllister, Keith. "The ASD-friendly classroom: Design complexity, challenge and characteristics." In *Design research society conference.* Retrieved from http://www. designresearchsociety.org/docs-procs/DRS2010/PDF/084.pdf. 2010.

4. Tomchek, Scott D., and Winnie Dunn. "Sensory processing in children with and without autism: A comparative study using the short sensory profile." *American journal of occupational therapy* 61, no. 2 (2007): 190–200.

5. Ashburner, Jill, Jenny Ziviani, and Sylvia Rodger. "Sensory processing and classroom emotional, behavioral, and educational outcomes in children with autism spectrum disorder." *American journal of occupational therapy* 62, no. 5 (2008): 564–573.

11.15 (top) Communal Living Example: Kitchen,
open concept to dining and staff area example

11.16 (bottom) Communal Living Example:
Residential: Private space—Design Concept
Bedroom and bathroom layout

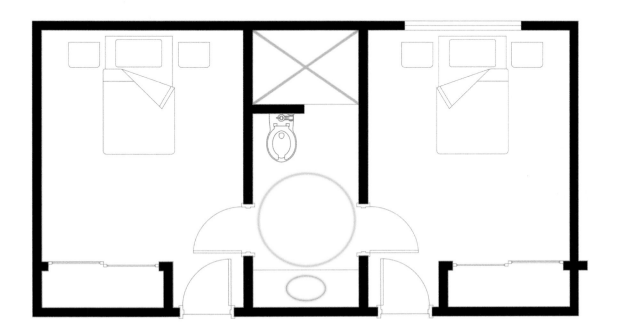

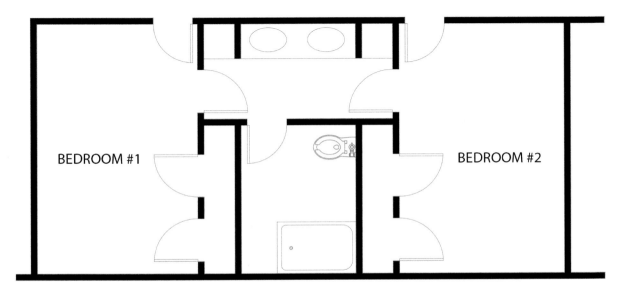

BEDROOM #1

BEDROOM #2

6. Myles, Brenda Smith, Winnie Dunn, Louann Rinner, Taku Hagiwara, Matthew Reese, Abby Huggins, and Stephanie Becker. "Sensory issues in children with Asperger syndrome and autism." *Education and training in developmental disabilities* 39, no. 4 (2004): 283–290.

7. Mostafa, Magda. "An architecture for autism: Concepts of design intervention for the autistic user." *Archnet-IJAR: International journal of architectural research* 2, no. 1 (2008): 189–211.

8. Winterbottom, Mark, and Arnold Wilkins. "Lighting and discomfort in the classroom." *Journal of environmental psychology* 29, no. 1 (2009): 63–75.

9. Winterbottom, Mark, and Arnold Wilkins. "Lighting and discomfort in the classroom." *Journal of environmental psychology* 29, no. 1 (2009): 63–75.

10. Boyce, Peter R. "Review: The impact of light in buildings on human health." *Indoor and built environment* 19, no. 1 (2010): 8–20.

11. Mostafa, Magda. "An architecture for autism: Concepts of design intervention for the autistic user." *Archnet-IJAR: International journal of architectural research* 2, no. 1 (2008): 189–211.

12. Mostafa, Magda. "An architecture for autism: Concepts of design intervention for the autistic user." *Archnet-IJAR: International journal of architectural research* 2, no. 1 (2008): 189–211.

13. Dawson, Geraldine, and Renee Watling. "Interventions to facilitate auditory, visual, and motor integration in autism: A review of the evidence." *Journal of autism and developmental disorders* 30, no. 5 (2000): 415–421.

14. Cascio, Carissa, Francis McGlone, Stephen Folger, Vinay Tannan, Grace Baranek, Kevin A. Pelphrey, and Gregory Essick. "Tactile perception in adults with autism: A multidimensional psychophysical study." *Journal of autism and developmental disorders* 38, no. 1 (2008): 127–137.

15. Tomchek, Scott D., and Winnie Dunn. "Sensory processing in children with and without autism: A comparative study using the short sensory profile." *American journal of occupational therapy* 61, no. 2 (2007): 190–200.

16. Cascio, Carissa, Francis McGlone, Stephen Folger, Vinay Tannan, Grace Baranek, Kevin A. Pelphrey, and Gregory Essick. "Tactile perception in adults with autism: A multidimensional psychophysical study." *Journal of autism and developmental disorders* 38, no. 1 (2008): 127–137.

17. Tomchek, Scott D., and Winnie Dunn. "Sensory processing in children with and without autism: A comparative study using the short sensory profile." *American journal of occupational therapy* 61, no. 2 (2007): 190–200.

18. Alcántara, José I., Emma J. L. Weisblatt, Brian C. J. Moore, and Patrick F. Bolton. "Speech-in-noise perception in high-functioning individuals with autism or Asperger's syndrome." *Journal of child psychology and psychiatry* 45, no. 6 (2004): 1107–1114.

19. Ashburner, Jill, Jenny Ziviani, and Sylvia Rodger. "Sensory processing and classroom emotional, behavioral, and educational outcomes in children with autism spectrum disorder." *American journal of occupational therapy* 62, no. 5 (2008): 564–573.

20. Tomchek, Scott D., and Winnie Dunn. "Sensory processing in children with and without autism: A comparative study using the short sensory profile." *American journal of occupational therapy* 61, no. 2 (2007): 190–200.

21. Ashburner, Jill, Jenny Ziviani, and Sylvia Rodger. "Sensory processing and classroom emotional, behavioral, and educational outcomes in children with autism spectrum disorder." *American journal of occupational therapy* 62, no. 5 (2008): 564–573.

22. Tomchek, Scott D., and Winnie Dunn. "Sensory processing in children with and without autism: A comparative study using the short sensory profile." *American journal of occupational therapy* 61, no. 2 (2007): 190–200.

23. Sánchez, Pilar Arnaiz, Francisco Segado Vázquez, and Laureano Albaladejo Serrano. *Autism and the built environment*. INTECH Open Access Publisher, 2011.

24. Weimer, Amy K., Amy M. Schatz, Alan Lincoln, Angela O. Ballantyne, and Doris A. Trauner. "'Motor' impairment in Asperger syndrome: Evidence for a deficit in proprioception." *Journal of developmental & behavioral pediatrics* 22, no. 2 (2001): 92–101.

25. Sánchez, Pilar Arnaiz, Francisco Segado Vázquez, and Laureano Albaladejo Serrano. *Autism and the built environment*. INTECH Open Access Publisher, 2011.

26. Davies, Fran, and S. Clayton. "Even the ants are noisy: Sensory perception in people with autism spectrum disorder." Presentation at NAS Regional Conference in London, 2008.

27. Ahrentzen, S., and K. Steele. *Advancing full spectrum housing: Designing for adults with autism spectrum disorders*. Tempe, AZ: Arizona Board of Regents, 2010.

28. "Klinger Wins $450K Grant to Measure Outcomes for Adults with ASD." UNC Healthcare Newsroom, 2013. http://news.unchealthcare.org/news/2013/january/klinger, accessed December 21, 2015.

29. Regnier, Victor, and Alexis Denton. "Ten new and emerging trends in residential group living environments." *Neurorehabilitation* 25, no. 3 (2008): 169–188.

30. Ahrentzen, S., and K. Steele. *Advancing full spectrum housing: Designing for adults with autism spectrum disorders.* Tempe, AZ: Arizona Board of Regents, 2010.

31. Maslow, Abraham H., and Norbett L. Mintz. "Effects of esthetic surroundings: I. Initial effects of three esthetic conditions upon perceiving 'energy' and 'well-being' in faces." *The journal of psychology* 41, no. 2 (1956): 247–254.

32. Thompson, Travis, Julia Robinson, Mary Dietrich, Marilyn Farris, and Valerie Sinclair. "Architectural features and perceptions of community residences for people with mental retardation." *American journal of mental retardation: AJMR* 101, no. 3 (1996): 292–314.

33. Day, Kristen, Daisy Carreon, and Cheryl Stump. "The therapeutic design of environments for people with dementia: A review of the empirical research." *The gerontologist* 40, no. 4 (2000): 397–416.

34. Meyers-Levy, Joan, and Rui Juliet Zhu. "The influence of ceiling height: The effect of priming on the type of processing that people use." *Journal of consumer research* 34, no. 2 (2007): 174–186.

35. Sloane, Philip D., C. Madeline Mitchell, John S. Preisser, Charles Phillips, Charlotte Commander, and Eileen Burker. "Environmental correlates of resident agitation in Alzheimer's disease special care units." *Journal of the American geriatrics society* 46, no. 7 (1998): 862–869.

36. Garce, Melinda La. "Control of environmental lighting and its effects on behaviors of the Alzheimer's type." *Journal of interior design* 28, no. 2 (2002): 15–25.

37. Regnier, Victor, Jennifer Hamilton, and Suzie Yatabe. *Assisted living for the aged and frail: Innovations in design, management, and financing.* Columbia University Press, 1995.

38. Kozma, Agnes, Jim Mansell, and Julie Beadle-Brown. "Outcomes in different residential settings for people with intellectual disability: A systematic review." *American journal on intellectual and developmental disabilities* 114, no. 3 (2009): 193–222.

39. Regnier, Victor, and Alexis Denton. "Ten new and emerging trends in residential group living environments." *Neurorehabilitation* 25, no. 3 (2008): 169–188.

40. Emerson, Eric. "Cluster housing for adults with intellectual disabilities." *Journal of intellectual and developmental disability* 29, no. 3 (2004): 187–197.

41. Braddock, David, Richard Hemp, Susan Parish, and James Westrich. *The state of the states in developmental disabilities. Fifth Edition.* Washington, DC: American Association on Mental Retardation, Research Monographs and Book Publication Program, 1998.

Work Environments

CHAPTER

12

The transition to adulthood is challenging for most people, and it is exceptionally challenging for those with ASD. This can be contributed to the fact that many of their support networks dissolve and they are left on their own to build new relationships. Moving onto higher education, training, and work means (in most cases) they will not know the people they will be interacting with, nor will they be familiar with the settings they experience.

Vocational training, life skills, and employment opportunities are increasing for this population. The American Disabilities Act (ADA) and the Vocational Rehabilitations Act (VRA) have put in place various programs to support the needs of individuals with ASD and provide them with equal opportunities. However, there is still a lack of appropriate work that is readily accessible to individuals on the spectrum even though education, life skills training, employment, and public transportation are four of the key areas identified by the National Institutes of Health (NIH).[1]

The authors of this book acknowledge that many individuals with ASD obtain advanced educational degrees and work in the same types of jobs as NT people. However, the focus of this chapter is to provide recommendations for ND individuals who may benefit most from design interventions. With adequate and focused training, the challenges this group faces in the workplace can be accommodated. Several businesses are acknowledging this and have started to provide training to individuals for jobs in retail, hospitality, packaging and manufacturing units, computer programming, with animals, and in creative fields such as composing music, painters, and craftsmen.

The retail industry, such as supermarkets, clothing stores, and home improvement stores, are progressively hiring people with ASD to stock shelves and keep track of inventory. These businesses realize that individuals on the spectrum have the ability to keep things orderly, and business owners and managers see this as an asset to their business. The restaurant industry has also found success with individuals with autism by assigning them to food prep, washing dishes, and keeping ingredients stocked. Packaging companies are also increasing the staffing of people with ASD as the repetitive work of creating boxes, stuffing envelopes, and preparing mailers requires patience and attention to detail, which are all common traits of adults with intellectual developmental disabilities.

Because of the social deficits and differentiated perceptions frequently noted in people with ASD, they rarely enjoy people-oriented jobs. However, they tend to exhibit a different relationship with animals. This makes them ideal candidates for jobs working with animals, such as veterinarians, veterinarian assistants, pet keepers, working at dog kennels, pet grooming, and working on farms. Supportive communities like this acknowledge the benefits working with animals can have on the well-being of this population and engage the resident in meaningful farm work such as caring for horses, cattle, pigs, and chickens. The immediate, positive response of seeing results is encouraging and fosters engagement and the development of self-esteem. This type of work may also provide an outlet for an individual's emotions and instill in them a sense of purpose that they wouldn't get from engaging with people.

Education

Many of the same interventions that worked in the classroom are effective for adults. Many adults with autism continue to demonstrate the same difficulty that they did as children in understanding the world and others' expectations.[2] Hence, their distractibility and organizational and sequencing difficulties interfere with their ability to function independently.

Over the years, the basic TEACCH philosophy has been used to teach children with ASD, and it has been adapted and applied to the work with adolescents and adults. The TEACCH system supports a structured educational strategy and serves as a method for preventing behavior problems in individuals with ASD.[3] The tools that are a part of this philosophy are currently being used to teach literacy skills classes, communication training, leisure and social skill development, and stress reduction in residential, vocational, and recreational settings. Based on the needs, skills, and deficits of individuals, the TEACCH philosophy provides a system of organizing the physical environment, developing appropriate activities, and helping individuals of all ages understand what is expected of them and how to function independently. Visual skills and routines are utilized to create meaningful environments that people with ASD can understand.

Behavioral difficulties are assumed to be the result of an individual's inability to understand and successfully cope with their environment. Therefore, teaching and training adults with ASD focuses on developing and retaining skills cultivated in their earlier years so that adjustments to new situations such as job opportunities

and more independent lifestyles can be successful. Treatment processes involve recognizing the strengths, interests, emerging skills, and work habits of individuals. Strengths are utilized to help compensate for the deficits of this population. Taking individual interests and preferences into account has been shown to provide them with opportunities to excel and demonstrate special talents.

In a comparison study between adults with autism and adults with mental retardation without autism living in group home settings, Van Bourgondien, Reichle, Campbell, and Mesibov found that adults with autism had significantly more problems with ritualistic behaviors and dealing with change than did those without autism.[4] The case studies examined in this research have created programs that emphasize the development of independent skills in a wide variety of areas. Communication, social, leisure, vocational, self-help, and domestic skills are addressed in both structured classes and daily activities.

Training

Working in a community is difficult for people with autism due to their problems with social skills and self-initiative. Some jobs need to be specifically arranged for a person with ASD to allow them to "fit" with the norms of an organization. Support workers and managers at intentional work/live communities invest energy in employee/employer match, as they understand the special needs of the autistic population. Supportive companies such as those that hire residents at the Marbridge foundation, a residential community for individuals with cognitive disabilities, organize both off-campus and on-campus work opportunities for their residents and young adults who live with their families.

Scott McAvoy, Vice President of Operations at the Marbridge Foundation, Manchaca, Texas, and other similar organizations, plan their curriculum in detail to prepare their students for the workplace. They start by developing the person with ASD's activities of daily living (ADL) and undertake habilitation training. Habilitation is the process of supplying a person with the means to develop maximum independence in activities of daily living through training. Although adults with ASD can continue to learn new skills as they progress through their adult years, many of their perceptions and behaviors challenge the rehabilitation efforts of support workers.

Giddan and Obee from Bittersweet Farms advocate for supportive farm community models for people with ASD and recommend four behavioral setting modification approaches to encourage habilitation.[5] They include (1) meaningful activities, (2) structured programming, (3) managing repetitive behaviors, and (4) enhanced interaction. All of these influence the design of the physical space used for teaching, training, and behavioral management.

1. **Meaningful Activities**

   In order to sustain attention and involvement, activities are best presented in meaningful contexts, and the impact of the work should be seen at some point.[6] For example, settings that include horticulture businesses enable this group to plant seeds, watch them grow, weed the gardens, harvest the vegetables, and then cook the food. Stages of this process are observable, concrete, and fully experienced by each person.

2. **Structured Programming**

   Program activities are guided by carefully planned schedules presented with strong visual cues. Mesibov et al. recommend the use of visual cues, such as those used in the TEACCH program that is commonly used to teach children with ASD.[7]

3. **Managing Repetitive Behaviors**

   A variety of strategies have been shown over time to be useful in dealing with the interfering, perseverative behaviors seen in individuals on the spectrum, such as diverting and redirecting perseverative responses toward similar motor movements into constructive and useful purposes.[8] For example, for people who have a tendency to pace, mowing grass may help temper their behaviors. People who show attention to small details may enjoy weeding gardens or working with textiles and crafts. People who like to flail their arms may be comforted when washing windows.

4. **Enhanced Interaction**

   To overcome social isolation, typical of adults with ASD, a range of interactive activities can be encouraged. Meaningful physical and social interactions can be structured into tasks to enhance sharing and interdependence among residents and peers (i.e. sharing household chores and meal preparation).[9]

Someone with autism may simultaneously encounter difficulties with "executive function," which is traditionally used as an umbrella term for functions such as planning, working memory, impulse control, inhibition, and the initiation and monitoring of action.[10] Difficulty with executive function can make organizing and remembering the steps involved in carrying out an everyday activity very challenging. In order to manage these behaviors, the environment for training and teaching needs to be orderly and predictable, acoustically sound, and clearly organized with workplace tools to support learning.

Learning Styles

"Learning styles" is a theory that describes the methods by which people gain information about their environment. The concept is that people can learn through: seeing (visually), hearing (auditory), and/or through touching or manipulating an object (kinesthetically, or "hands-on" learning). Generally, most people learn using two to three of these learning styles.

One's learning style can affect how well a person performs in an educational or training setting. Individuals who are kinesthetic learners may tend to have occupations involving their hands, such as shelf stockers, mechanics, or sculptors. Others may be visual learners that choose occupations that involve processing visual information, such as data processors, artists, architects, or manufacturing part sorters. Auditory learners may gravitate toward jobs that involve processing auditory information, such as sales people, judges, musicians, 9-1-1 operators, and waiters or waitresses.

Temple Grandin states that visual thinking tends to be the most prominent manner in which this population tends to gravitate.[11] As noted by the NIH, in order for an adult with autism to develop skills to live/function semi-independently, they need to develop vocational training, life skills, have mental and physical health support, and have help finding employment, public transportation, and public housing. Attempts, although limited, are being made to address this group's needs as adults. Supportive communities, such as those referenced and profiled in this book, pay close attention to the needs of people with ASD by providing holistic training. This community accommodates their residents/students/employees' abilities and manages their learning and workplace challenges by working with each individual's learning style. They also create intellectually challenging work opportunities that are meaningful and purposeful and try to manage their physical property layout so that each individual can get to their place of work as independently

12.1 Aerial view of the buildings at an intentional work/residential community for people with intellectual development diversities. Red = residential; yellow = work, recreational

as possible. At the Brookwood Community, residents can walk to their place of work (shown in yellow in Figure 12.1). Training can take place from their homes, shown in red. This is an integral part of the community's initiative to address the whole person's well-being.

The Fourth Teacher

Brookwood Community Layout

The work opportunities in the Brookwood Community (shown in Figure 12.1) include working in small business enterprises such as pottery making, preserving fruit, gardening and greenhouse work, property maintenance, office work, and the up-keep of the campus homes. The up-keep of the homes is one of the first jobs residents participate in upon joining the community. Daily jobs

related to the running of the homes such as cleaning, cooking, and food preparation are taught to the residents, and each person is expected to participate in keeping the home in order.

In 2010, a book titled *The Third Teacher* was published.[12] The book was developed by an international team of architects and designers and was concerned with the failing education system and studied links between school environments and how children learn. The authors discuss how the built environment affects learning, and present numerous practical design ideas to help designers improve schools. Like the structured classroom, one of the most important places to teach and learn is in the home. The title of the book is based on a perspective of Italian psychologist Loris Malaguzzi's work in the schools of Reggio Emilia following WWII. Malaguzzi asserted that students encounter three teachers: (1) the adult instructor(s), (2) their peers, and (3) the school environment itself.[13]

Borrowing from O'Donnell et al.'s[14] idea of the classroom as the third teacher, this writing proposes the home could be the fourth teacher. The tasks of daily living are taught to residents and used as foundations for preparation to work in a work setting. These transferable skills are often learned in childhood and are reinforced in adulthood. Many residences where people with ASD live, including their birth homes, use images of activities required to complete ADL.

Teaching activities of daily living (ADL) helps enable individuals with autism to live semi-independently and, in some cases, independently. According to Lawton and Brody, ADL includes the basic tasks of dressing, bathing, grooming and using the toilet, eating, walking, and getting in and out of bed.[15] Instrumental activities of daily living (IADL) are more complex tasks such as cooking and cleaning. Performing these activities demands a considerable amount of body coordination, including small and large motor skills, manual dexterity, acute proprioception, and vestibular stability. Additionally, they require self-motivation, the ability to plan, organize, communicate verbally, and understand social norms.

Given the range of cognitive, sensory, and human factors in individuals on the spectrum, some people may need help in one particular area more than another. Smith, Maenner, and Seltzer studied the effects of early intervention of teaching life skills and concluded that with consistent training, a person with ASD's abilities may improve during adolescence, and proficiency could develop through early adulthood.[16] However, this is not true for all people on the spectrum.

A recent study, "Designing Everyday Activities: Living Environments for Adults with Autism," conducted by the Helen Hamlyn Centre for Design at the Royal College of Art, examined how people with ASD perceived ADL, and strived to find out how design can enhance the life experiences of people with ASD.[17] They found that this group has very different perceptions of the processes and products used to complete tasks of daily living. Some were fearful of tools and equipment, and others were intrigued and wanted to engage at an intense level. Since everyday environments are furnished with a variety of items that stimulate an assortment of sensations, it is important to access and edit spaces for those who find it difficult to filter. If spaces are not edited properly, process stimuli can trigger enjoyment or anxiety.

Individuals with ASD can be hyper- or hypo-sensitive to multiple sensory experiences, which makes supportive design complex. Gaudion reported on a methodology for developing objects and spaces to support users with ASD.[18] She suggests that design can influence how people direct their negative reactions and can beneficially exploit positive reactions. The four key findings from the study are as follows:

1. Extend: This refers to taking a sensation that is enjoyed in one context (for example, the "spinning" of a washing machine) and extending it to a new context or activity (for example, a salad spinner or rotating shoe rack).
2. Tailor: This is about tailoring activities to avoid those things that a person dislikes (for example, choosing a quieter manual lawn mower over a loud electrical one, if a person is hyper-sensitive to sound), or choosing and tailoring the color of everyday objects to a person's preference.
3. Embrace: This refers to embracing the way people with autism like to do things, rather than conforming to social norms (for example, support staff sitting down to watch the spinning washing machine with the person they are supporting).
4. Create: This is about creating new activities to enhance particular sensory preferences and interests (for example, if a person likes listening to the sound of a washing machine, place a bell into a pair of socks to create new interesting sounds).

Gaudion's study made it clear that in order to have successful training experiences, the spaces that activities take place in and the tools needed to perform tasks need to acknowledge the individuals' sensory sensitivities. These spaces also need to differentiate neurological processing and include personal preferences and interests to be successful. The group home living facilities in the adult communities study in this book included rooms and spaces that encouraged residents to participate in activities of daily living (ADL). The spaces and activities were planned to engage the residents. The floor plans were spacious and free of clutter and included labels on cabinetry that identified its contents and sequence of the task required to perform the ADL. The setup helped the residents develop their independence and skill sets that they could use for work opportunities outside their home (Figures 12.2 and 12.3, overleaf).

12.2 (top)
Large laundry rooms with a sequential layout
help individuals with ASD learn how to manage
activities of daily living

12.3 (bottom)
Kitchens free from clutter with simple designs
encourage participation

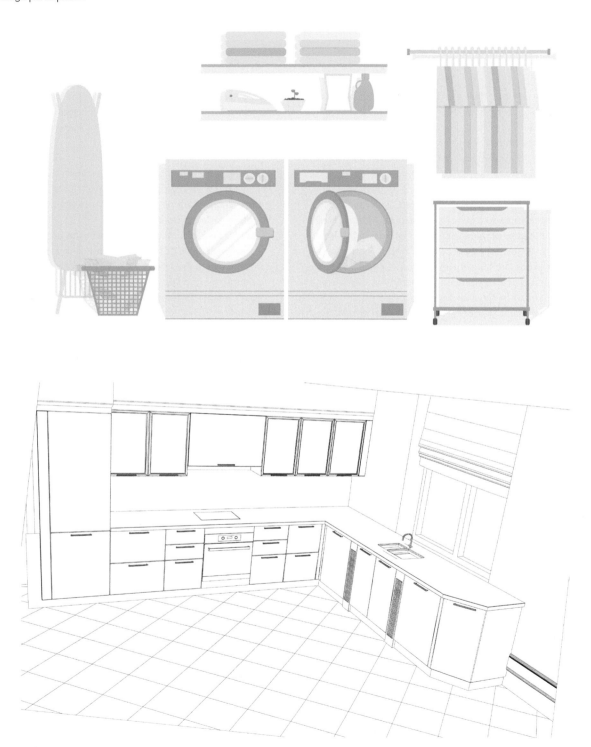

12.4 The Brookwood Community includes a commercial kitchen canning enterprise where residents have enough space to function and feel comfortable while completing canning tasks

Practical Applications for Design

Training for individuals with ASD can take many forms. Typically, training people with ASD emphasizes a habilitation approach whereby great effort is made to help an individual acquire, keep, or improve their skills, talents, and aptitudes. The focus is on providing support systems through co-habilitation (team work) that encourage competencies and abilities needed for the person to optimally function and interact with their environments and other people.

Two well-known work/live communities that were intentionally built for people with ASD, Bittersweet Farms (BSF) in Ohio, USA, and Brookwood Community (BWC) in Texas, USA, advocate for a habilitation approach to training. BSF systematically follows a behavioral modification approach (MAPS) and the BWC uses a system called Behavioral Environmental Structured Teaching Technologies (BESTT). Both approaches accommodate the changing needs of people with ASD, particularly their aging needs and varied physical, emotional, or mental challenges. BWC's program operates out of a dedicated space (learning lab) and provides residents the opportunity to develop skills at their own pace in a supportive small group setting. The BESTT teachers share these students' progress with the internal work place teachers to help integrate these individuals into larger work group settings. This successful program is augmented through the use of their "Snoezelen Room". This room provides the program

participants with a therapeutic space where they can rejuvenate and escape. Both training programs focus on an individual's strengths and attempt to find a match between a person's learning style, personality, and work opportunities. Each individual's needs vary; sometimes the trainers will go back and provide remedial academic training in order to bridge the gap in some training requirements. Other individuals have the skills and education to seamlessly be integrated into training.[19]

Bittersweet Farms' approach to successful habilitation is based on four behavioral setting modifications.[20] They include:

1. Environmental organization meaningful activities
2. Structured programming-MAPS
3. Managing repetitive behaviors
4. Enhanced interaction

All of these modifications can be facilitated by careful manipulation of the physical environment.

1. Environmental Organization

The environment needs to be clearly defined and highly organized.[21] This applies to the physical setting, roles of personnel, and program format. The physical space must accommodate specific daily tasks and activities and allow enough room for each person to function and feel comfortable.

2. Structured Programming

A successful approach to training used by Jan Cline,[22] the training manager at Bittersweet Farms, and her colleagues is an approach based on a format that includes:

- Meaning and Motivation
- Aerobic and Active Engagement
- Partnership and Purpose
- Structure and Support

BSF advocates for a pyramid structure, whereby the foundation of the process, which is the most critical and first to apply, is structure and support (Figure 12.5).

S=Structure and Support

Consistently structured routines, work areas, and social interactions (utilizing individualized supports) help people with ASD understand the order of activities, how to make choices, and how to communicate interests and needs. Visual schedules (written or pictured) are prosthetic aids that allow each individual to understand what is happening, what is expected of them, and what is coming next.

BSF's approach echoes Mesibov, Shea, and Schopler's view that program activities are guided by carefully planned schedules, presented with strong visual cues like the TEACCH method.[23] Using the TEACCH method enables the service worker to clearly lay out tasks to enhance the independence of individuals with ASD. The system helps develop skills of self-maintenance and to teach steps to completing ADL. The familiar images of activities and the tools associated with completing activities help trigger memory and enable people with ASD to conceptualize what they are to do and act on their interpretations (Figure 12.6).

The Bittersweet Farms structure of breaking long tasks into smaller steps, rehearsing, and preparing for changes while being considerate of sensory needs/concerns, helps develop clear lines of positive communication. Their approach focuses on mastery and then builds on learning. Careful consideration is given to engaging one's tactile senses. Hands-on work is at the root of BSF's philosophies. BWC also takes this approach in their horticulture enterprise. They first introduce the students to the tools and processes in smaller settings and "show and tell" by using visual aids that illustrate the individual steps and

12.5 Bittersweet Farms Training System—M.A.P.S.

samples of completed work for preparing a pot for a plant to be planted. These visual tools are also useful for helping students to understand what behaviors are expected of them. Regardless of the type of vocation or job one is preparing for, the teaching process requires spaces that allow for one-on-one and small group training.

P=Partnership and Purpose

The next level of the pyramid is partnership and purpose, which encourages working as a team with a mutual goal that is understood by each partner. When instructors share all of the work and teach by modeling, social "inter-dependence" is built with each individual on the spectrum. In this engagement, the service worker needs to remember the person with ASD is learning from their interactions and the supports they provide. This model encourages instructors to embrace teachable moments and remember that learning happens everywhere, not just in structured, classroom settings.

Adult educators and support workers, like Jan Cline at Bittersweet Farms, recommend that the staff work collaboratively

12.6 Sample of a TEACCH Visual Aid Schedule

and cooperatively. They should take time to prepare their participants before they engage in a task by helping them create a mental image of what their job might entail. They also recommend that participants start to engage in coaching by expressing a shared vision. For example, if a participant sees blooms on a tomato plant, the instructor should encourage them to return to the plant a few days later to see if it forms into a tomato. Developing this sense of inquiry helps to build comprehension of patterns and growth as well as the understanding of time and change. This process communicates that it takes time for things to develop properly. In order to physically enable a person with ASD to get the full experience of a situation and develop their own sense of inquiry, the area where the plant is growing needs to be accessible and have interest. Accessibility and interest will encourage the individual to visit the plant on their own and see the entire process from planting to harvest.

A=Aerobic and Active Engagement

Exercise is associated with a variety of physical and psychological benefits, including improved cardiovascular health and reduced depression among adults and children.[24] The Bittersweet Farms staff state that to "get the person moving, doing healthy exercise/activity throughout the course of the day/shift, design or set up simple physical movement within an activity such as walking, bending, stretching, reaching, etc. Think of it as a sensory banquet designed for each person's likes and needs; engaging participation as much as possible in all activities." Facilities, grounds, and between space can facilitate this by ensuring in-between space in the exterior, such as gardens, are equipped with materials and finishes to allow someone with ASD to express themselves verbally and physically such as by swinging arms, twirling, snapping fingers, and engaging in repetitive movement. These behaviors are common occurrences in this population when they are over-stimulated. Aerobic activity can be accommodated and encouraged by increasing the volume of rooms. Larger-than-normal corridors designed in segments with varying ceiling heights can help to create transition spaces.

Spaces should also be designed with active lifestyles in mind. Creating pathways and corridors that connect spaces allow people to walk and get to where they want to go on their own. These pathways and corridors can also create opportunities for the individual to temper emotions by engaging in points of interest. Points could include galleries of creative works, displays of natural life, or aspiring architecture. The contrasting volumes of space should create a sense of awe and evoke memorable experiences that are visible in textures, forms, and artifacts that activate one's memory.

M=Meaning and Motivation

The top level of the pyramid, meaning and motivation, seeks to provide opportunities for individuals to see the beginning, middle, and end of a process. When an individual sees the results of their work and effort, it is both motivating and develops a sense of accomplishment. Additionally, emphasizing an individual's needs is motivating because most people like to feel they are treated as individuals. Personalization can be achieved in the built environment by providing ample personal space and allowing individuals to personalize their work areas. Personalization of space can enable a person to establish their individual identity, thereby positively contributing to their self-worth. Personal spaces such as lockers, designated chairs, and work surfaces let people with ASD claim control over their workspace and feel important.

3. Managing Repetitive Behaviors

A variety of strategies have been shown over time to be useful in dealing with the interfering, pervasive behaviors seen in individuals with autism. Schopler and Mesibov recommend diverting and redirecting pervasive responses toward similar motor movements that are constructive and useful.[25] As mentioned earlier, it is useful to redirect these behaviors into productive actions such as mowing the lawn, weeding gardens, or cleaning windows.

4. Enhanced Interaction

As noted earlier, horticulture work is good to teach process and product relationships. It has also proven to increase self-esteem and self-confidence, encourage social interaction, improve productivity in work tasks, improve literacy and numeracy skills, increase general well-being, and develop independence. Sempik, Aldridge, and Becker found students with learning disabilities increased their feelings of value and worth in that they considered themselves more desirable after participating in horticulture activities.[26] They also noted that therapeutic horticulture provides individual students/residents with the opportunity to express themselves in a positive way.

These examples illustrate the complicated nature of developing training and teaching plans for individuals on the spectrum. They also stress the need for designers and architects to design spaces that accommodate a wide range of opportunities for teaching and training within the built environment. Incorporating elements into the design of spaces that support structure, order, consistency, and predictability can help a person with ASD attain an optimum environmental and personal fit in workplace settings.[27]

ASD in the Workplace

Many high-functioning individuals with ASD may be able to secure jobs in a more public work environment. However, the transition into this type of environment may still be very challenging due to communication and social difficulties. Common workplace challenges faced by people with autism, in particular, include:

- problems fitting in the general workplace environment, as many have not been exposed to a variety of workplaces
- lack of comprehension of others' emotions and providing inappropriate responses
- difficulty understanding verbal instruction
- adhering to standard work schedules of the company
- managing repetitive and obsessive behaviors
- heightened sensory-processing issues

Visual distractions are a problem for many on the spectrum because they process more visual information than people without autism.[28] Hence, they are easily visually distracted and need clearly defined, organized, and neatly arranged work spaces. Providing opportunities for individuals to organize their work space in an orderly fashion by using bins, baskets, or storage cupboards moves clutter out of sight and provides a clean work surface where an employee can concentrate. Compartmentalization of work allows people on the spectrum to dedicate specific areas in their workspace to specific tasks. This also encourages and maintains routines, something that is very important to many people with autism. It is also important to minimize the use of repetitive patterns, grids, and colors within a work area. Creating an environment with low visual complexity eliminates unnecessary environmental stimuli and can help a person focus on a given task.

The lighting used in work areas is also important for people with ASD, as they can become easily agitated by shadows and glare. Purposeful task lighting and the ability to manage natural light is essential. Additionally, ensuring the lighting design within the work area includes more than one light source is essential for eliminating shadows. Subdued, indirect, flexible lighting that creates a calm effect is always ideal.

Many people with ASD are sensitive to sounds and can hear sounds that most NT people cannot. Background noises are especially problematic. The sounds made by HVAC systems, for example, are of particular concern, as they are most likely sensed in work environments as they go on and off intermittently. If possible, the individual should be located far away from the HVAC unit to reduce the amount of noise they can hear. Sounds made by other office equipment such as photocopiers, shredders, and printers can also be an issue. In this case, it is best to locate the worker with ASD as far away from noisy equipment as possible.

Whether individuals with ASD are high-functioning members of the public workforce or live in a supportive community where they have working responsibilities, it is important that their sensitivities to environmental stimuli be considered. The education and training process for a working individual on the spectrum is also important to understand. Employers that are committed to understanding the ways they can help these individuals will have fewer difficulties caring for and supervising these essential employees. Whatever their job might be, people with autism most certainly have something to contribute to the workforce and should be given every opportunity to flourish and succeed.

Notes

1. National Institutes of Health. "Autism spectrum disorders (ASDs)." Eunice Kennedy Shriver: National Institute of Child Health and Human Development, November 15, 2011. http://www.nichd.nih.gov/health/topics/asd.cfm.
2. Braddock, D., R. Hemp, M. C. Rizzolo, E. S. Tanis, L. Haffer, and J. Wu. *The state of the states in intellectual and developmental disabilities: Emerging from the great recession.* Washington DC: American Association on Intellectual and Developmental Disabilities (AAIDD), 2015.
3. Mesibov, Gary B., Victoria Shea, and Eric Schopler. *The TEACCH approach to autism spectrum disorders.* Springer Science & Business Media, 2004.
4. Van Bourgondien, Mary E., Nancy C. Reichle, Duncan G. Campbell, and Gary B. Mesibov. "The environmental rating scale (ERS): A measure of the quality of the residential environment for adults with autism." *Research in developmental disabilities* 19, no. 5 (1998): 381–394.
5. Giddan, Jane J., and Victoria L. Obee. "Adults with autism: Habilitation challenges and practices." *Journal of rehabilitation* 62, no. 1 (1996): 72.
6. Giddan, Jane J., and Victoria L. Obee. "Adults with autism: Habilitation challenges and practices." *Journal of rehabilitation* 62, no. 1 (1996): 72.
7. Mesibov, Gary B., Victoria Shea, and Eric Schopler. *The TEACCH approach to autism spectrum disorders.* Springer Science & Business Media, 2004.
8. Schopler, Eric, and Gary B. Mesibov. *Autism in adolescents and adults.* Springer Science & Business Media, 1983.
9. Giddan, Jane J., and Victoria L. Obee. "Adults with autism: Habilitation challenges and practices." *Journal of rehabilitation* 62, no. 1 (1996): 72.
10. Rabbitt, P. "Introduction: Methodologies and models in the study of executive function." In *Methodology of frontal and executive function,* (pp. 1–38). Taylor & Francis, 1997.
11. Grandin, Temple. *Thinking in pictures: My life with autism* (expanded edition). New York: Vintage, 2006.
12. O'Donnell Wicklund Pigozzi and Peterson, Architects Inc, V. S. Furniture, and Bruce Mau Design. *The third teacher: 79 ways you can use design to transform teaching & learning.* New York: Abrams, 2010.
13. Strong-Wilson, Teresa, and Julia Ellis. "Children and place: Reggio Emilia's environment as third teacher." *Theory into practice* 46, no. 1 (2007): 40–47.
14. O'Donnell Wicklund Pigozzi and Peterson, Architects Inc, V. S. Furniture, and Bruce Mau Design. *The third teacher: 79 ways you can use design to transform teaching & learning.* New York: Abrams, 2010.

15. Lawton, M. P., and E. M. Brody. "Assessment of older people: Self-maintaining and instrumental activities of daily living." *The gerontologist* 9, no. 3 (1969): 179–186.

16. Smith, Leann E., Matthew J. Maenner, and Marsha Mailick Seltzer. "Developmental trajectories in adolescents and adults with autism: The case of daily living skills." *Journal of the American Academy of Child & Adolescent Psychiatry* 51, no. 6 (2012): 622–631.

17. Gaudion, Katie. *Designing everyday activities: Living environments for adults with autism*. Helen Hamlyn Centre for Design, 2013.

18. Gaudion, Katie. *Designing everyday activities: Living environments for adults with autism*. Helen Hamlyn Centre for Design, 2013.

19. Bourne, Angela, personal communication with Rick DeMunbrun and Carol Whitmore at Brookwood Community, Brookshire, Texas, June 2013.

20. Giddan, Jane J., and Victoria L. Obee. "Adults with autism: Habilitation challenges and practices." *Journal of rehabilitation* 62, no. 1 (1996): 72.

21. Van Bourgondien, Mary E., Nancy C. Reichle, Duncan G. Campbell, and Gary B. Mesibov. "The environmental rating scale (ERS): A measure of the quality of the residential environment for adults with autism." *Research in developmental disabilities* 19, no. 5 (1998): 381–394.

22. Giddan, Jane J., and Victoria L. Obee. "Adults with autism: Habilitation challenges and practices." *Journal of rehabilitation* 62, no. 1 (1996): 72.

23. Mesibov, Gary B., Victoria Shea, and Eric Schopler. *The TEACCH approach to autism spectrum disorders*. Springer Science & Business Media, 2004.

24. Brannon, Linda, and Jess Feist. *Health psychology: An introduction to behavior and health* (3rd ed.). Pacific Grove, CA: Brooks/Cole, 1997.

25. Schopler, Eric, and Gary B. Mesibov. *Autism in adolescents and adults*. Springer Science & Business Media, 1983.

26. Sempik, Joe, Jo Aldridge, and Saul Becker. *Social and therapeutic horticulture: Evidence and messages from research*. Thrive, 2003.

27. Autism Society Ontario. *Our most vulnerable citizens: A report of the Adult Task Force, Autism Society Ontario*. Guelph, Ontario: s.n., 1991.

28. Remington, Anna, John Swettenham, Ruth Campbell, and Mike Coleman. "Selective attention and perceptual load in autism spectrum disorder." *Psychological science* 20, no. 11 (2009): 1388–1393.

Therapeutic Environments

Design for health and wellness is in the midst of a great change. Prior to WWII, health was based on a pathogenic model known as an absence of disease.[1] In the past, identifying and classifying the illness of the patient was the focus of the care received in healthcare settings. After WWII, the aim of healthcare was to provide "a state of complete physical, mental, and social well-being and not merely the absences of disease and infirmity."[2] By the 1970s, a new paradigm evolved known as "a model of salutogenesis" (by Aaron Antonovsky). The Model of Salutogenesis viewed health as "a continuum on an axis between total ill health (dis-ease) to total health (ease)."[3]

Designing for wellness and health is necessary for an individual with ASD due to the number of psychological and physiological factors to consider when designing a therapeutic environment. The seven dimensions of The Wellness Model provide a broader perspective for designing spaces. The model's seven dimensions are as follows: [4]

- **Physical Wellness:** involves engaging in physical activity; consuming a healthy diet; avoiding harmful behaviors; having a self-awareness of physical body, understanding of the health hazards associated with environmental issues and self-actualization
- **Emotional/Psychological Wellness:** involves positive mental health; awareness of self in relationship to others; investing and committing to meaningful relationships; and engaging in self-regulation in stressful situations
- **Social Wellness:** participating appropriately in comfortable and intimate interactions with others; expressing oneself emotionally or managing conflict resolution; participating in community activities; initiating and following through with social and support networks; respect for others' opinions
- **Spiritual Wellness:** having a belief and value system that is self-nurturing; appreciating the spiritual preferences others may have
- **Environmental Wellness:** monitoring work–life balance; respecting and participating in preservation of nature and built environment resources
- **Intellectual Wellness:** involves engaging in stimulating and thought-provoking activities to expand one's knowledge; developing abilities, skills, and global awareness
- **Occupational Wellness:** involves engaging in meaningful work that one can self-express and having their contributions valued

Martin Seligman, a psychologist, advocates for a positive approach to well-being with a focus on behavioral adaptation.[5] Seligman notes that in order to achieve mental wellness, care and support must focus on positive factors and behaviors. Focusing on the positive aspects is especially important when creating environments that nurture the sensory sensitivities of those with ASD. Caregivers should focus on working with the behaviors of people with ASD, and designers should seek to provide an environment that accommodates caregiver and patient needs.

Features of the Therapeutic Environment

A relationship exists between the mental and physical health of an individual and the built environment. Smyth states that healing properties are associated with the environment of the user.[6] Environmental psychology (psycho-social effects of the environment), psychoneuroimmunology (the effects of the environment on the immune system), and neuroscience (how the brain perceives architecture) contribute to Therapeutic Environment Theory.[7] Four key factors of Therapeutic Environment Theory are

- reducing or eliminating environmental stressors
- providing positive distractions
- enabling social support
- providing a sense of control

Smith and Watkins give the following examples of ways to achieve the key factors of the therapeutic environment in healthcare design.[8] These examples may also be applied to other environments such as school or residential spaces. The design features of a supportive therapeutic environment should include:

- acoustical separation from sources of noise
- acoustical treatment of corridors
- appropriate lighting systems
- natural daylighting where possible
- comfortable furnishings and comfortable layouts
- good indoor air quality
- appropriate use of color

Layout

One space that is typically "therapeutic" is a healthcare environment. Healthcare environments, specifically hospitals, are often large, wide-open volumes of space that can be extremely difficult for individuals with ASD to understand. Individuals have difficulty processing information from the environment because of the large, unsegmented amounts of stimulation and information they experience.[9] Smaller spaces that are easier to navigate provide a more therapeutic space for neurodiverse (ND) individuals. Areas should be clearly defined by furniture placement, flooring, finishes, and other physical or visual dividers.

The design of the reception area in the Village Family Health offices by ARK, shown in Figure 13.1, clearly indicates the purpose of each space. The visual transparency from space to space allows the vulnerable population they serve to scan the environment and establish their bearings as they adjust to a new setting. The repetition of the clean architectural forms in the walls, ceiling, and millwork create a uniform setting that eases comprehension. The neutral color scheme enhances the continuity of the space and provides an appropriate backdrop for the large nature scenes behind the reception desk. The expansive images provide a positive distraction to patients. Allowing patients to have a connection with the nature scenes provides a calming atmosphere that may reduce a patient's anxiety.

The waiting area adjacent to the reception desk is made up of therapeutic design elements that relate to a person with intellectual challenges. The predictable arrangement of modular seating reflects the horizontal lines in Figure 13.1 and reinforces the continuity of the space. This continuity provides comfort for vulnerable populations, such as those with ASD, given their preference for order.

Scale

Scale is an important factor for both the overall physical design of a space as well as the furniture and other items that are incorporated. In healthcare environments, the scale of a patient room should be designed with the patient in mind. For example, a room for a grown adult and a room for a pediatric patient should be designed at two different scales. An adult would need a larger bed and furniture,

which would in turn require a larger amount of square footage. A child may feel overwhelmed in a room that is designed for someone two to three times their size. Providing comfortable, appropriately selected furniture leads to a higher level of patient satisfaction. While the first priority should be enabling caregivers to provide the best care to the patient, the scale of the room and furniture should also cater to the comfort of the patient.

The award-winning firm, ARK, realizes the importance of scale in a space and has successfully integrated forms, shapes, and visuals in the reception space shown in Figure 13.2. The reception desk illustrates a conscientious approach to scale for a variety of users. An individual in a wheelchair can maintain eye contact with the receptionist and feel engaged in a conversation. Additionally, the artwork behind the desk spans from the counter to the ceiling,

13.3 (facing page, top)
Corridor, view to the distance. Mount Sinai Hospital, Sherman Health and Wellness Center at the UJA Federation Lebovic Community Campus, Vaughan, Canada

13.4 (facing page, bottom)
Entrance and reception view—close-up patient interaction. Village Family Health Team clinic, partner of the Centre for Addiction and Mental Health, Toronto, Canada

thereby providing visual appeal at any eye level and allowing visitors to have a positive distraction from any negative emotions they may feel.

Stress

According to Kopec, stress is defined as a "psychological or physiological response to a stimulus or stressor" that may come from internal or external sources.[10] External sources of stress for individuals with ASD may include physical environmental features such as crowding, noise, fluorescent lights, spatial disorganization, and others. Individuals with ASD may be more prone to external stressors due to a greater sensitivity to environmental stimuli, especially within healthcare environments. The unpredictability that patients feel within hospitals, either due to inhabiting a complex, unfamiliar environment or one's ailing health, can also contribute significantly to stress and suppression of the immune system.[11] Smith and Watkins point out that it is the responsibility of all designers to incorporate design interventions that significantly improve patient outcomes.[12] Internal sources of stress may be reduced through choice and control. Several theorists believe that when people have the control and opportunity to make choices about their environment, they will experience greater well-being. Psychology researchers have examined the relationship between happiness, life satisfaction, positive mental health, depression, and sense of control for over 30 years.[13] Due to impaired adaptive behaviors, neurodiverse (ND) individuals often do not have as much control over their lives as neurotypical (NT) people. As a result, they are at special risk for negative outcomes from stressful experiences. Cohen, Glass, and Phillips have called groups with diminished control over their environments "susceptible populations."[14] This understanding should influence the design of interventions that enhance control and contribute to the well-being of people on the spectrum.[15] Providing escape spaces, such as sensory rooms, music rooms, and safe exercise rooms, can help relieve stress in individuals with ASD. Access to nature, such as healing or walking gardens, can also alleviate stress in people with autism.[16, 17, 18]

Views of Nature and Biophilic Design

Researchers have written extensively about therapeutic environments, primarily in relation to outdoor environments, and question how well the indoor environment can provide users with desirable experiences.[19, 20, 21] Factors that may positively or negatively affect a user's experience could include how attractive the environment is, how comfortable it is, and how easy is it to get through or around a space.

Therapeutic environments should be both restorative and instorative.[22] A restorative environment provides an individual the prospect to recover through a "restorative" experience. A restorative experience creates a sense of being away, fascination, extent, and compatibility.[23] Additonally, Ulrich's theory of supportive gardens indicates that healthcare environments have the ability to improve health when they provide restorative resources such as sense of control, access to privacy, social support, physical movement and exercise, and access to nature and other positive distractions.[24, 25]

Environments are considered to be instorative when the experiences and activities in the environment are in harmony with the user's background and character health and when well-being and drive are promoted.[26] An instorative environment strengthens identity and self-esteem and helps individuals feel like they are part of a meaningful context. According to Kaplan and Kaplan, restorative and instorative environments offer more than recovery and provide something of existential value and reorientation in life.[27]

Biophilia is a term coined by Harvard University professor E. O. Wilson. He postulates that humans are naturally attracted to nature-like forms and emphasizes that biophilia "is the innately emotional affiliation of human beings to other living organisms. Innate means hereditary and hence part of ultimate human nature."[28]

Evidence of the emotional and psychological benefits of nature is rising. Studies indicate that contact with nature is critical to human health and well-being and that *nature* has a major influence in identifying ways to make buildings: more enjoyable and pleasing (therapeutic), relate to the sensory sensitivities and neurological needs (prosthetic), and promote new skill sets and experiences (instorative) for individuals with autism. Kellert argues that visual representations of nature, symbols of nature, views to nature, and indoor plants and other natural design elements appeal to one's innate affinity and can evoke positive experiences in the built environment.[29]

Examining nature relative to one's cognitive processing is appropriate given that many people with ASD have differentiated or delayed cognitive processing. Kahn and Kellert determined that the direct experience of nature greatly enhances cognitive processing and termed the process *cognitive biophilia*.[30] In their view, the natural world affords numerous opportunities for stimulation and engagement. Various elements of nature, such as trees, bushes, plants, flowers, birds, and landscapes, can be incorporated into interior environments to mimic this type of stimulation and engagement. Incorporating these elements can be accomplished through architecture, finishes, artwork, furnishings, and accessories.

Photographs of nature scenes, like those displayed in the corridor at the Sherman Health and Wellness Centre (Figure 13.3 and Figure 13.4) represent a form of cognitive biophilia. These authentic photographs allow visitors to create mental cues by relating the scenes to their own experiences. This may allow patients to have a better understanding of their environment and enjoy a restorative moment.

13.5 Nature scene with water, rocks, and vegetation-inspired signage.
Mount Sinai Hospital, Sherman Health and Wellness Center at the
UJA Federation Lebovic Community Campus, Vaughan, Canada

The signage in Figure 13.5 illustrates how graphic forms of nature images can be incorporated into interior spaces. The scale and proportion and real-life imagery depicted in the photography serves as an instorative design intervention.

Designing with Biophilia

Fostering satisfying contact between people and nature in the built environment is called *positive environmental impact* and supports a biophilic design approach. Kellert explains that there are two dimensions to biophilic design.[31] They include:

1. organic (or naturalistic) design and vernacular (or place-based) design. Organic design includes forms and shapes, lines, colors, pattern, and textures found in natural materials like plants and trees. When used in buildings and landscape design they can directly, indirectly, or symbolically elicit people's attention and tap into their inherent affinity for the natural environment.

This effect can be achieved through the use of natural lighting, ventilation, and materials; the presence of water and vegetation; and decoration or ornamentation that mimics natural forms and processes.

2. Vernacular design refers to buildings and landscapes that represent a connection to a place. The relationship may be to one's culture, history, or the ecology within a geographic context.

Designing places for adults and children with ASD that include a *positive environmental impact* can be achieved by building homes, schools, and places of work that connect the individuals to their cultural surroundings. The group living communities such as Bittersweet Farms, Brookwood Community, Marbridge Foundation, Campill Community, and TERI Inc.'s new campus of life are all geographically located in rural areas and reflect vernacular design.

Building exteriors, interiors, and outdoor spaces for schools and healthcare centers designed by architects and designers noted throughout this book, such as GA Architects, Baskervill Architects, Design Plus Inc., VisonScape Landscape Architects, and Office of Cheryl Barton Architects/Chrisitine Reed, incorporate a variety of organic design principles to foster *positive environmental impact*.

Designing with an emphasis on natural elements is referred to as restorative design. Restorative design is a design approach that focuses on minimizing harm to humankind and natural systems as well as designing to enrich the human body, mind, and spirit. The approach advocates for a design plan that promotes positive experiences between people and the built environment. Design elements of restorative environmental design include low environmental impact and organic and vernacular biophilic design.

1. Low environmental impact design sustains various ecosystem services on which human existence relies.
2. Organic design fosters various benefits that people derive from their tendency to value nature (biophilia).
3. Vernacular design enables a satisfying connection to the places where people live.[32]

Kellert, Heerwagen, and Mador identify six elements of biophilic design.[33] They are:

1. *Environmental features.* Characteristics and features of the natural environment such as sunlight, fresh air, plants, animals, water, soils, landscapes, natural colors, and natural materials such as wood and stone.
2. *Natural shapes and forms.* The simulation and mimicking of shapes and forms found in nature. These include botanical and animal forms such as leaves, shells, trees, foliage, ferns, honeycombs, insects, other animal species, and body parts. Examples include tree-like columns rising in a building interior to support a roof that projects the feeling of a forest canopy; building shapes that simulate the appearance of bird wings; ornamentation suggestive of a natural shape like a crystal or geological feature.
3. *Natural patterns and processes.* Functions, structures, and principles characteristic of the natural world, especially those that have been instrumental in human evolution and development. For example, designs that stimulate a variety of senses, simulate the qualities of organic growth, facilitate the organization of complexity, or reflect the processes of aging and the passage of time.
4. *Light and space.* Spatial and lighting features that evoke the sense of being in a natural setting. These include natural lighting, a feeling of spaciousness, and more subtle expressions such as sculptural qualities of light and space, and the integration of light, space, and mass.
5. *Place-based relationships.* Connections between buildings and the distinctive geographical, ecological, and cultural characteristics of particular places and localities. This can be achieved through incorporating geological and landscape features, the use of local and indigenous materials, and connections to particular historic and cultural traditions.
6. *Evolved human relationships to nature.* Basic inborn inclinations to affiliate with nature such as the feeling of being in a coherent and legible environment, the sense of prospect and refuge, the simulation of living growth and development, and evoking various biophilic values.[34]

Each of these elements can be incorporated into the environment in a variety of ways. Views of nature and incorporating biophilic design can increase the therapeutic qualities within a space and may put an individual on the spectrum at ease. Biophilic design may be especially helpful in a healthcare environment where people with

ASD may experience high levels of stress. However, it is important to note that these design interventions are not limited to healthcare spaces. These design approaches can be incorporated in schools, homes, workplaces, and other public environments.

Attention to other details in the environment, such as scale, layout, and stress are also important when designing healthcare and therapeutic spaces. The scale of environments for individuals with ASD should be smaller and segmented, but most importantly, the scale should relate to the user. The layout of spaces in a therapeutic environment should promote wayfinding and provide areas of comfort and relaxation. Stress levels should be reduced whenever possible. This can be accomplished by eliminating the amount of stimuli in the environment and providing control for individuals with ASD. Each of these design suggestions aims to promote the overall health and well-being of individuals on the spectrum and should be implemented whenever possible to increase the therapeutic qualities of spaces.

Biophilia Design, Health, and Well-Being

Biophilic design has been promoted by designers and architects who focus on designing healthy spaces. In their work, such as the examples in Figures 13.1–13.5, ARK architects illustrate the passive appreciation of landscape and the active participation in natural scenes. Landscape architects Christine Reed and Virginia Burt incorporate an active form of architecture by including horticulture and gardening spaces in their designs. Several principles identified in the Health and Well-Being through Nature and Horticulture model (Figure 13.6) interrelate. Active processes and activities provide rehabilitation, habitation, acceptance, and inclusion. Passive processes and activities provide tranquility, peace, and spirituality.[35] Although these terms are represented here as two distinct groupings, they are similar in that they have the potential to aid well-being. Active activities can be implemented by providing access to gardens and outdoor recreation areas or facilitating horticulture activities. Passive activities may include views to nature, nature-inspired artwork, or incorporating a water element (real or pictorial image, as in Figure 13.5) within the built environment.

Therapeutic Horticulture

The "active" and "passive" approaches have the ability to provide rehabilitation, habitation, acceptance, and inclusion on one side and tranquillity, peace, and spirituality on the other.[36] Although they are represented here as two distinct groupings, they are nonetheless connected in that they have the potential to aid overall well-being. The passive aspect aids in healing, and the active aspect promotes cognitive enrichment, self-worth, productivity, and social connectedness. Most biophilia activists consider the two groups of attributes as interconnected given one can enhance the other. Regardless of the application or intensity of implanting an active and/or passive biophilia practice, in most cases, this exchange is desirable and leads to peace, tranquillity, support, acceptance, inclusion, and rehabilitation and is used to enrich the lives of many people with cognitive challenges. Figure 13.6 illustrates the interconnectedness of all elements promoted by social and therapeutic horticulture as described above.

Practical Applications for Design

Case Study 1

The waiting room of the Medical Investigations for Neurological Disorders (MIND) Institute at UC Davis in California, a collaborative international research center, is an example of a therapeutic environment. HGA Minneapolis, an architecture and design firm, designed this project in collaboration with A. J. Paron-Wildes, an interior design consultant. The spatial layout and building materials used in this purposeful design reduce environmental stressors, provide positive distractions, facilitate opportunities for socialization, and give users a sense of control.

Waiting Room Design

The lobby design was intended to provide privacy for patient families as they wait to see a care specialist. The layout was strategically planned to include nooks and niches created by quarter-height custom millwork units. The modular format of the units allow children to engage in an activity without being distracted. Often,

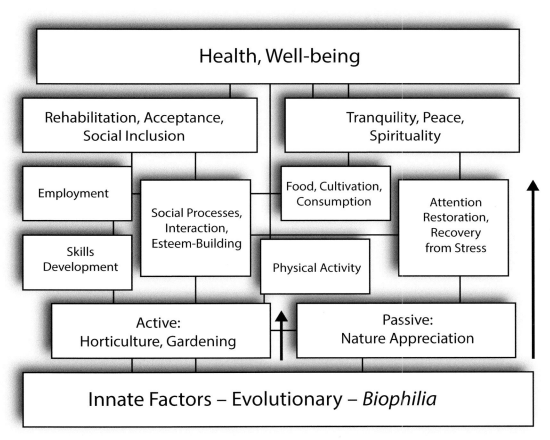

13.6   Health and Well-Being through Nature and Horticulture

families with children with ASD are more disturbed by seeing other children with ASD if they are acting out or displaying bad behavior. This is especially true for young families that are experiencing the diagnosis of their toddler. It may be detrimental for these families to observe negative behaviors that their own child may exhibit in the future.[37] Providing privacy for families was very important in the design of this waiting room, as it may provide individuals with a sense of control.

The neutral color of the units contributes to the overall subtle color palette in the space. The configuration and position of the modular divider units make a repetitive form that resonates with a child on the spectrum's need for predictability. In order to ensure the space did not feel closed in, seating areas were seamlessly incorporated into the end of the units. The cushioned seating areas allow for "prospect," and the niche areas provide "refuge" for the visitors with ASD and enable them to adjust to their new surroundings. Given that the divider units do not extend to the ceiling, the airflow and lighting can be evenly distributed, reducing the prevalence for shadows and thereby limiting confusion for the visitors.

13.7 (top) The waiting room is segregated into privacy units at the Medical Investigations for Neurological Disorders (MIND) Institute at UC Davis in California

13.8 (middle) The waiting room window view and access to outside of the Medical Investigations for Neurological Disorders (MIND) Institute at UC Davis in California

13.9 (bottom) Outdoor, secured courtyard that is connected to the waiting room. Medical Investigations for Neurological Disorders (MIND) Institute at UC Davis in California

Materials and Finishes

This clinic incorporates broadloom carpet throughout all of the public spaces. There is no pattern in the carpet, reducing distractions for individuals with ASD.

Color

The color scheme is neutral. The only primary colors present are in the toys, which can be stored away in a storage area. Magazines are also stored up high and out of reach of children to avoid the possibility of negative reactions.

Views and Access to the Outdoors (Positive Distractions)

Indirect lighting is built into the crossbeams and creates a canopy effect (refuge) for the area and cocoons the users in the space (Figure 13.7). Natural lighting generously lights the space. The waiting room looks out onto a gated courtyard, which can be accessed from the waiting room (Figure 13.8). If a child is overly anxious and needs an escape space to expel energy between appointments or therapy, they can go outside to the courtyard on their own while their parents stay inside and observe (Figure 13.9).

Staircase

The stairs were strategically designed to provide a strong sensory awareness and give children on the spectrum a sense of control as they strive to build independence. The stairway is clearly defined through contrasting accent materials adhered to the front edge of the tread. The visual cues remind the patients where a step begins and ends (Figure 13.10 and Figure 13.11). The frosted glazing on the stairway railing provides transparent views into surrounding spaces. The clarity the design provides helps children manage their proprioception by enabling them to make connections between materials, themselves, and their body movement. The semi-transparent glazing also allows the child to manage their emotions as they search for coherence when transferring from one level to another.

13.10 (top) The staircase of the Medical Investigations for Neurological Disorders (MIND) Institute at UC Davis in California

13.11 (bottom) The staircase of the Medical Investigations for Neurological Disorders (MIND) Institute at UC Davis in California

13.12 (bottom) The third-story walkway at the Medical Investigations for Neurological Disorders (MIND) Institute at UC Davis in California

Transition Area/Corridor

This third-story walkway was designed to be wider than normal and includes extra support to limit the amount of vibration that can happen when children rambunctiously walk over a cantilevered floor area. Extra care was taken to make the walkway feel secure and sustain full views to the outdoors by widening the walkway and extending windows close to the floor (Figure 13.12). Providing ergonomically friendly handrails with opaque panel inserts provides security and enables children to independently move through the space with confidence (Figure 13.12).

To date, there is limited information on how to design therapeutic environments for people with ASD. However, the ideas presented in this chapter can help direct the development of new spaces to help people with autism manage their daily lives.

Notes

1. World Health Organization. "Preamble to the constitution of The World Health Organization as adopted by the International Health Conference." [Official Records of the World Health Organization, no. 2, p. 100.] New York, 1946. pp. 19–22.

2. World Health Organization. "Preamble to the constitution of the World Health Organization as adopted by the International Health Conference." [Official Records of the World Health Organization, no. 2, p. 100.] New York, 1946. pp. 19–22.

3. Lindström, Bengt, and Monica Eriksson. "Salutogenesis." *Journal of epidemiology and community health* 59, no. 6 (2005): 440–442.

4. Myers, Jane E., Thomas J. Sweeney, and J. Melvin Witmer. "The wheel of wellness counseling for wellness: A holistic model for treatment planning." *Journal of counseling & development* 78, no. 3 (2000): 251–266.

5. Seligman, Martin. "The new era of positive psychology." *Ted Conference.* 2004.

6. Smyth, Fiona. "Medical geography: Therapeutic places, spaces and networks." *Progress in human geography* 29, no. 4 (2005): 488–495.

7. Smith, Ron, and Nicholas Watkins. "Therapeutic environments." Washington, DC: Academy of Architecture for Health, 2008.

8. Smith, Ron, and Nicholas Watkins. "Therapeutic environments." Washington, DC: Academy of Architecture for Health, 2008.

9. Stokes, S. "Structured teaching: Strategies for supporting students with autism." *USA: CESA* 7 (2001).

10. Kopec, David Alan. *Environmental psychology for design.* New York: Fairchild, 2006.

11. Smith, Ron, and Nicholas Watkins. "Therapeutic environments." Washington, DC: Academy of Architecture for Health, 2008.

12. Smith, Ron, and Nicholas Watkins. "Therapeutic environments." Washington, DC: Academy of Architecture for Health, 2008.

13. Thompson, Suzanne C., and Shirlynn Spacapan. "Perceptions of control in vulnerable populations." *Journal of social issues* 47, no. 4 (1991): 1–21.

14. Cohen, Sheldon, D. C. Glass, and Susan Phillips. "Environment and health." In H. Freeman, S. Levine, and L. G. Reeder, *Handbook of medical sociology* (pp. 134–149). Englewood Cliffs, NJ: Prentice-Hall, 1979.

15. Thompson, Suzanne C., and Shirlynn Spacapan. "Perceptions of control in vulnerable populations." *Journal of social issues* 47, no. 4 (1991): 1–21.

16. Hildebrand, Grant. *Origins of architectural pleasure.* University of California Press, 1999.

17. Kaplan, Rachel, and Stephen Kaplan. *The experience of nature: A psychological perspective.* CUP Archive, 1989.

18. Ulrich, Roger S. "Effects of gardens on health outcomes: Theory and research." In C. C. Marcus and M. Barnes, *Healing gardens: Therapeutic benefits and design recommendations* (pp. 27–86). New York: John Wiley & Sons, 1999.

19. Kaplan, Rachel, and Stephen Kaplan. *The experience of nature: A psychological perspective.* CUP Archive, 1989.

20. Ulrich, Roger S. "Effects of gardens on health outcomes: Theory and research." In C. C. Marcus and M. Barnes, *Healing gardens: Therapeutic benefits and design recommendations* (pp. 27–86). New York: John Wiley & Sons, 1999.

21. Ulrich, Roger S. "Effects of healthcare environmental design on medical outcomes." In *Design and health: Proceedings of the second international conference on health and design* (pp. 49–59). Stockholm, Sweden: Svensk Byggtjanst, 2001.

22. Grahn, Patrik, and Ulrika A. Stigsdotter. "Landscape planning and stress." *Urban forestry & urban greening* 2, no. 1 (2003): 1–18.

23. Kaplan, Rachel, and Stephen Kaplan. *The experience of nature: A psychological perspective.* CUP Archive, 1989.

24. Ulrich, Roger S. "Effects of gardens on health outcomes: Theory and research." In C. C. Marcus and M. Barnes, *Healing gardens: Therapeutic benefits and design recommendations* (pp. 27–86). New York: John Wiley & Sons, 1999.

25. Ulrich, Roger S. "Effects of healthcare environmental design on medical outcomes." In *Design and health: Proceedings of the second international conference on health and design* (pp. 49–59). Stockholm, Sweden: Svensk Byggtjanst, 2001.

26. Grahn, Patrik, and Ulrika A. Stigsdotter. "Landscape planning and stress." *Urban forestry & urban greening* 2, no. 1 (2003): 1–18.

27. Kaplan, Rachel, and Stephen Kaplan. *The experience of nature: A psychological perspective.* CUP Archive, 1989.

28. Wilson, E. O. "Biophilia and the conservation ethic." In S. R. Kellert and E. O. Wilson, *The biophilia hypothesis*, Island Press, 1993.

29. Kellert, S. R. *Building for life: Designing and understanding the human-nature connection.* Island Press, 2005.

30. Kahn, Peter H., and Stephen R. Kellert. *Children and nature: Psychological, sociocultural, and evolutionary investigations.* MIT Press, 2002.

31. Kellert, S. R. *Building for life: Designing and understanding the human-nature connection.* Island Press, 2005.

32. Kellert, S. R., J. Heerwagen, and Martin Mador. *Biophilic design: The theory, science, and practice of bringing buildings to life.* Chichester, UK: John Wiley & Sons Ltd., 2008.

33. Kellert, S. R., J. Heerwagen, and Martin Mador. *Biophilic design: The theory, science, and practice of bringing buildings to life.* Chichester, UK: John Wiley & Sons Ltd., 2008.

34. Kellert, S. R., J. Heerwagen, and Martin Mador. *Biophilic design: The theory, science, and practice of bringing buildings to life.* Chichester, UK: John Wiley & Sons Ltd., 2008.

35. Jarrott, Shannon E., Hye Ran Kwack, and Diane Relf. "An observational assessment of a dementia-specific horticultural therapy program." *Horttechnology* 12, no. 3 (2002): 403–410.

36. Jarrott, Shannon E., Hye Ran Kwack, and Diane Relf. "An observational assessment of a dementia-specific horticultural therapy program." *Horttechnology* 12, no. 3 (2002): 403–410.

37. A. J. Paron-Wildes, personal interview, July 28, 2015.

Connections to the Outdoors

CHAPTER

14

Direct access to nature can help individuals with autism spectrum disorders manage their behaviors, encourage learning, and improve their sense of well-being. According to University of Illinois environment and behavior researcher Frances "Ming" Kuo, access to nature and green environments yields improved cognitive functioning, more self-discipline and impulse control, and greater overall mental health. Lack of nature is linked to worsened outcomes including attention deficit/hyperactivity disorder symptoms, higher rates of anxiety, and higher rates of clinical depression.[1]

Gardens and Outdoor Living Spaces

Access to the outdoors provides an opportunity for restoration, calming views of nature, and stress reduction. Gardens may also provide areas for social support, positive escape, or a feeling of control.[2, 3] Evidence suggests an appropriately designed garden will encourage daily, habitual interaction with nature and provide measurable therapeutic benefit for individuals with autism. Table 14.1 illustrates elements that can be included and considered during the design of outdoor areas to improve social, psychological, or cognitive well-being.

The inclusion of a garden or outdoor space should be a thoughtful process, especially when designing for an individual with ASD. The materials, plants, and spaces should take into consideration the many sensitivities individuals with ASD often experience (i.e. sensitivities to textures, light, sound, etc.). The garden should be designed in an area that is more than leftover space and work in conjunction with the design of the interior of the building. Ideally the space would be tranquil and quiet. Careful consideration should be given to the design of the garden to avoid or reduce exterior noises such as traffic or air conditioning units. Incorporating items such as talking tubes, wind chimes, or other movement-simulated sounds creates the opportunity for children with ASD to simulate aspects of real-world sounds in a controlled environment.

Because individuals with ASD are often texture sensitive and light sensitive (Chapters 6 and 7), it is important to consider the materials used to create the garden. For example, a pathway with small modular pavers could create a vibration in wheelchairs that might be over-stimulating. Some materials that may be more appropriate

Table 13.1 Elements to incorporate and consider during the design of outdoor areas to improve social, psychological, or cognitive well-being.

SOCIAL, PSYCHOLOGICAL, AND COGNITIVE WELL-BEING	OUTDOOR DESIGN FEATURES
1. Social engagement	<ul><li>comfortable outdoor meeting places</li><li>layouts that support informal interaction in the space</li><li>inspiring, engaging spaces that encourage conversation (Kaplan, 1995)</li></ul>
2. Cultural and collective meaning	<ul><li>gardens that include artifacts and symbols of cultural and group identity</li><li>sense of uniqueness</li></ul>
3. Relaxation and psychological restoration	<ul><li>quiet spaces with low sensory stimulation</li><li>distant views</li></ul>
4. Visual and aural privacy as needed; movement between interaction and solitude	<ul><li>outdoor seating or walking paths in visually appealing landscapes</li><li>enclosure or screening</li><li>distance from others</li><li>ability to regulate the desired degree of social interaction by moving between spaces or by manipulating personal space</li><li>variety of informal social spaces to encourage relationship development</li></ul>
5. Learning and information sharing	<ul><li>multisensory environments, where the sounds, textures, colors, and patterns of nature can be appreciated as much as the visual</li><li>provide opportunities to observe, touch, and be in the presence of natural forms, shapes, and materials</li></ul>
6. Connection to nature and natural processes	<ul><li>daylight, views of nature outdoors, careful use of indoor sunlight, natural ventilation, interior plantings, nature décor, and nature patterns in spatial layouts, furnishings, fitments, and finishes—for those with limited mobility and or sensory issues, include vicarious opportunities—viewing from inside through large windows</li></ul>
7. Sensory variability	<ul><li>include natural elements that feature organic shapes and movements; provide shapes that offer multi-sensory stimulation and patterning through variations in color and texture; finally, provide access to daylighting and natural ventilation</li></ul>
8. Sound levels similar to nature	<ul><li>operable windows to allow connection to positive outdoor sounds; acoustic conditioning to reduce equipment and industrial noise, yet allowing for some human sound ("buzz") that is energizing; maximize decibels similar to those found in nature—bird chatter, breeze, etc.</li></ul>
9. Interesting visual environment with aesthetic integrity	<ul><li>adoption of naturalistic, bio-inspired design; patterned complexity; reduced monochromatic environments; more organic layouts and forms, fractal patterning—organized complexity</li></ul>
10. Wayfinding and making sense	<ul><li>Landmarks, variability of space to serve as location cues, windows to orient by outdoor views, use of color and pattern on walls or carpeting to provide location and movement cues; also appropriate signage and visual displays to develop overall sense of space</li></ul>
11. Exercise	<ul><li>outdoor bike and hiking paths, open stairways to promote interaction and walking, visually interesting landscape to entice exploration</li></ul>
12. Sense of equity	<ul><li>design of spaces and allocation of amenities that show concern for the health and well-being of all occupants, visitors, and other users of the space</li><li>provide opportunities to be productive and contribute in meaningful ways—gardens for food, farming, animals for food, horticulture production, sell goods</li></ul>

14.1 A garden pathway filled with a bench and a large, smooth walkway provides an area for rest and relaxation

include smooth, non-glare paving made from concrete with integral color tinting, asphalt, or rubberized paving.

The incorporation of clear, simple photographs or pictograms to communicate ideas or intended use of certain play areas can be helpful to a person with ASD. As discussed in Chapter 2, an individual with ASD often requires clear and consistent orientation, as they are uncomfortable with change and unpredictability. When designing for this population, inclusion of an orientation map to illustrate the layout of the garden or play space allows users to know where they are and what to expect next.

A garden should provide a variety of seating areas, for both individual exploration and larger, social groupings (Figure 14.1). Providing areas to sit throughout the garden can reinforce the sense of security and predictability. For example, the first time walking through a garden a person may only feel comfortable to get as far as the first bench. Each additional visit, he or she may venture further knowing they are safe, secure, and able to process the environment. Individuals who are hyper-sensitive to movement may benefit from a cocoon-like space, which may be created with a swing that tightly embraces them, or a hammock. Cave-like spaces

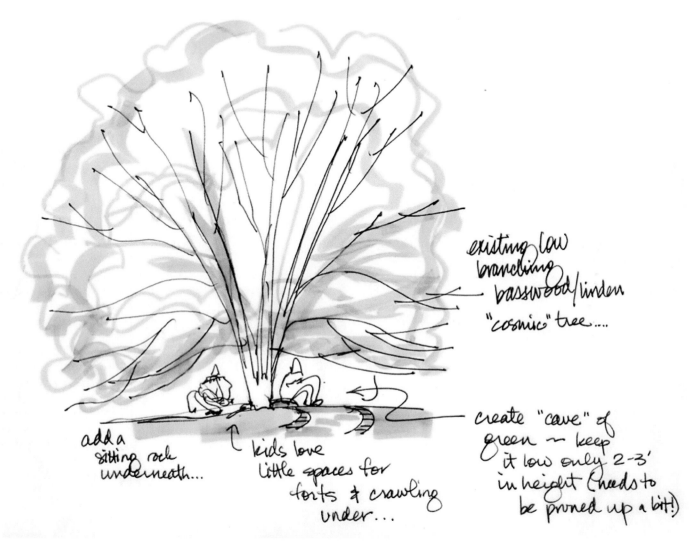

existing low
branching
basswood/linden
"cosmic" tree.....

create "cave" of
green ~ keep
it low only 2-3'
in height (needs to
be pruned up a bit!)

add a
sitting rock
underneath...

kids love
little spaces for
forts & crawling
under...

14.2 The low-hanging tree provides a place for an individual to relax in
a "cave of green." This provides one a space to go and see out
(prospect) without necessarily being seen (refuge)

are soothing to people with ASD and help reduce sensory input and
allow them to relax. These might be created under a low-hanging
tree or perhaps a rock enclosure (Figure 14.2).

Literature suggests that children enjoy nature because it
provides a place for active play and exploration. Children often
find gardens are a place to get "away" and can provide them
with a sense of refuge.[4] One of the goals of creating an outdoor
environment for the ASD population is to reinforce and apply
lessons often learned in the classroom. Access to a garden or
outdoor area, specifically in an education setting, provides coping
skills outside of the classroom.

Playgrounds

Play is important to the social, intellectual, physical, and emotional
growth of developing children. Play also provides learning
opportunities in self-mastery, skills in environmental experience,
reality-testing, coordination versus passivity, fulfillment, and, most
importantly, spontaneous free fun. Play for all children is a tool for
learning, and self-directed play is the best learning tool. A growing
body of research has shown that all children learn and develop
cognitively, physically, and socially through play in the outdoors.
More specifically, for children with autism, supportive environments

and healing gardens designed in response to this spectrum can create opportunities for richer learning experiences.

Play can occur individually or within groups, indoors or outdoors. One area that is most typical for play is playgrounds. Universally designed playgrounds provide an environment for children of all abilities to play together.[5] A universal playground is defined as one where children who use wheelchairs, walkers, or canes or who have sensory or developmental disabilities can use at least 70 percent of the play equipment. There are a number of environments that could and should incorporate some form of a play space for children, including school, healthcare, and home environments.

Considering the amount of time a child or adolescent will spend in a classroom setting, the environment should be therapeutic, and a therapeutic environment should provide for external access. Learning should take place in a school's external environment as well as the interior environment. Outdoor spaces should be provided for recreation and physical education, social development, and academic learning. Pathways, gardens, seating, ball fields, covered porches, and playgrounds contribute to optimal learning. Children with views of and contact with nature score higher on tests of concentration and self-discipline. The greener the spaces, the better the scores.[6] Urban schools should incorporate interior courtyards or play areas above parking lots or lunch rooms.[7] Children are experiencing a lack of exercise outside of the classroom, which is contributing to hyperactivity in the classroom.[8] For optimal benefit, outdoor activity areas should be placed on the south side of the building to take advantage of sunlight. Cragmont School in Berkeley, California, was designed using an environmental focus. Every classroom has an adjacent outdoor patio for small group teaching.[9]

Another area where playgrounds could greatly benefit the user is within healthcare environments. MacCarthy said: "Second to the continuing presence of the mother or another supporting figure, play can be an important factor in diminishing the harmful effects of stress in hospitalized children."[10] When in hospital environments, play helps pediatric patients adjust to common stresses and anxiety associated with hospitalization,[11] as well as cope with the admission process.[12] Providing opportunities and areas for pediatric patients to interact or play with other pediatric patients can have a number of benefits on the patient, including positive impacts on social skills, communication skills, self-confidence, and independence.[13] While some pediatric patients have reported that seeing others with visible signs of illness distressed them, the majority enjoyed

social interactions with other patients.[14] Providing a space that encourages positive feelings and feels child friendly may promote siblings and friends to visit the patient in the hospital. Having visitors similar in age may promote the amount of play the patient experiences.

In residential settings, the backyard and other outdoor spaces where the child will be exposed to nature and sunlight are excellent spaces for sensory integration activities, not to mention exercise and fresh air. A sandbox or a kiddie pool filled with preferred objects are an excellent source for tactile experiences. A hammock or swing could provide solutions for vestibular movement. Activities for the sensory integration space should be selected based entirely off of an individual child's symptoms and interests.

When designing a playground to meet the needs of an individual with ASD, there are several features to consider. Firstly, children with ASD require clear and consistent orientation, as they are uncomfortable with change and unpredictability. An orientation map to illustrate the layout of the play space allows users to know where they are and what to expect next. Indication of transitions between spaces allows individuals to orient themselves and creates understanding and sense-making of the environment. Both lower-functioning and higher-functioning children tend to prefer soft play areas.

Because the scale and proportion of outside spaces are often much larger than inside spaces, there is more opportunity for physical activity and utilization of large motor skills. The encouragement of physical activity may contribute to improved health-related outcomes. Research has shown environments with less green space are associated with greater rates of childhood obesity; higher rates of 15 out of 24 categories of physician-diagnosed diseases, including cardiovascular diseases; and higher rates of mortality in younger and older adults.[15]

Views to Nature

Simply viewing nature has consistently been found to have a number of stress-reducing benefits as well as a number of positive emotional and physiological changes. In fact, as few as three to five minutes of exposure to nature can provide individuals with the positive physiological effects of nature.[16] Providing visual access to nature allows a person to feel connected to activities taking

14.3 (facing page)
Example of a sitting room that would provide an
individual with the ability to see nature outside
of a window view

place if they are not able or comfortable being outside. Simmel (1950) says providing nature-filled views allows "inhabitants to have the outside world at their visual disposal and at the same time provides control over their accessibility to the world" (p. 68).[17] Schwartz (1968) also reported that an important part of residential privacy is the feeling of safety by being inside and looking out[18] (Figure 14.3).

As discussed in Chapter 10, views of nature within classroom environments can provide a number of benefits. Overall, the natural light brought into a room by windows has a positive influence on the users within a classroom, including higher scores on tests of concentration and self-discipline. The greener the environment, the higher the scores.[19, 20]

Cognitive Biophilia

The taxonomy of cognitive processing, which was developed by psychologist Benjamin Bloom (1981) and colleagues, identified six stages in a child's normal intellectual development.[21] The development moves from simple to more complex levels of understanding and includes problem solving, the formation of basic understandings of facts and terms, creating rudimentary classifications, and discerning causal relationships. In review of Bloom's theory, Kahn and Kellert (2002) theorized that the direct experience of nature greatly enhances cognitive processing and termed the process *cognitive biophilia*.[22] In their view, the natural world greatly aids emerging capacities because it affords numerous opportunities for stimulation and engagement for ordering basic information and ideas. At an early age, most children encounter, either vicariously or in natural settings, an opportunity to distinguish and label a variety of features and properties of items found in nature, i.e. trees, bushes, plants, flowers, birds, mammals, habitats, and landscapes. Wells and Evans's (2003) research provides convincing evidence of the more profound benefits of experiences in nature for children due to their greater plasticity and vulnerability.[23] The findings of the research indicate that:

- Children with symptoms of Attention Deficit Hyperactivity Disorder (ADHD) are better able to concentrate after contact with nature.[24]

- Children with views of and contact with nature score higher on tests of concentration and self-discipline. The greener, the better the scores.[25, 26]
- Exposure to natural environments improves children's cognitive processing by improving their awareness, reasoning, and observational skills.[27]
- Nature buffers the impact of life stress on children and helps them deal with adversity. The greater the amount of nature exposure, the greater the benefits.[28]
- Nature helps children develop powers of observation and creativity and instills a sense of peace and being at one with the world.[29]
- Natural environments stimulate social interaction between children.[30, 31]
- Outdoor environments are important to children's development of independence and autonomy.[32]

Safety and Comfort

Depending upon the mobility of garden users, visual monitoring by staff or family members is critical. Including views from an interior allows caregivers the ability to keep an eye on the individual while he or she explores on their own.

Furthermore, caregivers may find reassurance knowing the garden contains non-poisonous plants, accessible surfaces, and safe materials.

Creation of a secure space becomes important in order to ensure that caregivers feel comfortable allowing participants to experience the garden on their own whenever possible. This includes, when appropriate, creating a minimum five-foot-high perimeter fence and secure gates that are difficult to climb. Maintenance and access from other exterior spaces on the site also need to be considered, specifically in relation to possible key card access, lock/latch types, and monitoring with security cameras as required.

Virginia T. Burt, an award-winning therapeutic garden designer from Virginia Burt Designs, believes that the healing environment begins as soon as one turns into the driveway of a facility. Burt recommends that the point of arrival should include designated drop-off and pick-up areas that are covered by a portico. Parking should be clearly labeled and include designated wheelchair areas

14.4 (facing page)
Example of barrier-free garden entrance

and safe interconnecting walkways made of paving materials that conform to building code standards. Walkway path widths should be wider than normal to accommodate vestibular and proprioceptive variations. Door widths should be barrier-free and thresholds clearly defined to encourage independence (Figure 14.4).

Conclusion

Creating thoughtful healing gardens and outdoor play environments that incorporate the design characteristics described above will encourage children with ASD, their loved ones, and caregivers to attend to nature's natural healing abilities. Connecting people to nature, regardless of age and stage, has been proven to lower heart rates, decrease stress, and improve neurological brain function. It is an antidote-stimulating development, including cognitive power and increasing the efficiency of exercise and physical therapy, and connecting us to our intrinsic bond with nature.

Practical Applications for Design— Pacific Autism Center for Education (PACE)

Pacific Autism Center for Education is located in Santa Clara County, California. PACE owns and operates two children group homes and four adult group homes. On site, there are two backyards that have been designed to serve as a therapeutic oasis for its residents (see below).

Case Study 1: Lamar Garden: A Case Study Garden Design at a Residential Group Home for Severely Autistic Adults

Lamar Garden (Figure 14.5) is located at one of the PACE homes and was designed by Christine Reed, a registered landscape architect and Associate Principal at OICB in San Francisco. The design was developed for a residential group home in which the residents are severely autistic adults. The garden was developed to encourage daily, habitual interaction with nature for the residents. In addition,

the design of the garden was used as a case study for researchers to gain understanding on needs of those with autism, develop design strategies, and provide sensory integration opportunities. The researchers assessed the impact of the Lamar Garden on behavior patterns and stress levels of the residents through the use of pre-development interviews, questionnaires, use-pattern diagrams, and post-occupancy evaluations. Researchers found residents used the garden more frequently, for longer periods of time, and had less frenetic movement patterns than with pre-design use. In addition to serving the residents, the garden provides a place of respite for live-in caregivers, serves as a gathering place for visiting friends and family, and hosts group events for socialization of residents. Working with PACE staff, the landscape architect developed the following design recommendations:

- Encourage outdoor use by creating a range of safe and comfortable spaces to accommodate individual preference
- Allow a sense of privacy and independence for the users while providing visibility for adequate supervision (Figure 14.6)
- Accommodate activities particular to the individual residents and for autistic individuals in general: swinging, bouncing, shooting hoops, pacing, sitting and lying on the ground, and walking barefoot
- Accommodate a wide range of activities with varying levels of physicality (activities requiring ranges of intense movement to minimal movement) in a small space without compromising the experiential quality of each particular activity and individual
- Create a garden with a clear and intentional organizational structure, clear visual cues related to circulation, and activities to facilitate wayfinding and spatial orientation (Figure 14.7)
- Facilitate perceptual focus by associating different activities with distinct spaces within the garden
- Provide physically protected spaces that create a calming experience of reduced sensory input and a retreat from sensory-rich environments
- Avoid elements with strong or perceptually demanding qualities such as bright colors, intense contrast, or strong fragrances
- Design all structures and features to be very durable and able to withstand heavy impact as well as repetitive picking or grasping
- Incorporate elements with potential stress relieving qualities such as white noise, tactile engagement, physically supportive, and constant-pressure applying (also known as "postural security") structures

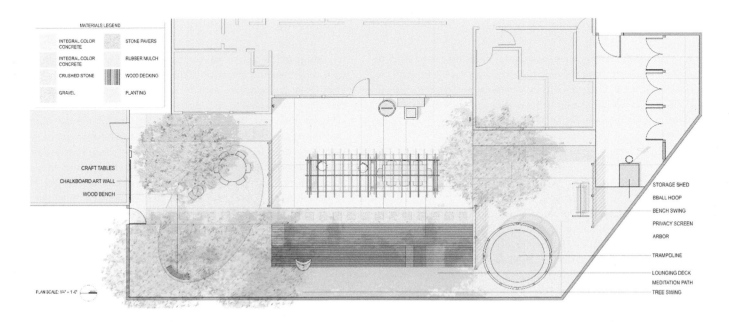

14.5 Lamar Garden. A Case Study Garden Design at a Residential Group Home for Severely Autistic Adults. The garden design incorporates strategic site planning principles, such as spatial organization for intuitive wayfinding, and physical transitions between spaces and activities

- Provide a safe, barrier-free garden to accommodate restricted motor-skill function
- Encourage and accommodate safe outdoor use at night
- Provide a low-maintenance and low-water-use garden
- Accommodate the needs of live-in caretakers
- Create an amenable setting for visiting family and friends
- Provide a place for group events for inter-socialization of residents with other autistic and typical adults

Key features implemented by the landscape architect in this garden (Figure 14.5) include accommodating activities that resonate with people with autisms' desire to move their bodies in active ways and rest in positions that are comforting. Equipment, finish materials, and plantings have been positioned to offer individual choice and keep the residents safe. Residents can bounce, swing, sway, pace, and sit or lie on the ground as they choose. The area

also is designed with a variety of microclimates in mind to suit the variations of thermal sensitivities of the individuals. Strategic placement of lighting that can be independently controlled has also been integrated into the design.

In this design (Figure 14.6), resident privacy was accommodated in the shaded seating areas that seat both small groups and individuals. The layout affords individuals an opportunity to choose the level of privacy they desire and at the same time transparency for the caregivers to monitor the residents' well-being.

The architect also organized the space to include garden rooms (Figure 14.7) treated with materials, built structures, and equipment that clearly define their purpose. The rooms accommodate both active and passive experiences and serve as social centers for group gatherings. The defined pathways enhance mobility and provide for cognitive clarity to encourage independent wayfinding.

14.6 (top) Lamar Garden. A Case Study Garden Design at a Residential Group Home for Severely Autistic Adults. Spatial Zoning to promote engagement and respond to the behavioral needs of people with ASD

14.7 (bottom) Lamar Garden. A Case Study Garden Design at a Residential Group Home for Severely Autistic Adults. Purposeful Spaces and Clear Wayfinding to accommodate the needs of people with ASD

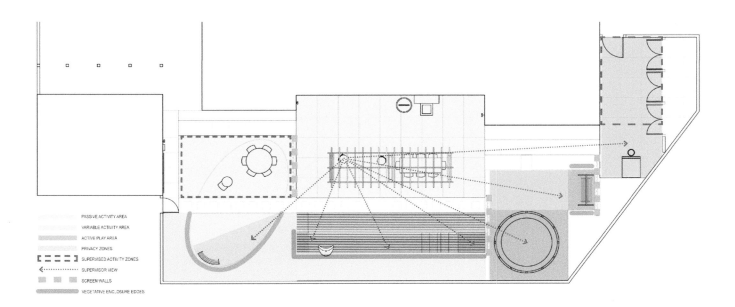

PASSIVE ACTIVITY AREA
VARIABLE ACTIVITY AREA
ACTIVE PLAY AREA
PRIVACY ZONES
SUPERVISED ACTIVITY ZONES
SUPERVISOR VIEW
SCREEN WALLS
VEGETATIVE ENCLOSURE EDGES

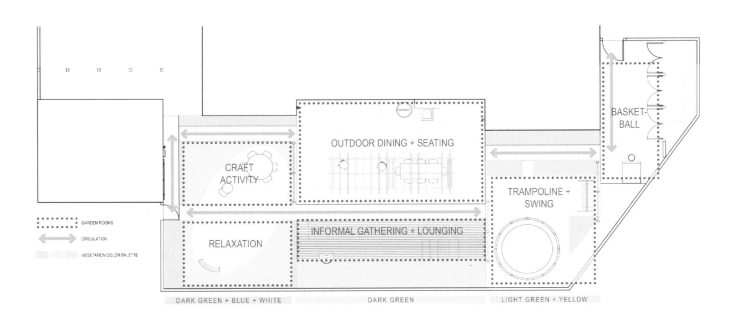

GARDEN ROOMS
CIRCULATION
VEGETATION COLOR PALETTE

CRAFT ACTIVITY

OUTDOOR DINING + SEATING

BASKET-BALL

TRAMPOLINE + SWING

RELAXATION

INFORMAL GATHERING + LOUNGING

DARK GREEN + BLUE + WHITE   DARK GREEN   LIGHT GREEN + YELLOW

LAMAR GARDEN: A CASE STUDY

The design of LaMar Garden addresses the challenge of creating outdoor spaces to meet the specific and specialized needs of individuals with Autism and Developmental Disorders.

Careful documentation of the process from design through implementation and use will contibute to the growing body of knowledge and understanding of Autism; and facilitate the creation of guidelines for design of the home environment for Autistic individuals.

Design guidelines, with an emphasis on safety, accessibility, comfort, accomodation of restricted motor-skill function and stress reduction, may be used to create other gardens like LaMar and have potential to improve the quality of life for other individuals living with Autism.

ESTABLISHING AN ACTIVITY GRADIENT

- Accommodate a wide range of activities in a small space without compromising the experiential quality of each particular activity
- Accommodate activities particular to the individual residents and autistic individuals in general: swinging, bouncing, shooting hoops, pacing, sitting and lying on the ground and walking barefoot
- Create a range of safe and comfortable spaces with modulated microclimates to encourage outdoor use for relaxation and passive activities
- Provide circulation and area lighting for safe outdoor use at night

MICROCLIMATE + COMFORT

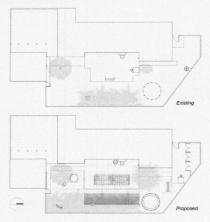

Existing

Proposed

BALANCING VISIBILITY / PRIVACY

- Allow a sense of privacy and independence for the residents while providing visibility for adequate supervision
- Provide physically protected places that create a calming experience of reduced sensory input
- Incorporate elements with stress relieving qualities, such as physically supportive and constant-pressure applying structures, shading and cooling vegetation, and engaging tactile materials
- Accommodate the needs of live-in caretakers by providing comfortable and shaded outdoor seating for relaxation

TACTILE MATERIALS

Rubber Mulch   *Gravel*   *Plastic Wood*   *Concrete*   *Crushed Stone*

COLOR GRADIENT PLANTING

Agapanthus   *Fortnight Lily*   *Licorice Plant*   *Myrtle*   *Phormium 'Tiny Tiger'*   *Kangaroo Paw*   *Euphorbia characias*

ORGANIZING AROUND GARDEN ROOMS

- Facilitate perceptual focus by associating different activities with distinct spaces within the garden
- Create a garden with a clear and intentional organizational structure to facilitate way-finding and spatial orientation
- Provide low-maintenance and low water use planting that responds to the garden room activity gradient
- Associate different materials with each room, while avoiding elements with strong or perceptually demanding qualities: bright colors, intense contrast, strong fragrances
- Provide safe, barrier-free pathways and structures to accommodate restricted motor-skill function

c.e.reed.studio.
landscape architecture

Pacific Autism Center for Education
Connect ·Support ·Educate

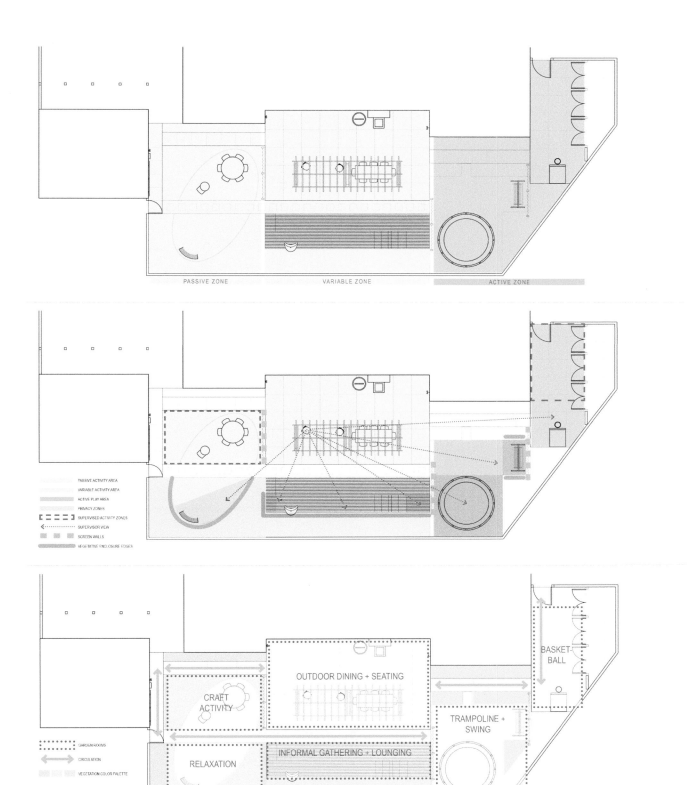

PASSIVE ZONE   VARIABLE ZONE   ACTIVE ZONE

PASSIVE ACTIVITY AREA
VARIABLE ACTIVITY AREA
ACTIVE PLAY AREA
PRIVACY ZONES
SUPERVISED ACTIVITY ZONES
SUPERVISOR VIEW
SCREEN WALLS
VEGETATIVE ENCLOSURE EDGES

GARDEN ROOMS
CIRCULATION
VEGETATION COLOR PALETTE

CRAFT ACTIVITY

OUTDOOR DINING + SEATING

BASKET-BALL

TRAMPOLINE + SWING

RELAXATION

INFORMAL GATHERING + LOUNGING

DARK GREEN + BLUE + WHITE   DARK GREEN   LIGHT GREEN + YELLOW

14.8 Lamar Garden. A Case Study Garden Design at a Residential Group Home for Severely Autistic Adults

LAMAR GARDEN

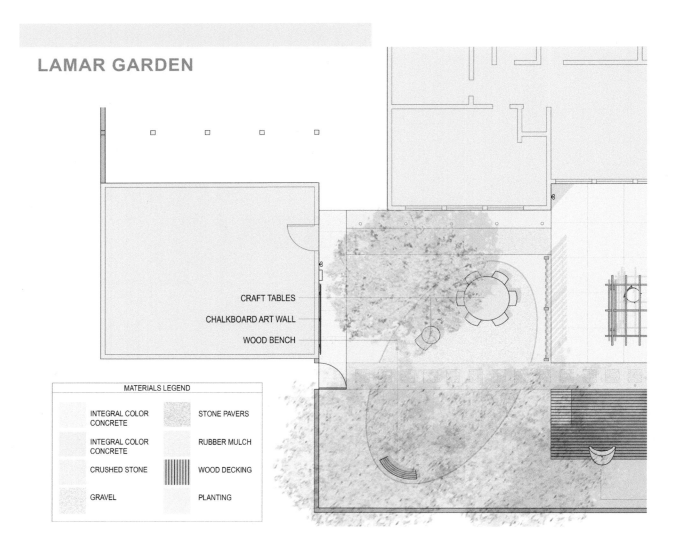

CRAFT TABLES

CHALKBOARD ART WALL

WOOD BENCH

MATERIALS LEGEND		
INTEGRAL COLOR CONCRETE		STONE PAVERS
INTEGRAL COLOR CONCRETE		RUBBER MULCH
CRUSHED STONE		WOOD DECKING
GRAVEL		PLANTING

GARDEN FEATURES

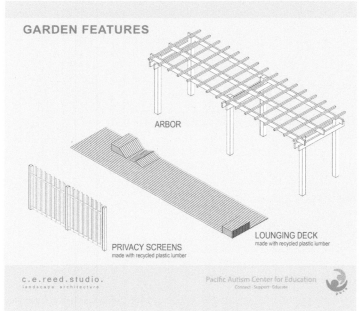

ARBOR

PRIVACY SCREENS
made with recycled plastic lumber

LOUNGING DECK
made with recycled plastic lumber

c.e.reed.studio.
landscape architecture

Pacific Autism Center for Education
Connect · Support · Educate

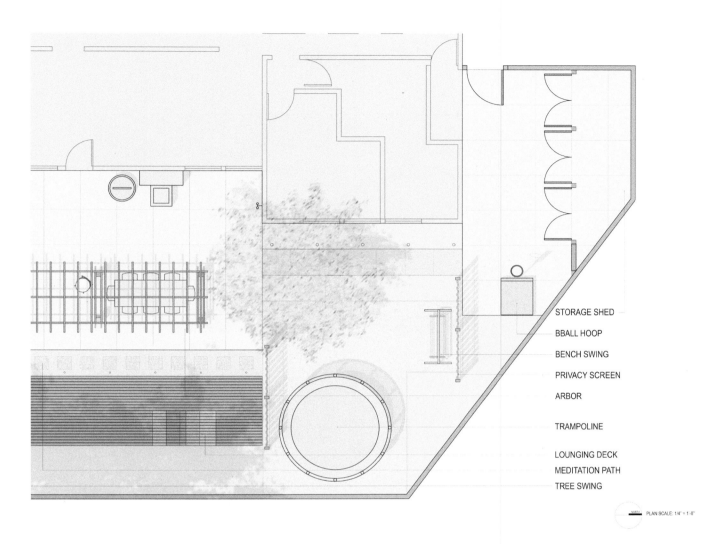

STORAGE SHED

BBALL HOOP

BENCH SWING

PRIVACY SCREEN

ARBOR

TRAMPOLINE

LOUNGING DECK

MEDITATION PATH

TREE SWING

NORTH PLAN SCALE: 1/4" = 1'-0"

View of the Craft Activity and Relaxation Room

View from the Meditation Path of the arbor and lounging deck

14.9 Lamar Garden. A Case Study Garden Design at a Residential Group Home for Severely Autistic Adults

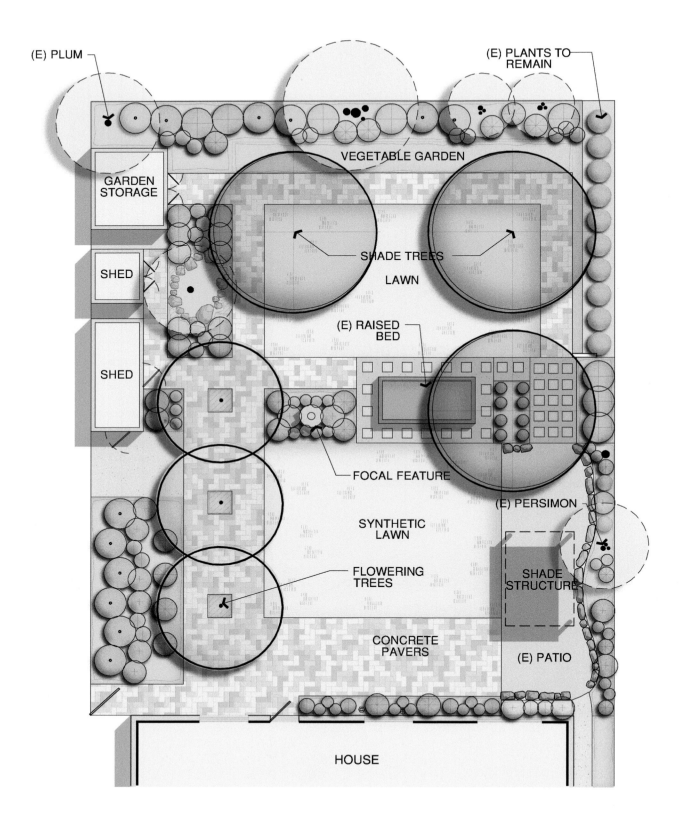

(E) PLUM

(E) PLANTS TO REMAIN

GARDEN STORAGE

SHED

SHED

VEGETABLE GARDEN

SHADE TREES

LAWN

(E) RAISED BED

FOCAL FEATURE

(E) PERSIMON

SYNTHETIC LAWN

FLOWERING TREES

SHADE STRUCTURE

CONCRETE PAVERS

(E) PATIO

HOUSE

14.10 (facing page)
The design and layout of Mahola Group Home Garden for people with Autism

14.11 Example of a raised planter bed to accommodate vestibular and proprioception needs

herbs
scented
when
crushed....

rosemary.

sniff!

Raised timber
beds for hort.therapy
& getting your hands
in the dirt!

Case Study 2: Mahola Group Home Garden

The second garden space at CASE is the Mahola Group Home garden designed by Paul Reed from Reed Associates Landscape Architecture. Similar to the Lamar Garden, the Mahola Group Home garden was designed to respond to the various sensory sensitivities individuals with ASD often experience. In addition, the garden was designed with the goal of enabling the residents to participate in gardening.

The design of the garden (Figure 14.10) features a layout that encourages resident interaction and includes lawns for mowing, raised planter beds, and shaded areas to protect residents from the sun. The planter beds feature plants that are intriguing to the senses. Visually, the plants are interesting and include colorful flowers, foliage, and a variation of textures and patterns. Vegetable and herb gardens were integrated into the design to appeal to the olfactory and gustation senses (Figure 14.11). The incorporation of small crop planting enables the users to develop a care for understanding and an appreciation for life cycles and nutriment.

Notes

1. University of Illinois College of Agricultural, Consumer and Environmental Sciences. "Green environments essential for human health, research shows." ScienceDaily. www.sciencedaily.com/releases/2011/04/110419151438.htm, accessed November 11, 2015.

2. Marcus, Clare Cooper, and Marni Barnes. *Gardens in healthcare facilities: Uses, therapeutic benefits, and design recommendations.* Center for Health Design, 1995.

3. Ulrich, Roger S. "Effects of gardens on health outcomes: Theory and research." In C. C. Marcus and M. Barnes, *Healing gardens: Therapeutic benefits and design recommendations* (pp. 27–86). New York: John Wiley & Sons, 1999.

4. Whitehouse, Sandra, James W. Varni, Michael Seid, Clare Cooper Marcus, Mary Jane Ensberg, Jenifer R. Jacobs, and Robyn S. Mehlenbeck. "Evaluating a children's hospital garden environment: Utilization and consumer satisfaction." *Journal of environmental psychology* 21, no. 3 (2001): 301–314.

5. National Institutes of Health. "Autism spectrum disorders (ASDs)." Eunice Kennedy Shriver: National Institute of Child Health and Human Development, November 15, 2011. http://www.nichd.nih.gov/health/topics/asd.cfm.

6. Taylor, Andrea Faber, Frances E. Kuo, and William C. Sullivan. "Coping with ADD: The surprising connection to green play settings." *Environment and behavior* 33, no. 1 (2001): 54–77.

7. Wagner, Cheryl. "Planning School Grounds for Outdoor Learning." *National clearinghouse for educational facilities* (2000).

8. Freed, Jeffrey, and Laurie Parsons. *Right-brained children in a left-brained world: Unlocking the potential of your ADD child.* Simon and Schuster, 1998.

9. Rudd, Tim, and Futurelab. *Reimagining outdoor learning spaces: Primary capital, co-design and educational transformation: A Futurelab handbook.* Bristol: Futurelab, 2008. p. 23.

10. MacCarthy, D. *The under fives in hospital.* London: National Association for the Welfare of Children in Hospital, 1979.

11. Peterson, G. "Let the children play." *Nursing* 3, no. 41 (1989): 22–25.

12. Delpo, E., and S. Frick. "Directed and non-directed play as therapeutic modality." *Children's health care* 16, no. 4 (1988): 261–267.

13. Fels, Deborah I., Judith K. Waalen, Shumin Zhai, and P. Weiss. "Telepresence under exceptional circumstances: Enriching the connection to school for sick children." In *Human–computer interaction, Interact '01,* (pp. 617–624). International Federation for Information Processing, 2001.

14. Adams, Annmarie, David Theodore, Ellie Goldenberg, Coralee McLaren, and Patricia McKeever. "Kids in the atrium: Comparing architectural intentions and children's experiences in a pediatric hospital lobby." *Social science & medicine* 70, no. 5 (2010): 658–667.

15. University of Illinois College of Agricultural, Consumer and Environmental Sciences. "Green environments essential for human health, research shows." ScienceDaily. www.sciencedaily.com/releases/2011/04/110419151438.htm, accessed November 11, 2015.

16. Parsons, Russ, and Terry Hartig. "Environmental psychophysiology." In *Handbook of psychophysiology* (2nd ed.) (pp. 815–846). New York: Cambridge University Press, 2000.

17. Simmel, Georg, and Kurt H. Wolff. *The sociology of Georg Simmel.* Vol. 92892. Simon and Schuster, 1950.

18. Schwartz, Barry. "The social psychology of privacy." *American journal of sociology* 73, no. 6 (1968): 741–752.

19. Taylor, Andrea Faber, Frances E. Kuo, and William C. Sullivan. "Coping with ADD: The surprising connection to green play settings." *Environment and behavior* 33, no. 1 (2001): 54–77.

20. Wells, A. *Emotional disorders and metacognition: Innovative cognitive therapy.* Chichester, UK: John Wiley & Sons, 2000.

21. Bloom, Benjamin Samuel. *All our children learning: A primer for parents, teachers, and other educators.* McGraw-Hill Companies, 1981.

22. Kahn, Peter H., and Stephen R. Kellert. *Children and nature: Psychological, sociocultural, and evolutionary investigations.* MIT Press, 2002.

23. Wells, Nancy M., and Gary W. Evans. "Nearby nature: A buffer of life stress among rural children." *Environment and behavior* 35, no. 3 (2003): 311–330.

24. Taylor, Andrea Faber, Frances E. Kuo, and William C. Sullivan. "Coping with ADD: The surprising connection to green play settings." *Environment and behavior* 33, no. 1 (2001): 54–77.

25. Taylor, Andrea Faber, Frances E. Kuo, and William C. Sullivan. "Coping with ADD: The surprising connection to green play settings." *Environment and behavior* 33, no. 1 (2001): 54–77.

26. Wells, A. *Emotional disorders and metacognition: Innovative cognitive therapy.* Chichester, UK: John Wiley & Sons, 2000.

27. Pyle, Robert Michael. "Eden in a vacant lot: Special places, species, and kids in the neighborhood of life." In Peter H. Kahn and Stephen R. Kellert, *Children and nature: Psychological, sociocultural, and evolutionary investigations* (pp. 305–327). MIT Press, 2002.

28. Wells, Nancy M., and Gary W. Evans. "Nearby nature: A buffer of life stress among rural children." *Environment and behavior* 35, no. 3 (2003): 311–330.

29. Crain, Margaret Ann. "Looking at people and asking 'why?': An ethnographic approach to religious education." *Religious education* 96, no. 3 (2001): 386–394.

30. Moore, R. *Children's domain: Play and play space in child development.* London: Croom Helm, 1986.

31. Bixler, Robert D., Myron F. Floyd, and William E. Hammitt. "Environmental socialization quantitative tests of the childhood play hypothesis." *Environment and behavior* 34, no. 6 (2002): 795–818.

32. Bartlett, Sheridan. "Access to outdoor play and its implications for healthy attachments." Unpublished article, Putney, VT, 1996.

Glossary

Accessibility (ADA): The Americans with Disabilities Act of 1990 prohibits employers from discriminating against individuals with disabilities. The Act, which was amended in 2003, also states that employers must make certain accommodations for qualified employees including making existing facilities accessible for all and other adjustments to fit the employee's needs.[1]

Adaptable Environments (AE): refers to spaces that are favorable or even minimally adequate; it represents a state of relative "adaptedness."[2] Adaptedness reflects generally positive person–environment exchanges over time.

Advocacy/Participatory Research efforts are directed toward producing and fostering research and initiatives that act as catalysts for debate, action, and innovation.

The American Association on Intellectual and Developmental Disabilities (AAI/DD): Formerly the American Association on Mental Retardation (AAMR), it is an American non-profit professional organization that advocates on behalf of those with mental retardation.

Asperger's Syndrome: A subtype of pervasive developmental disorder (PDD) defined by distinguishable difficulties in social reciprocation and communication, impaired speech, and unusual obsessions or interests.[3]

Attention Deficit/Hyperactivity Disorder: This syndrome is characterized by short attention span, hyperactivity, and poor concentration. The commonality of characteristics between autism and ADD/ADHD has caused some to believe that ADD/ADHD should be considered a part of the autism spectrum.[4]

Auditory Stimuli/Triggers: A stimulus perceived through the sense of hearing that initiates or precipitates a reaction or series of reactions. Shabha identified a variety of auditory triggers in his study.[5] These include:

- Unduly harsh and lengthy echoes caused by large un-curtained window areas and/or hard floors and/or ceiling in larger areas
- Higher pitch sound (e.g. drilling and hammering sound, vacuum cleaner, fire alarm, siren)
- Low-pitch sound from the main road traffic
- Low-pitch sound from fans
- Background noise from adjacent rooms and corridors
- Higher background noise levels from group activity (e.g. discussion, practical sessions, etc.)
- Sudden unexpected sound (e.g. banging, cracking sound)
- Noise from flickering fluorescent light

Autism Spectrum Disorders (ASD): Autism Spectrum Disorders are complex developmental disorders marked by social and communication deficits, repetitive behaviors, sensory processing difficulties, and cognitive inflexibility.[6] ASD is referred to as a spectrum disorder because each individual varies in types of symptoms, severity, and level of functioning.[7]

Behavior: Behavior includes anything that an organism does involving action and response to stimulation. This includes the response of an individual, group, or species to its environment.[8]

Biophilia Design: is the deliberate attempt to translate an understanding of the inherent human affinity with natural systems and processes[9] into the built environment.[10]

Built Environment: refers to the human-made surroundings that provide the setting for human activity, ranging in scale from buildings and parks or green space to neighborhoods and cities that can often include their supporting infrastructure.[11]

Cognitive Processing: The term "cognition" is a group of mental processes that includes attention, memory, producing and understanding language, learning, reasoning, problem solving, and decision making.[12]

Ecological Perspective: The term "ecology" designates a science that deals with the interrelationships between organisms (people) and their surroundings.[13]

Elements and Principles of Design: The elements and principles of design are fundamental guidelines used by architects and interior designers. These basic concepts cover a range of small pieces that make up a whole creation. The comprehension of these pieces allows an interior designer or architect to complete a work that is technically correct and appreciated by critics.

Environment: Environment is defined as the aggregate of surrounding things, conditions, or influences; surroundings; milieu.[14] For this study, environment refers to the built environment.

Environment Behavior Theory: is a conceptual model recognizing the relationship between an individual and his or her environment.[15]

Environmental Perception: The way in which an individual perceives the environment, the process of evaluating and storing information received about the environment.[16]

Environment Preference Theory: is based on the idea that people prefer scenes that are engaging and involving rather than simple and boring.[17]

Environmental Press: refers to the interplay between individuals and their environment. The theory relates to a degree of person–environment match in terms of competence.[18]

Evidence-Based Design: The process of making design choices about a space, including schools, hospitals, restaurants, residences, etc. based on research and data.[19, 20]

Gestalt Theory: The whole is greater than the sum of its parts. It employs a visual perception of putting components together.[21]

Hearing: One of the five main senses, by which sound waves are perceived by the organ of hearing—the ear—in vertebrate animals. The process of sound perception is called audition. The physical stimulus of auditory sensation is the vibration of some material object. The vibration is transmitted from the object to the ear, under ordinary conditions, by a wave movement of air particles.[22]

Hyper-Sensitive: Individuals with ASD that have hyper-arousal toward or are over-reactive to stimuli pertaining to the five senses. Children that are hyper-sensitive are more easily aroused by their environment and are much slower to adjust to the environment than other children.[23]

Hypo-Sensitive: Individuals with ASD that have hypo-arousal toward or are under-reactive to stimuli pertaining to the five senses. Children with hypo-sensitive autism often appear to have visual or hearing impairments, as they sometimes do not respond to stimuli at all.[24]

Independence: is the ability to be in control of one's self, no matter what the situation. It indicates a willingness to take complete responsibility for one's thoughts, feelings, actions, and circumstances; in fact, life itself.[25]

Independent Living: A multi-unit housing development that may provide supportive services such as meals, housekeeping, social activities, and transportation.[26]

Interdependence: takes the stance that we are mutually responsible for each other, and it is essential that we share a common set of principles with others.[27]

Independence through Interdependence: Whether one realizes it or not, one does rely on others for one's self-esteem and emotional needs, and one's general state of well-being is assured only if one is comfortable in the interdependent, interconnected world.[28]

Instorative Environments: The creation of therapeutic environments that are instorative recognizes one's personality, and supports compatibility to stimulate abilities and give possibilities for development.[29]

Intellectual Disabilities: Previously referred to as mental retardation, these are disabilities characterized by significant limitations both in intellectual functioning and in adaptive behavior.[30]

Neurological Nourishment: Kellert, Heerwagen, and Mador argue that humans have an emotional relationship with nature elements and that by being in environments that reflect the intrinsic characteristics of nature, people function better psychologically, physiologically, and cognitively.[31]

Normalization: refers to a model of inclusion that is process driven.[32]

Personal Space: is a territory that humans carry with themselves and is not related to a particular physical place.[33]

Proprioception: The sense of proprioception provides the brain information about the location or movement of the body in space.[34]

Quality of Life: Quality of Life is associated with human values including happiness, satisfaction, general feelings of well-being, and opportunities to achieve personal potential.[35]

Repetitive Behaviors: include stereotyped and repetitive body movements, compulsive or ritualized behaviors, insistence on sameness in the environment and routines; strict focus on parts or details, narrow interests, and self-injurious behaviors.[36]

Restorative Environments: Restorative environment gives opportunity for recovery through the restorative experiences of being away, Extent, Fascination and Compatibility.[37]

Self-Determination (SD): is a combination of skills, knowledge, and beliefs that enable a person to engage in goal-directed, self-regulated, autonomous behavior. [38]

Sensory Design: Sensory design means designing for all the senses. Sound, touch, and odor are treated as equally important as sight.[39]

Sensory Integration Theory (SIT): is a neurobiological process that refers to the detection, assimilation, organization, and use of sensory information to allow an individual to interact effectively with the environment in daily activities.[40]

Sensory Seeking: The attempt to either create predictable, repetitive sensory input to block out unpleasant sensory stimuli when over-stimulated or to derive pleasure from predictable, repetitive sensory input when under-stimulated.[41]

Sensory Overload: An overwhelming sensory experience that occurs when an individual with ASD is trying to process too much sensory information or attempting to use more than one of the senses at a time. Sensory overload usually results in the use of a coping mechanism, in the form of repetitive behaviors, in an attempt to maintain some control over the environment.[42]

Smell: One of the five special senses, by which odors are perceived. The nose, equipped with olfactory nerves, is the special organ of smell. The olfactory nerves also account for differing tastes of substances taken into the mouth, that is, most sensations that appear introspectively as tastes are really smells.[43]

Snoezelen Rooms: Also referred to as multi-sensory rooms or sensory integration spaces, Snoezelen rooms are highly simulative environments that allow individuals to engage with the space through different smells, sights, tastes, and sounds.[44]

Spatial Sequencing: Zoning or spatial sequencing involves reorganizing a space into different "zones" or "spaces," each with its own singular function or activity in order to promote routine and preserve predictability.[45]

Stimming: A repetitive behavior, usually a physical movement, that engages the individual and gives pleasure because of its predictability.[46]

Taste: One of the five senses in humans and other animals, by which four gustatory qualities (sweetness, sourness, saltiness, and bitterness) of a substance are distinguished. Taste is determined by receptors, called taste buds, the number and shape of which may vary greatly between one person and another.[47]

TEACCH: is Treatment and Education of Autistic and Related Communication Handicapped Children. TEACCH is a service, training, and research program for individuals of all ages and skill levels with autism spectrum disorders.

Theory of Mind: Thought to explain some of the difficulties with social interaction among individuals with autism, Theory of Mind refers to the ability of an individual to recognize the mental states of others, including deciphering beliefs, desires, intentions, imagination, and emotions.[48]

Therapeutic Environment: Smyth (2005) states that healing properties are associated with the environment.[49] The fields of environmental psychology (psycho-social effects of the environment), psychoneuroimmunology (the effects of the environment on the immune system), and neuroscience (how the brain perceives architecture) contribute to Therapeutic Environment Theory.[50]

Touch: One of the five senses in humans and other animals, by which the body perceives contact with substances. In humans, touch is accomplished by nerve endings in the skin that convey sensations to the brain via nerve fibers. Nerves end in or between the cells of the epidermis, the outer layer of the skin, in all parts of the body. In one complex form of nerve ending, the terminals form tiny swellings, or end bulbs; characteristic of this form are the Pacinian corpuscles found in the sensitive pad of each finger. Touch is the least specialized of the senses, but acuteness can be sharpened by use.[51]

Vestibular Movement: There are three sensory systems that contribute to balance—the visual system, the sense of proprioception, and the vestibular system, which senses movement and imbalance in the body.[52]

Vision: Ability to see the features of objects we look at, such as color, shape, size, details, depth, and contrast. Vision is achieved when the eyes and brain work together to form pictures of the world around us. Vision begins with light rays bouncing off the surface of objects. These reflected light rays enter the eye and are transformed into electrical signals. Millions of signals per second leave the eye via the optic nerve and travel to the visual area of the brain. Brain cells then decode the signals into images, providing us with sight.[53]

Wayfinding: The process of navigating an environment and finding a desired point of destination.

Weak Central Coherence Theory: One of the theories thought to explain unusual attention to details; a common symptom among individuals with ASD, weak central coherence refers to a bias toward local or piecemeal information rather than global or configurationally processing.[54]

Notes

1. U.S. Equal Employment Opportunity Commission. "Facts about the Americans with Disabilities Act." The U.S. Equal Employment Opportunity Commission, 2008.

2. Dubos, Rene. "Health and creative adaptation." *Human nature* 1, no. 1 (1978): 75–82.

3. Szatmari, Peter, Susan E. Bryson, David L. Streiner, Freda Wilson, Lynda Archer, and Cynthia Ryerse. "Two-year outcome of preschool children with autism or Asperger's syndrome." *American journal of psychiatry* 157, no. 12 (2014): 1980–1987.

4. Kennedy, Diane M. *The ADHD-autism connection.* Colorado Springs: Waterbrook Press, 2002.

5. Shabha, Ghasson. "An assessment of the impact of the sensory environment on individuals' behaviour in special needs schools." *Facilities* 24, no. 1/2 (2006): 31–42.

6. Landrigan, Philip J. "What causes autism? Exploring the environmental contribution." *Current opinion in pediatrics* 22, no. 2 (2010): 219–225.

7. National Institutes of Health. "Autism spectrum disorders (ASDs)." Eunice Kennedy Shriver: National Institute of Child Health and Human Development, November 15, 2011. http://www.nichd.nih.gov/health/topics/asd.cfm.

8. *Merriam-Webster's Medical Dictionary.* s.v. "Behavior." Retrieved April 19, 2008, http://dictionary.reference.com/browse/behavior.

9. Kellert, S. R. *"Building for life: Designing and understanding the human-nature connection."* Island Press, 2005.

10. Kellert, S. R., J. Heerwagen, and Martin Mador. *Biophilic design: The theory, science, and practice of bringing buildings to life.* Chichester, UK: John Wiley & Sons Ltd., 2008.

11. Caan, Shashi. *Rethinking design and interiors.* Laurence King, 2011.

12. Sternberg, Robert J. *Cognitive psychology.* Fort Worth: Harcourt Brace College Publishers, 1996.

13. Bronfenbrenner, Urie. *The ecology of human development: Experiments by design and nature.* Harvard University Press, 1979.

14. *Dictionary.com Unabridged* (v1.1), s.v. "Environment." Retrieved April 16, 2008, http://dictionary.reference.com/browse/environment.

15. Lewin, Kurt. *Field theory in social science.* Harper, 1951.

16. Saarinen, Thomas Frederick, David Seamon, and James L. Sell. *Environmental perception and behavior: An inventory and prospect.* Chicago: University of Chicago, Department of Geography, 1984.

17. Kaplan, Rachel, and Stephen Kaplan. *The experience of nature: A psychological perspective.* CUP Archive, 1989.

18. Lawton, M. P., and B. Simon. "The ecology of social relationships in housing for the elderly." *The gerontologist* 8, no. 2 (1968): 108–115.

19. Malkin, Jain. *A visual reference for evidence-based design.* Center for Health Design, 2008.

20. Whitemyer, David. "The future of evidence-based design." *International interior design association.* 2010. See http://www. iida.org/content. cfm/the-future-of-evidence-based-design (accessed January 17, 2014).

21. Köhler, Wolfgang. *Gestalt psychology.* Liveright Publishing Corporation, 1929.

22. *MSN Encarta,* s.v. "Sense Organs," Retrieved April 16, 2008, http://encarta.msn.com/encyclopedia_761565821/Sense_Organs.html.

23. Volkmar, Fred R., Rhea Paul, Ami Klin, and Donald J. Cohen, eds. *Handbook of autism and pervasive developmental disorders, diagnosis, development, neurobiology, and behavior.* Vol. 1. John Wiley & Sons, 2005.

24. Volkmar, Fred R., Rhea Paul, Ami Klin, and Donald J. Cohen, eds. *Handbook of autism and pervasive developmental disorders, diagnosis, development, neurobiology, and behavior.* Vol. 1. John Wiley & Sons, 2005.

25. Felce, David. *A comprehensive guide to intellectual and developmental disabilities.* Ivan Brown and Maire Ede Percy, eds. PH Brookes, 2007.

26. Regnier, Victor, Jennifer Hamilton, and Suzie Yatabe. *Assisted living for the aged and frail: Innovations in design, management, and financing.* Columbia University Press, 1995.

27. Welch, Polly, Valerie Parker, and John Zeisel. *Independence through interdependence: Congregate living for older people.* Office of Policy and Planning, Department of Elder Affairs, 1984.

28. Welch, Polly, Valerie Parker, and John Zeisel. *Independence through interdependence: Congregate living for older people.* Office of Policy and Planning, Department of Elder Affairs, 1984.

29. Kaplan, S., and R. Kaplan. *Cognition and environment: Functioning in an uncertain world.* Praeger, 1982.

30. American Association on Mental Retardation (AAMR). *Diagnostic and Statistical Manual of Mental Disorders. Fifth Ed.* Washington, DC: American Psychiatric Association, 2013.

31. Kellert, S. R., J. Heerwagen, and Martin Mador. *Biophilic design: The theory, science, and practice of bringing buildings to life.* Chichester, UK: John Wiley & Sons Ltd., 2008.

32. Murray, Christopher J., and Alan D. Lopez. *Global burden of disease.* Vol. 1. Cambridge, MA: Harvard University Press, 1996.

33. Sommer, Robert. *Personal space. The behavioral basis of design.* Prentice-Hall, 1969.

34. Myles, Brenda Smith. *Asperger syndrome and sensory issues: Practical solutions for making sense of the world.* AAPC Publishing, 2000.

35. Brown, Roy I., Robert L. Schalock, and Ivan Brown. "Quality of life: Its application to persons with intellectual disabilities and their families—Introduction and overview." *Journal of policy and practice in intellectual disabilities* 6, no. 1 (2009): 2–6.

36. Gabriels, Robin L., John A. Agnew, Lucy Jane Miller, Jane Gralla, Zhaoxing Pan, Edward Goldson, James C. Ledbetter, Juliet P. Dinkins, and Elizabeth Hooks. "Is there a relationship between restricted, repetitive, stereotyped behaviors and interests and abnormal sensory response in children with autism spectrum disorders?" *Research in autism spectrum disorders* 2, no. 4 (2008): 660–670.

37. Kaplan, Rachel, and Stephen Kaplan. *The experience of nature: A psychological perspective.* CUP Archive, 1989.

38. Field, Sharon, James Martin, Robert Miller, Michael Ward, and Michael Wehmeyer. "Self-determination for persons with disabilities: A position statement of the division on career development and transition." *Career development for exceptional individuals* 21, no. 2 (1998): 113–128.

39. Malnar, Joy Monice. *Sensory design.* University of Minnesota Press, 2004.

40. Ayres, A. J. *Sensory integration and learning disabilities.* Los Angeles: Western Psychological Services, 1972.

41. Ashburner, Jill, Jenny Ziviani, and Sylvia Rodger. "Sensory processing and classroom emotional, behavioral, and educational outcomes in children with autism spectrum disorder." *American journal of occupational therapy* 62, no. 5 (2008): 564–573.

42. Gabriels, Robin L., John A. Agnew, Lucy Jane Miller, Jane Gralla, Zhaoxing Pan, Edward Goldson, James C. Ledbetter, Juliet P. Dinkins, and Elizabeth Hooks. "Is there a relationship between restricted, repetitive, stereotyped behaviors and interests and abnormal sensory response in children with autism spectrum disorders?" *Research in autism spectrum disorders* 2, no. 4 (2008): 660–670.

43. *MSN Encarta*, s.v. "Sense Organs," Retrieved April 16, 2008, http://encarta.msn.com/encyclopedia_761565821/Sense_Organs.html.

44. May, Michael E. *Comparison of living unit, Snoezelen room, and outdoor activities on stereotypic and engagement behavior with individuals with profound mental retardation.* Southern Illinois University at Carbondale, 1999.

45. May, Michael E. *Comparison of living unit, Snoezelen room, and outdoor activities on stereotypic and engagement behavior with individuals with profound mental retardation.* Southern Illinois University at Carbondale, 1999.

46. Baron-Cohen, S. "Autism: The empathizing-systemizing (ES) theory." *Annals of the New York Academy of Sciences* 1156 (2009): 68–80.

47. *MSN Encarta*, s.v. "Sense Organs," Retrieved April 16, 2008, http://encarta.msn.com/encyclopedia_761565821/Sense_Organs.html.

48. Bogdashina, Olga. *Sensory perceptual issues in autism and Asperger Syndrome: Different sensory experiences, different perceptual worlds.* Jessica Kingsley Publishers, 2003.

49. Mostafa, Magda. "An architecture for autism: Concepts of design intervention for the autistic user." *Archnet-IJAR: International journal of architectural research* 2, no. 1 (2008): 189–211.

50. Smith, Ron, and Nicholas Watkins. "Therapeutic environments." Washington DC: Academy of Architecture for Health, 2008.

51. *MSN Encarta*, s.v. "Sense Organs," Retrieved April 16, 2008, http://encarta.msn.com/encyclopedia_761565821/Sense_Organs.html.

52. Weimer, Amy K. *Motor impairment in Asperger Syndrome: Evidence for a deficit in proprioception.* No publisher information, 1999.

53. *MSN Encarta*, s.v. "Sense Organs," Retrieved April 16, 2008, http://encarta.msn.com/encyclopedia_761565821/Sense_Organs.html.

54. Brock, Jon, Caroline C. Brown, Jill Boucher, and Gina Rippon. "The temporal binding deficit hypothesis of autism." *Development and psychopathology* 14, no. 2 (2002): 209–224.

References

Adams, Annmarie, David Theodore, Ellie Goldenberg, Coralee McLaren, and Patricia McKeever. "Kids in the atrium: Comparing architectural intentions and children's experiences in a pediatric hospital lobby." *Social science & medicine* 70, no. 5 (2010): 658–667.

Affleck, James Q., Sally Madge, Abby Adams, and Sheila Lowenbraun. "Integrated classroom versus resource model: Academic viability and effectiveness." *Exceptional children* 54, no. 4 (1988): 339–348.

Ahrentzen, S., and K. Steele. *Advancing full spectrum housing: Designing for adults with autism spectrum disorders.* Tempe: Arizona Board of Regents, 2010.

Alcántara, José I., Emma J. L. Weisblatt, Brian C. J. Moore, and Patrick F. Bolton. "Speech-in-noise perception in high-functioning individuals with autism or Asperger's syndrome." *Journal of child psychology and psychiatry* 45, no. 6 (2004): 1107–1114.

Alexander, Christopher, Sara Ishikawa, and Murray Silverstein. *A pattern language: Towns, buildings, construction.* Vol. 2. Oxford University Press, 1977.

Altman, Irwin. "Privacy regulation: Culturally universal or culturally specific?" *Journal of social issues* 33, no. 3 (1977): 66–84.

Altman, Irwin. *The environment and social behavior: Privacy, personal space, territory, and crowding.* Brooks/Cole Publishing, 1975.

American Association on Mental Retardation (AAMR). *Diagnostic and Statistical Manual of Mental Disorders* (5th ed.). Washington, DC: American Psychiatric Association, 2013.

Americans with Disabilities Act of 1990 (ADA)—42 U.S. Code Chapter 126, 1990.

Appleton, Jay. *The experience of landscape.* New York: John Wiley & Sons, 1975.

Armstrong, Thomas. *The power of neurodiversity: Unleashing the advantages of your differently wired brain.* Da Capo Press, 2011.

Ashburner, Jill, Jenny Ziviani, and Sylvia Rodger. "Sensory processing and classroom emotional, behavioral, and educational outcomes in children with autism spectrum disorder." *American journal of occupational therapy* 62, no. 5 (2008): 564–573.

Asperger, H. "Die Bautistischen Psychopathen" [im Kindesalter.] Archiv fur Psychiatrie und Nervenkrankheiten, 117, 76–136. Translated by U. Frith in U. Frith (Ed.) (1991) *Autism and Asperger syndrome*, pp. 36–92. Cambridge, 1944.

Augustin, Sally. *Place advantage: Applied psychology for interior architecture.* John Wiley & Sons, 2009.

Autism Society of Delaware. "Best practices for serving adults with autism: Results of the study on services and support for adults on the autism spectrum across the United States." Full Research Report. (n.d.) Retrieved from: http://www.delautism.org/POW&R/servingadults.html.

Autism Society Ontario. *Our most vulnerable citizens: A report of the Adult Task Force, Autism Society Ontario.* Guelph, Ontario: s.n., 1991.

Ayres, A. J. *Sensory integration and learning disabilities.* Los Angeles: Western Psychological Services, 1972.

Babyparenting.com. "The tactile defensive child." (n.d.). Retrieved June 3, 2003, from http.//babyparentingabout.com.

Baker, Edward T. "The effects of inclusion on learning." *Educational leadership* 52, no. 4 (1995): 33–35.

Baker, E.T., M.C Wang, and H.J. Walberg. "Synthesis of research/The effects of inclusion on learning." Educational Leadership 52, no.4 (December 1994/January 1995): 33-35.

Banaschewski, Tobias, Sinje Ruppert, Rosemary Tannock, Björn Albrecht, Andreas Becker, Henrik Uebel, Joseph A. Sergeant, and Aribert Rothenberger. "Colour perception in ADHD." *Journal of child psychology and psychiatry* 47, no. 6 (2006): 568–572.

Banerji, Madhabi, and Ronald A. Dailey. "A study of the effects of an inclusion model on students with specific learning disabilities." *Journal of learning disabilities* 28, no. 8 (1995): 511–522.

Baron-Cohen, S. "Autism: the empathizing-systematizing (ES) theory." *Annals of the New York Academy of Sciences* 1156 (2009): 68–80.

Bartlett, Sheridan. "Access to outdoor play and its implications for healthy attachments." Unpublished article, Putney, VT, 1996.

Baum, Andrew, and Glenn E. Davis. "Reducing the stress of high-density living: An architectural intervention." *Journal of personality and social psychology* 38, no. 3 (1980): 471.

Baumers, Stijn, and Ann Heylighen. "Beyond the designers' view: How people with autism experience space." In *Design and complexity. Proceedings of the Design Research Society Conference 2010*. 2010.

Bechtel, Robert B. *Environment and behavior: An introduction*. Sage, 1997.

Bellizzi, Joseph A., Ayn E. Crowley, and Ronald W. Hasty. "The effects of color in store design." *Journal of retailing* 59, no. 1 (1983): 21–45.

Belmonte, Matthew. "What's the story behind 'theory of mind' and autism?" *Journal of consciousness studies* 16, no. 6–8 (2009): 118–139.

Benedyk, R., A. Woodcock, and A. Woolner. "Applying the hexagon-spindle model for educational ergonomics to the design of school environments for children with autistic spectrum disorders." *Work journal* 32 (2009): 249–259.

Bengtsson, Anna, and Gunilla Carlsson. "Outdoor environments at three nursing homes: Focus group interviews with staff." *Journal of housing for the elderly* 19, no. 3–4 (2006): 49–69.

Bixler, Robert D., Myron F. Floyd, and William E. Hammitt. "Environmental socialization quantitative tests of the childhood play hypothesis." *Environment and behavior* 34, no. 6 (2002): 795–818.

Blaxill, Mark F. "What's going on? The question of time trends in autism." *Public health reports* 119, no. 6 (2004): 536.

Bloom, Benjamin Samuel. *All our children learning: A primer for parents, teachers, and other educators*. McGraw-Hill Companies, 1981.

Bogdashina, Olga. *Autism and the edges of the known world: Sensitivities, language, and constructed reality*. Jessica Kingsley Publishers, 2010.

Bogdashina, Olga. *Sensory perceptual issues in autism and Asperger Syndrome: Different sensory experiences, different perceptual worlds*. Jessica Kingsley Publishers, 2003.

Bogdashina, Olga. *Theory of mind and the triad of perspectives on autism and Asperger syndrome: A view from the bridge*. Jessica Kingsley Publishers, 2006.

Bourassa, Steven C. *The aesthetic of landscape*. London & New York: Belhaven Press, 1991.

Bourne, Angela. "Neuro-considerate environments for adults with intellectual developmental diversities: An integrated design approach to support wellbeing." PhD diss., Texas Tech University, 2013.

Bourne, Angela, personal communication at Brookwood Community in Brookshire, Texas, June 2013.

Bourne, Angela, personal communication with Jan Cline, Bittersweet Farms, Whitehouse, Ohio, August, 2013.

Bourne, Angela, personal communication with Rick DeMunbrun and Carol Whitmore at Brookwood Community, Brookshire, Texas, June 2013.

Bourne, Angela. "Therapeutic environments for adults with intellectual developmental diversities." Master's Report, Texas Tech University, 2012.

Boyce, Peter R. "Review: The impact of light in buildings on human health." *Indoor and built environment* 19, no. 1 (2010): 8–20.

Braddock, David, Richard Hemp, Susan Parish, and James Westrich. *The state of the states in developmental disabilities* (5th ed.). Washington, DC: American Association on Mental Retardation, Research Monographs and Book Publication Program, 1998.

Braddock, D., R. Hemp, M. C. Rizzolo, E. S. Tanis, L. Haffer, and J. Wu. *The state of the states in intellectual and developmental disabilities: Emerging from the great recession*. Washington DC: American Association on Intellectual and Developmental Disabilities (AAIDD), 2015.

Bradley, John S. "Speech intelligibility studies in classrooms." *The journal of the acoustical society of America* 80, no. 3 (1986): 846–854.

Brandon, Kelly C. "Wayfinding." *Issues in graphic design*. 2014. http://www.kellybrandondesign.com/IGDWayfinding.html.

Brannon, Linda, and Jess Feist. *Health Psychology: An introduction to behavior and health* (3rd ed.). Pacific Grove, CA: Brooks/Cole, 1997.

Brock, Jon, Caroline C. Brown, Jill Boucher, and Gina Rippon. "The temporal binding deficit hypothesis of autism." *Development and psychopathology* 14, no. 2 (2002): 209–224.

Bronfenbrenner, Urie. *The ecology of human development: Experiments by design and nature*. Harvard University Press, 1979.

Brown, Roy I., Robert L. Schalock, and Ivan Brown. "Quality of life: Its application to persons with intellectual disabilities and their families— Introduction and overview." *Journal of policy and practice in intellectual disabilities* 6, no. 1 (2009): 2–6.

Burnette, Courtney P., Peter C. Mundy, Jessica A. Meyer, Steven K. Sutton, Amy E. Vaughan, and David Charak. "Weak central coherence and its relations to theory of mind and anxiety in autism." *Journal of autism and developmental disorders* 35, no. 1 (2005): 63–73.

Caan, Shashi. *Rethinking design and interiors*. Laurence King, 2011.

Carbo, Marie, and Helene Hodges. "Learning styles strategies can help students at risk." *Teaching exceptional children* 20, no. 4 (1988): 55–58.

Carmody, Dennis P., Melvin Kaplan, and Alexa M. Gaydos. "Spatial orientation adjustments in children with autism in Hong Kong." *Child psychiatry and human development* 31, no. 3 (2001): 233–247.

Cascio, Carissa, Francis McGlone, Stephen Folger, Vinay Tannan, Grace Baranek, Kevin A. Pelphrey, and Gregory Essick. "Tactile perception in adults with autism: A multidimensional psychophysical study." *Journal of autism and developmental disorders* 38, no. 1 (2008): 127–137.

Castell, Lindsay. "Building access for the intellectually disabled." *Facilities* 26, no. 3/4 (2008): 117–130.

Castle, Steven. "LED lighting creates nurturing environment for autistic students." *K-12 Tech Decisions.* 2014. http://www.k-12techdecisions. com/article/led_lighting_saves_one_school_money_and_creates_a_ better_learning_environme.

Centers for Disease Control and Prevention. "Diagnostic Criteria." November 1, 2011. Accessed August 1, 2014. http://www.cdc.gov/ncbddd/autism/ hcp-dsm.html.

Childers, T. L., and J. Peck. "Informational and affective influences of haptics on product evaluation: Is what I say how I feel?" In *Sensory marketing: Research on the sensuality of products* (pp. 63–72). New York: Routledge/ Taylor & Francis Group, 2010.

Clark, Greg. "The ears have it." *American school & university* 76, no. 3 (2003): 298–301.

Clay, R. A. "No more Mickey Mouse design: Child's environments require unique considerations." *ASID ICON* (2004): 43–47.

Cohen, Sheldon, D. C. Glass, and Susan Phillips. "Environment and health." In H. Freeman, S. Levine, and L. G. Reeder, *Handbook of medical sociology* (pp. 134–149). Englewood Cliffs, NJ: Prentice-Hall, 1979.

Cohen, Uriel, and Gerald D. Weisman. *Holding on to home: Designing environments for people with dementia.* Johns Hopkins University Press, 1991.

Courchesne, Eric, Jeanne Townsend, Natacha A. Akshoomoff, Osamu Saitoh, Rachel Yeung-Courchesne, Alan J. Lincoln, Hector E. James, Richard H. Haas, Laura Schreibman, and Lily Lau. "Impairment in shifting attention in autistic and cerebellar patients." *Behavioral neuroscience* 108, no. 5 (1994): 848.

Crain, Margaret Ann. "Looking at people and asking 'why?': An ethnographic approach to religious education." *Religious education* 96, no. 3 (2001): 386–394.

Davies, F., and S. Clayton. "Even the ants are noisy: Sensory perception in people with autism spectrum disorder." Presentation at NAS Regional Conference in London, 2008.

Dawson, Geraldine, and Renee Watling. "Interventions to facilitate auditory, visual, and motor integration in autism: A review of the evidence." *Journal of autism and developmental disorders* 30, no. 5 (2000): 415–421.

Day, Kristen, Daisy Carreon, and Cheryl Stump. "The therapeutic design of environments for people with dementia: A review of the empirical research." *The gerontologist* 40, no. 4 (2000): 397–416.

De Charms, Richard. *Personal causation: The internal affective determinants of behavior.* Academic Press, 1968.

Delaney, David. *Territory: A short introduction.* John Wiley & Sons, 2008.

Delpo, E., and S. Frick. "Directed and non-directed play as therapeutic modality." *Children's health care* 16, no. 4 (1988): 261–267.

Dictionary.com Unabridged (v1.1), s.v. "Environment." Retrieved April 16, 2008, http://dictionary.reference.com/browse/environment.

Dubos, Rene. "Health and creative adaptation." *Human nature* 1, no. 1 (1978): 75–82.

Dunn, Rita and Kenneth Dunn. "Learning styles/teaching styles: Should they... can they... be matched?" *Educational leadership* 36, no. 4 (1979): 238–244.

Dunn, Rita, Shirley A. Griggs, Jeffery Olson, Mark Beasley, and Bernard S. Gorman. "A meta-analytic validation of the Dunn and Dunn model of learning-style preferences." *The journal of educational research* 88, no. 6 (1995): 353–362.

Edwards, L., and Paul A. Torcellini. *A literature review of the effects of natural light on building occupants.* Golden, CO: National Renewable Energy Laboratory, 2002.

Emerson, Eric. "Cluster housing for adults with intellectual disabilities." *Journal of intellectual and developmental disability* 29, no. 3 (2004): 187–197.

Engelbrecht, K. "The impact of color on learning." *NeoCON2003*, 2003.

Evans, Gary W., Stephen J. Lepore, and Alex Schroeder. "The role of interior design elements in human responses to crowding." *Journal of personality and social psychology* 70, no. 1 (1996): 41.

Felce, David. *A comprehensive guide to intellectual and developmental disabilities.* Ivan Brown and Maire Ede Percy, eds. PH Brookes, 2007.

Fels, Deborah I., Judith K. Waalen, Shumin Zhai, and P. Weiss. "Telepresence under exceptional circumstances: Enriching the connection to school for sick children." In *Human–computer interaction, Interact '01* (pp. 617–624). International Federation for Information Processing, 2001.

Ferguson, J. "Sensory Integration Therapy." 2003. Retrieved June 3, 2003. Available at http://memorialhospital.org/sensoryintegration.htm.

Field, Sharon, James Martin, Robert Miller, Michael Ward, and Michael Wehmeyer. "Self-determination for persons with disabilities: A position statement of the division on career development and transition." *Career development for exceptional individuals* 21, no. 2 (1998): 113–128.

Fielding, Randall. "Learning, lighting and color: Lighting design for schools and universities in the 21st century." *Designshare (NJ1)*. 2006.

Fisher, A. G., E. A. Murray, and A. C. Bundy. *Sensory integration: Theory and practice.* F. A. Davis, 1991.

Fore III, Cecil, Shanna Hagan-Burke, Mack D. Burke, Richard T. Boon, and Steve Smith. "Academic achievement and class placement in high school: Do students with learning disabilities achieve more in one class placement than another?" *Education and treatment of children* 31, no. 1 (2008): 55–72.

Frankel, Frederick D., Clarissa M. Gorospe, Ya-Chih Chang, and Catherine A. Sugar. "Mothers' reports of play dates and observation of school playground behavior of children having high-functioning autism spectrum disorders." *Journal of child psychology and psychiatry* 52, no. 5 (2011): 571–579.

Frederick, Matthew. *101 things I learned in architecture school.* Cambridge: MIT Press, 2007.

Freed, Jeffrey, and Laurie Parsons. *Right-brained children in a left-brained world: Unlocking the potential of your ADD child.* Simon and Schuster, 1998.

Frith, Uta. *Autism: Explaining the enigma.* Wiley-Blackwell, 1989.

Frith, U. *Autism: Explaining the enigma. Volume 2: Cognitive development.* Hoboken, NJ: Wiley, 2003.

Frith, Uta. *Autism: Towards an explanation of the enigma* (2nd ed.) Madrid: Alianza Editorial, 2006. p. 170.

Frith, Uta. "Mind blindness and the brain in autism." *Neuron* 32, no. 6 (2001): 969–979.

Frith, Uta, and Francesca Happé. "Theory of mind and self-consciousness: What is it like to be autistic?" *Mind & language* 14, no. 1 (1999): 82–89.

Gabriels, Robin L., John A. Agnew, Lucy Jane Miller, Jane Gralla, Zhaoxing Pan, Edward Goldson, James C. Ledbetter, Juliet P. Dinkins, and Elizabeth Hooks. "Is there a relationship between restricted, repetitive, stereotyped behaviors and interests and abnormal sensory response in children with autism spectrum disorders?" *Research in autism spectrum disorders* 2, no. 4 (2008): 660–670.

Gaines, Kristi. "Brain compatible learning environments for students with autism spectrum disorders." PhD diss., Texas Tech University, 2008.

Gaines, Kristi S., and Zane D. Curry. "The inclusive classroom: The effects of color on learning and behavior." *Journal of family & consumer sciences education* 29, no. 1 (2011): 46–57.

Gaines, Kristi S., Zane Curry, JoAnn Shroyer, Cherif Amor, and Robin H. Lock. "The perceived effects of visual design and features on students with autism spectrum disorder." *Journal of architectural and planning research* 31, no. 4 (2014): 282–298.

Gaines, Kristi, and S. Sancibrian. "The effects of environmental noise on the behavior of children with ASD." *The international journal of architectonic, spatial, and environmental design* 7, no. 2 (2014): 51–64.

Garce, Melinda La. "Control of environmental lighting and its effects on behaviors of the Alzheimer's type." *Journal of interior design* 28, no. 2 (2002): 15–25.

Gaudion, Katie. *Designing everyday activities: Living environments for adults with autism.* Helen Hamlyn Centre for Design, 2013.

Gibson, James J. "The concept of the stimulus in psychology." *American psychologist* 15, no. 11 (1960): 694.

Giddan, Jane J., and Victoria L. Obee. "Adults with autism: Habilitation challenges and practices." *Journal of rehabilitation* 62, no. 1 (1996): 72.

Grahn, Patrik, and Ulrika A. Stigsdotter. "Landscape planning and stress." *Urban forestry & urban greening* 2, no. 1 (2003): 1–18.

Grandin, Temple. "Calming effects of deep touch pressure in patients with autistic disorder, college students, and animals." *Journal of child and adolescent psychopharmacology* 2, no. 1 (1992): 63–72.

Grandin, Temple. *Thinking in pictures: My life with autism* (expanded edition). New York: Vintage, 2006.

Gresham, Frank M. "Assessment of children's social skills." *Journal of school psychology* 19, no. 2 (1981): 120–133.

Groat, L. "Contextual compatibility in architecture: An issue of personal taste." In *Environmental aesthetics: Theory, research, and applications* (pp. 228–254). Cambridge University Press, 1988.

Hall, Edward T. *The hidden dimension.* Garden City, NY: Doubleday, 1966.

Hall, Edward T. *The silent language.* Garden City, NY: Doubleday, 1959.

Hall, Kenneth B., and Gerald A. Porterfield. *Community by design: New urbanism for suburbs and small communities.* McGraw Hill Professional, 2001.

Happé, Francesca, and Uta Frith. "The weak coherence account: Detail-focused cognitive style in autism spectrum disorders." *Journal of autism and developmental disorders* 36, no. 1 (2006): 5–25.

Hatch-Rasmussen, Cindy. "Sensory integration." Center for the Study of Autism at www.autism.org/si.html. 1995.

Heaton, Pamela, Beate Hermelin, and Linda Pring. "Autism and pitch processing: A precursor for savant musical ability?" *Music perception* 15, no. 3 (1998): 291–305.

Heller, Tamar, Alison B. Miller, and Kelly Hsieh. "Eight-year follow-up of the impact of environmental characteristics on well-being of adults with developmental disabilities." *Mental retardation* 40, no. 5 (2002): 366–378.

Herzog, Thomas R., and Olivia L. Leverich. "Searching for legibility." *Environment and behavior* 35, no. 4 (2003): 459–477.

Hildebrand, Grant. *Origins of architectural pleasure.* University of California Press, 1999.

Hobson, R. Peter. "The autistic child's appraisal of expressions of emotion." *Journal of child psychology and psychiatry* 27, no. 3 (1986): 321–342.

Holloway, John H. "Inclusion and students with learning disabilities." *Educational leadership* 58, no. 6 (2001): 86–88.

Humphreys, Lee. "Cellphones in public: Social interactions in a wireless era." *New media & society* 7, no. 6 (2005): 810–833.

Iarocci, Grace, and John McDonald. "Sensory integration and the perceptual experience of persons with autism." *Journal of autism and developmental disorders* 36, no. 1 (2006): 77–90.

International Interior Design Association (IIDA). "Multi-sensory environments for special populations—Live webinar." Healthcare Design Webinars. January 26, 2012.

Jackson, L. *Freaks, geeks, and Asperger Syndrome.* London: Jessica Kingsley Publishers, 2002.

Jacobs, Karen, and Nancy A. Baker. "The association between children's computer use and musculoskeletal discomfort." *Work* 18, no. 3 (2002): 221–226.

Jacobson, Max, Murray Silverstein, and Barbara Winslow. *Patterns of home: The ten essentials of enduring design*. Taunton Press, 2002.

Jarrott, Shannon E., Hye Ran Kwack, and Diane Relf. "An observational assessment of a dementia-specific horticultural therapy program." *Horttechnology* 12, no. 3 (2002): 403–410.

Jones, Robert, Ciara Quigney, and Jaci Huws. "First-hand accounts of sensory perceptual experiences in autism: A qualitative analysis." *Journal of intellectual and developmental disability* 28, no. 2 (2003): 112–121.

Jordan, Rita. "Social play and autistic spectrum disorders: A perspective on theory, implications and educational approaches." *Autism* 7, no. 4 (2003): 347–360.

Kahn, Peter H., and Stephen R. Kellert. *Children and nature: Psychological, sociocultural, and evolutionary investigations*. MIT Press, 2002.

Kanner, Leo. *Autistic disturbances of affective contact*. Publisher not identified, 1943.

Kaplan, Rachel. "The nature of the view from home psychological benefits." *Environment and behavior* 33, no. 4 (2001): 507–542.

Kaplan, Rachel, and Stephen Kaplan. *The experience of nature: A psychological perspective*. CUP Archive, 1989.

Kaplan, Rachel, Stephen Kaplan, and Robert Ryan. *With people in mind: Design and management of everyday nature*. Island Press, 1998.

Kaplan, Rachel, Stephen Kaplan, and Terry Brown. "Environmental preference: A comparison of four domains of predictors." *Environment and behavior* 21, no. 5 (1989): 509–530.

Kaplan, Stephen. "The restorative benefits of nature: Toward an integrative framework." *Journal of environmental psychology* 15, no. 3 (1995): 169–182.

Kaplan, S., and R. Kaplan. *Cognition and environment: Functioning in an uncertain world*. Praeger, 1982.

Kellert, S. R. *Building for life: Designing and understanding the human-nature connection*. Island Press, 2005.

Kellert, Stephen R., and Edward O. Wilson. *The biophilia hypothesis*. Island Press, 1995.

Kellert, S. R., J. Heerwagen, and Martin Mador. *Biophilic design: The theory, science, and practice of bringing buildings to life*. Chichester, UK: John Wiley & Sons Ltd., 2008.

Kennedy, Diane M. *The ADHD-autism connection*. Colorado Springs: Waterbrook Press, 2002.

Kern, Janet K., Madhukar H. Trivedi, Carolyn R. Garver, Bruce D. Grannemann, Alonzo A. Andrews, Jayshree S. Savla, Danny G. Johnson, Jyutika A. Mehta, and Jennifer L. Schroeder. "The pattern of sensory processing abnormalities in autism." *Autism* 10, no. 5 (2006): 480–494.

Khare, Rachna, and Abir Mullick. "Incorporating the behavioral dimension in designing inclusive learning environment for autism." *ArchNet-IJAR* 3, no. 3 (2009): 45–64.

Killeen, Jennifer Platten, Gary W. Evans, and Sheila Danko. "The role of permanent student artwork in students' sense of ownership in an elementary school." *Environment and behavior* 35, no. 2 (2003): 250–263.

Koegel, Lynn Kern, Anjileen K. Singh, and Robert L. Koegel. "Improving motivation for academics in children with autism." *Journal of autism and developmental disorders* 40, no. 9 (2010): 1057–1066.

Köhler, Wolfgang. *Gestalt psychology*. Liveright Publishing Corporation, 1929.

Konkle, Talia, Qi Wang, Vincent Hayward, and Christopher I. Moore. "Motion aftereffects transfer between touch and vision." *Current biology* 19, no. 9 (2009): 745–750.

Koomar, Jane, Carol Stock Kranowitz, Stacey Szklut, Lynn Balzer-Martin, Elizabeth Haber, and Deanna Iris Sava. *Answers to questions teachers ask about sensory integration: Forms, checklists, and practical tools for teachers and parents*. Future Horizons, 2001.

Kopec, David Alan. *Environmental psychology for design*. New York: Fairchild, 2006.

Kozma, Agnes, Jim Mansell, and Julie Beadle-Brown. "Outcomes in different residential settings for people with intellectual disability: A systematic review." *American journal on intellectual and developmental disabilities* 114, no. 3 (2009): 193–222.

Kranowitz, Carol, and Lucy Miller. *The out-of-sync child: Recognizing and coping with Sensory Processing Disorder*. Skylight Press, 2005.

Kuller, Rikard, and Thorbjorn Laike. "The impact of flicker from fluorescent lighting on well-being, performance and physiological arousal." *Ergonomics* 41, no. 4 (1998): 433–447.

Lackney, Jay. "School building design principles for an assessment program," (1998) in *School building assessment methods*, ed. Henry Sanoff. Washington, DC: National Clearing House for Educational Facilities, 2001.

Lackney, Jeffery A. "33 principles of educational design." Retrieved in 2008. http://schoolstudio.engr.wisc.edu.html.

Landrigan, Philip J. "What causes autism? Exploring the environmental contribution." *Current opinion in pediatrics* 22, no. 2 (2010): 219–225.

Lang, Peter J. "The application of psychophysiological methods to the study of psychotherapy and behavior modification." In *Handbook of psychotherapy and behavior change: An empirical analysis* (pp. 75–125). New York: Wiley, 1971.

Lawton, M. Powell. *Focus on the end of life: Scientific and social issues*. Vol. 20. Springer Publishing Company, 2001.

Lawton, M. P., and E. M. Brody. "Assessment of older people: Self-maintaining and instrumental activities of daily living." *The gerontologist* 9, no. 3 (1969): 179–186.

Lawton, M. P., and B. Simon. "The ecology of social relationships in housing for the elderly." *The gerontologist* 8, no. 2 (1968): 108–115.

Leekam, Susan R., Margot R. Prior, and Mirko Uljarevic. "Restricted and repetitive behaviors in autism spectrum disorders: A review of research in the last decade." *Psychological bulletin* 137, no. 4 (2011): 562.

Lercher, Peter, Gary W. Evans, and Markus Meis. "Ambient noise and cognitive processes among primary schoolchildren." *Environment and behavior* 35, no. 6 (2003): 725–735.

Lewin, Kurt. *Field theory in social science*. Harper, 1951.

Lind, Sophie E., David M. Williams, Jacob Raber, Anna Peel, and Dermot M. Bowler. "Spatial navigation impairments among intellectually high-functioning adults with autism spectrum disorder: Exploring relations with theory of mind, episodic memory, and episodic future thinking." *Journal of abnormal psychology* 122, no. 4 (2013): 1189.

Lindström, Bengt, and Monica Eriksson. "Salutogenesis." *Journal of epidemiology and community health* 59, no. 6 (2005): 440–442.

Lovelace, Maryann Kiely. "Meta-analysis of experimental research based on the Dunn and Dunn model." *The journal of educational research* 98, no. 3 (2005): 176–183.

Lowenthal, David, and Marquita Riel. "The nature of perceived and imagined environments." *Environment and behavior* 4, no. 2 (1972): 189–207.

Ludlow, Amanda K., and Arnold J. Wilkins. "Case report: Color as a therapeutic intervention." *Journal of autism and developmental disorders* 39, no. 5 (2009): 815–818.

Lynch, Kevin. *The image of the city.* Vol. 11. MIT Press, 1960.

Lyons, John B. "Do school facilities really impact a child's education." *CEFPI brief, issue Trak* (2001): 1–6.

MacCarthy, D. *The under fives in hospital.* London: National Association for the Welfare of Children in Hospital, 1979.

Maenner, Matthew J., and Maureen S. Durkin. "Trends in the prevalence of autism on the basis of special education data." *Pediatrics* 126, no. 5 (2010): e1018–e1025.

Malkin, Jain. *A visual reference for evidence-based design.* Center for Health Design, 2008.

Malnar, Joy Monice. *Sensory design.* University of Minnesota Press, 2004.

Manlove, Elizabeth E., Tom Frank, and Lynne Vernon-Feagans. "Why should we care about noise in classrooms and child care settings?" In *Child and youth care forum* (vol. 30, no. 1, pp. 55–64). Kluwer Academic Publishers-Plenum Publishers, 2001.

Mann, Rebecca Lyn. "The identification of gifted students with spatial strengths: An exploratory study." UMI ProQuest digital dissertations, 2005.

Manset, Genevieve, and Melvyn I. Semmel. "Are inclusive programs for students with mild disabilities effective? A comparative review of model programs." *The journal of special education* 31, no. 2 (1997): 155–180.

Marcus, Clare Cooper, and Marni Barnes. *Gardens in healthcare facilities: Uses, therapeutic benefits, and design recommendations.* Center for Health Design, 1995.

Maslow, Abraham H., and Norbett L. Mintz. "Effects of esthetic surroundings: I. Initial effects of three esthetic conditions upon perceiving "energy" and "well-being" in faces." *The journal of psychology* 41, no. 2 (1956): 247–254.

May, Michael E. *Comparison of living unit, Snoezelen room, and outdoor activities on stereotypic and engagement behavior with individuals with profound mental retardation.* Southern Illinois University at Carbondale, 1999.

May, Mike. *Sensation and perception.* Infobase Publishing, 2009.

Maxwell, Lorraine E. "A safe and welcoming school: What students, teachers, and parents think." *Journal of architectural and planning research* 17, no. 4 (2000): 271–282.

McAllister, Keith. "The ASD-friendly classroom: Design complexity, challenge and characteristics." In *Design research society conference.* Retrieved from http://www.designresearchsociety.org/docs-procs/DRS2010/PDF/084.pdf. 2010.

McAllister, Keith, and Barry Maguire. "A design model: The autism spectrum disorder classroom design kit." *British journal of special education* 39, no. 4 (2012): 201–208.

McAllister, Margaret. "Awake and aware: Thinking constructively about the world through transformative learning." In *Creative approaches in health and social care education* (pp. 157–172). London: Macmillan, 2010.

McDonnell, John, Nadine Thorson, Stephanie Disher, Connie Mathot-Buckner, Jerri Mendel, and Lavinia Ray. "The achievement of students with developmental disabilities and their peers without disabilities in inclusive settings: An exploratory study." *Education and treatment of children* 26, no. 3 (2003): 224–236.

Merriam-Webster's Medical Dictionary. s.v. "Behavior." Retrieved April 19, 2008, http://dictionary.reference.com/browse/behavior.

Merritt, Edwin T. *Magnet and specialized schools of the future: A Focus on change.* R&L Education, 2005.

Mesibov, Gary B., and Marie Howley. *Accessing the curriculum for pupils with autistic spectrum disorders: Using the TEACCH programme to help inclusion.* David Fulton Publishers, 2003.

Mesibov, Gary B., and Victoria Shea. "Evidence-based practices and autism." *Autism* 15, no. 1 (2011): 114–133.

Mesibov, Gary B., Victoria Shea, and Eric Schopler. *The TEACCH approach to autism spectrum disorders.* Springer Science & Business Media, 2004.

Meyers-Levy, Joan, and Rui Juliet Zhu. "The influence of ceiling height: The effect of priming on the type of processing that people use." *Journal of consumer research* 34, no. 2 (2007): 174–186.

Ministry of Education. Special Programs Branch. "Teaching students with autism: A resource guide for schools." 2000.

Mitchell, Peter, and Danielle Ropar. "Visuo-spatial abilities in autism: A review."*Infant and child development* 13, no. 3 (2004): 185–198.

Mitchell, Shelley, Jessica Brian, Lonnie Zwaigenbaum, Wendy Roberts, Peter Szatmari, Isabel Smith, and Susan Bryson. "Early language and communication development of infants later diagnosed with autism spectrum disorder." *Journal of developmental & behavioral pediatrics* 27, no. 2 (2006): S69–S78.

Montagu, Ashley. *Touching: The human significance of the skin.* Harper & Row, 1971.

Moore, R. *Children's domain: Play and play space in child development.* London: Croom Helm, 1986.

Moos, Rudolf H., and Sonne Lemke. "Assessing the physical and architectural features of sheltered care settings." *Journal of gerontology* 35, no. 4 (1980): 571–583.

Morgan, Debra G., and Norma J. Stewart. "Multiple occupancy versus private rooms on dementia care units." *Environment and behavior* 30, no. 4 (1998): 487–503.

Morton, Jill. *Color voodoo for the office*. Colorcom, 1998.

Mostafa, Magda. "An architecture for autism: Concepts of design intervention for the autistic user." *Archnet-IJAR: International journal of architectural research* 2, no. 1 (2008): 189–211.

Mostafa, Mohamed M. "A hierarchical analysis of the green consciousness of the Egyptian consumer." *Psychology & marketing* 24, no. 5 (2007): 445–473.

MSN Encarta, s.v. "Sense Organs," Retrieved April 16, 2008, http://encarta. msn.com/encyclopedia_761565821/Sense_Organs.html.

Murray, Christopher J., and Alan D. Lopez. *Global burden of disease*. Vol. 1. Cambridge, MA: Harvard University Press, 1996.

Myers, Jane E., Thomas J. Sweeney, and J. Melvin Witmer. "The wheel of wellness counseling for wellness: A holistic model for treatment planning." *Journal of counseling & development* 78, no. 3 (2000): 251–266.

Myles, Brenda Smith. *Asperger syndrome and sensory issues: Practical solutions for making sense of the world*. AAPC Publishing, 2000.

Myles, Brenda Smith, Winnie Dunn, Louann Rinner, Taku Hagiwara, Matthew Reese, Abby Huggins, and Stephanie Becker. "Sensory issues in children with Asperger syndrome and autism." *Education and training in developmental disabilities* 39, no. 4 (2004): 283–290.

Nanda, U. *Sensthetics: A crossmodal approach to sensory design*. Saarbrücken, Germany: Lighting Source, 2008. p. 48.

National Institutes of Health. "Autism spectrum disorders (ASDs)." Eunice Kennedy Shriver: National Institute of Child Health and Human Development, November 15, 2011. http://www.nichd.nih.gov/health/topics/asd.cfm.

Neisser, U. *Cognitive psychology*. New York: Appleton-Century-Crofts, 1966.

Nielson, Karla J. and David A. Taylor. *Interiors: An introduction*. New York: McGraw-Hill, 2007.

Nober, Linda W., and E. Harris Nober. "Auditory discrimination of learning disabled children in quiet and classroom noise." *Journal of learning disabilities* 8, no. 10 (1975): 656–659.

O'Donnell Wicklund Pigozzi and Peterson, Architects Inc, V. S. Furniture, and Bruce Mau Design. *The third teacher: 79 ways you can use design to transform teaching & learning*. New York: Abrams, 2010.

O'Neill, Jasmine Lee. *Through the eyes of aliens: A book about autistic people*. Jessica Kingsley Publishers, 1999.

O'Neill, Meena, and Robert S. P. Jones. "Sensory-perceptual abnormalities in autism: A case for more research?" *Journal of autism and developmental disorders* 27, no. 3 (1997): 283–293.

Odom, Samuel L., and Scott R. McConnell. *Social competence of young children with disabilities: Issues and strategies for intervention*. Paul H Brookes Pub Co, 1992.

Oldenburg, Ray. *The great good place: Café, coffee shops, community centers, beauty parlors, general stores, bars, hangouts, and how they get you through the day*. Paragon House Publishers, 1989.

Ottosson, Johan, and Patrik Grahn. "Measures of restoration in geriatric care residences: The influence of nature on elderly people's power of concentration, blood pressure and pulse rate." *Journal of housing for the elderly* 19, no. 3–4 (2006): 227–256.

Pallasmaa, Juhani. *The eyes of the skin: Architecture and the senses*. Chichester, UK: John Wiley & Sons Ltd., 2005.

Panerai, Simonetta, L. Ferrante, and M. Zingale. "Benefits of the Treatment and Education of Autistic and Communication Handicapped Children (TEACCH) programme as compared with a non-specific approach." *Journal of intellectual disability research* 46, no. 4 (2002): 318–327.

Parcells, Claudia, Manfred Stommel, and Robert P. Hubbard. "Mismatch of classroom furniture and student body dimensions: Empirical findings and health implications." *Journal of adolescent health* 24, no. 4 (1999): 265–273.

Parmelee, Patricia A., and M. Powell Lawton. "The design of special environments for the aged." In *Handbook of the psychology of aging* (pp. 464–488). Academic Press, 2013.

Parsons, Russ, and Terry Hartig. "Environmental psychophysiology." In *Handbook of psychophysiology* (2nd ed.) (pp. 815–846). New York: Cambridge University Press, 2000.

Peck, Charles A., Patricia Carlson, and Edwin Helmstetter. "Parent and teacher perceptions of outcomes for typically developing children enrolled in integrated early childhood programs: A statewide survey." *Journal of early intervention* 16, no. 1 (1992): 53–63.

Pellicano, Elizabeth, Alastair D. Smith, Filipe Cristino, Bruce M. Hood, Josie Briscoe, and Iain D. Gilchrist. "Children with autism are neither systematic nor optimal foragers." *Proceedings of the National Academy of Sciences* 108, no. 1 (2011): 421–426.

Perreault, Audrey, Rick Gurnsey, Michelle Dawson, Laurent Mottron, and Armando Bertone. "Increased sensitivity to mirror symmetry in autism." *PLoS one* 6, no. 4 (2011): e19519–e19519.

Peterson, G. "Let the children play." *Nursing* 3, no. 41 (1989): 22–25.

Polirstok, Susan Rovet, Lawrence Dana, Serafino Buono, Vita Mongelli, and Grazia Trubia. "Improving functional communication skills in adolescents and young adults with severe autism using gentle teaching and positive approaches." *Topics in language disorders* 23, no. 2 (2003): 146–153.

Porteous, John Douglas. *Environment & behavior: Planning and everyday urban life*. Reading, MA: Addison-Wesley, 1977.

Pyle, Robert Michael. "Eden in a vacant lot: Special places, species, and kids in the neighborhood of life." In Peter H. Kahn and Stephen R. Kellert *Children and nature: Psychological, sociocultural, and evolutionary investigations* (pp. 305–327). MIT Press, 2002.

Quill, Kathleen Ann. *Teaching children with autism: Strategies to enhance communication and socialization*. Cengage Learning, 1995.

Rabbitt, P. "Introduction: Methodologies and models in the study of executive function." In *Methodology of frontal and executive function* (pp. 1–38). Taylor & Francis, 1997.

Rapoport, Amos. *The meaning of the built environment: A nonverbal communication approach*. University of Arizona Press, 1982.

Rayneri, Letty J., Brian L. Gerber, and Larry P. Wiley. "Gifted achievers and gifted underachievers: The impact of learning style preferences in the classroom." *Prufrock journal* 14, no. 4 (2003): 197–204.

Rea, Patricia J., Virginia L. McLaughlin, and Chriss Walther-Thomas. "Outcomes for students with learning disabilities in inclusive and pullout programs." *Council for exceptional children* 68, no. 2 (2002): 203–222.

Read, Marilyn A., and Deborah Upington. "Young children's color preferences in the interior environment." *Early childhood education journal* 36, no. 6 (2009): 491–496.

Reed, Ron. *Color+design: Transforming interior space*. Fairchild Books, 2010.

Regnier, Victor. *Design for assisted living: Guidelines for housing the physically and mentally frail*. John Wiley & Sons, 2003.

Regnier, Victor, and Alexis Denton. "Ten new and emerging trends in residential group living environments." *Neurorehabilitation* 25, no. 3 (2008): 169–188.

Regnier, Victor, Jennifer Hamilton, and Suzie Yatabe. *Assisted living for the aged and frail: Innovations in design, management, and financing*. Columbia University Press, 1995.

Regnier, Victor, and Jon Pynoos. *Housing the aged: Design directives and policy considerations*. Elsevier Publishing Company, 1987.

Remington, Anna, John Swettenham, Ruth Campbell, and Mike Coleman. "Selective attention and perceptual load in autism spectrum disorder." *Psychological science* 20, no. 11 (2009): 1388–1393.

Rodiek, Susan, and Benyamin Schwarz. "Perceptions of physical environment features that influence outdoor usage at assisted living facilities." In *The role of the outdoors in residential environments for aging* (pp. 95–107). Binghamton, NY: Haworth Press, 2005..

Rogers, Sally J., and Sally Ozonoff. "Annotation: What do we know about sensory dysfunction in autism? A critical review of the empirical evidence." *Journal of child psychology and psychiatry* 46, no. 12 (2005): 1255–1268.

Rogers, Sally J., Susan Hepburn, and Elizabeth Wehner. "Parent reports of sensory symptoms in toddlers with autism and those with other developmental disorders." *Journal of autism and developmental disorders* 33, no. 6 (2003): 631–642.

Roweton, William E. and Murray-Seegert, C. *Nasty girls, thugs, and humans like us: Social relations between severely disabled and nondisabled students in high school*. Baltimore: Brookes, 1989.

Ruble, Lisa A., and Dana M. Robson. "Individual and environmental determinants of engagement in autism." *Journal of autism and developmental disorders* 37, no. 8 (2007): 1457–1468.

Rudd, Tim, and Futurelab. *Reimagining outdoor learning spaces: Primary capital, co-designing and educational transformation: A Futurelab handbook*. Bristol: Futurelab, 2008. p. 23.

Russell, Robert L. "Children's philosophical inquiry into defining art: A quasi-experimental study of aesthetics in the elementary classroom." *Studies in art education* 29, no. 3 (1988): 282–291.

Saarinen, Thomas Frederick, David Seamon, and James L. Sell. *Environmental perception and behavior: An inventory and prospect*. Chicago: University of Chicago, Department of Geography, 1984.

Salingaros, Nikos A., and Michael W. Mehaffy. *A theory of architecture*. UMBAU-VERLAG Harald Püschel, 2006.

Samuels, J., O. Joseph Bienvenu III, M. A. Riddle, B. A. M. Cullen, M. A. Grados, K-Y. Liang, R. Hoehn-Saric, and G. Nestadt. "Hoarding in obsessive compulsive disorder: Results from a case-control study." *Behaviour research and therapy* 40, no. 5 (2002): 517–528.

Sánchez, Pilar Arnaiz, Francisco Segado Vázquez, and Laureano Albaladejo Serrano. *Autism and the built environment*. INTECH Open Access Publisher, 2011.

Schopler, Eric, and Gary B. Mesibov. *Autism in adolescents and adults*. Springer Science & Business Media, 1983.

Schwartz, Barry. "The social psychology of privacy." *American Journal of Sociology* 73, no. 6 (1968): 741–752.

Scott, Fiona J., Simon Baron-Cohen, Patrick Bolton, and Carol Brayne. "Brief report: Prevalence of autism spectrum conditions in children aged 5–11 years in Cambridgeshire, UK." *Autism* 6, no. 3 (2002): 231–237.

Scott, J., C. Clark, and M. Brady. *Students with autism*. Canada: Thompson Wadsworth, 2000.

Scott, Suzanne C. "Visual attributes related to preference in interior environments." *Journal of interior design* 18, no. 1–2 (1993): 7–16.

Seep, Benjamin, Robin Glosemeyer, Emily Hulce, Matt Linn, and Pamela Aytar. "Classroom acoustics: A resource for creating environments with desirable listening conditions." *Acoustical society of America*. (2000).

Seligman, Martin. "The new era of positive psychology." *Ted Conference*. 2004.

Seligman, Martin E. P. *Helplessness: On depression, development, and death*. WH Freeman/Times Books/Henry Holt & Co, 1975.

Sempik, Joe, Jo Aldridge, and Saul Becker. *Social and therapeutic horticulture: Evidence and messages from research*. Thrive, 2003.

Shabha, Ghasson. "An assessment of the impact of the sensory environment on individuals' behaviour in special needs schools." *Facilities* 24, no. 1/2 (2006): 31–42.

Shabha, Ghasson, and Kristi Gaines. "A comparative analysis of transatlantic design interventions for therapeutically enhanced learning environments—Texas vs West Midlands." *Facilities* 31, no. 13/14 (2013): 634–658.

Shin, Su and Kristi Gaines. "Team of Texas Tech researchers create sensory clothing." *Lubbock avalanche journal (TX)*, May 26, 2015. http://lubbockonline.com/local-news/2015-05-25/team-texas-tech-researchers-create-sensory-clothing.

Siebein, Gary W., Martin A. Gold, Glenn W. Siebein, and Michael G. Ermann. "Ten ways to provide a high-quality acoustical environment in schools." *Language, speech, and hearing services in schools* 31, no. 4 (2000): 376–384.

Simmel, Georg, and Kurt H. Wolff. *The sociology of Georg Simmel*. Vol. 92892. Simon and Schuster, 1950.

Sloane, Philip D., C. Madeline Mitchell, John S. Preisser, Charles Phillips, Charlotte Commander, and Eileen Burker. "Environmental correlates of resident agitation in Alzheimer's disease special care units." *Journal of the American Geriatrics Society* 46, no. 7 (1998): 862–869.

Smith, Leann E., Matthew J. Maenner, and Marsha Mailick Seltzer. "Developmental trajectories in adolescents and adults with autism: The case of daily living skills." *Journal of the American Academy of Child & Adolescent Psychiatry* 51, no. 6 (2012): 622–631.

Smith, Ron, and Nicholas Watkins. "Therapeutic environments." Washington DC: Academy of Architecture for Health, 2008.

Smyth, Fiona. "Medical geography: Therapeutic places, spaces and networks." *Progress in human geography* 29, no. 4 (2005): 488–495.

Sommer, Robert. *Personal space. The behavioral basis of design.* Prentice-Hall, 1969.

Sternberg, Robert J. *Cognitive psychology.* Fort Worth: Harcourt Brace College Publishers, 1996.

Stewart-Pollack, Julie, and Rosemary Menconi. *Designing for privacy and related needs.* Fairchild Books, 2005.

Stokes, S. "Structured teaching: Strategies for supporting students with autism." *USA: CESA* 7 (2001).

Strong-Wilson, Teresa, and Julia Ellis. "Children and place: Reggio Emilia's environment as third teacher." *Theory into practice* 46, no. 1 (2007): 40–47.

Styne, A. F. "Making light and color work in office harmony." *The office.* (1990): 77–78.

Szatmari, Peter, Susan E. Bryson, David L. Streiner, Freda Wilson, Lynda Archer, and Cynthia Ryerse. "Two-year outcome of preschool children with autism or Asperger's syndrome." *American journal of psychiatry* 157, no. 12 (2014): 1980–1987.

Talay-Ongan, Ayshe, and Kara Wood. "Unusual sensory sensitivities in autism: A possible crossroads." *International journal of disability, development and education* 47, no. 2 (2000): 201–212.

Taylor, Andrea Faber, Frances E. Kuo, and William C. Sullivan. "Coping with ADD: The surprising connection to green play settings." *Environment and behavior* 33, no. 1 (2001): 54–77.

Terzigni, Mark. "HVAC-System Acoustics-Methods of reducing unwanted sound associated with mechanical systems in commercial buildings." *Heating/Piping/Air Conditioning engineering: HPAC* 80, no. 8 (2008): 18.

Thompson, Suzanne C., and Shirlynn Spacapan. "Perceptions of control in vulnerable populations." *Journal of social issues* 47, no. 4 (1991): 1–21.

Thompson, Travis, Julia Robinson, Mary Dietrich, Marilyn Farris, and Valerie Sinclair. "Architectural features and perceptions of community residences for people with mental retardation." *American journal of mental retardation: AJMR* 101, no. 3 (1996): 292–314.

Tomchek, Scott D., and Winnie Dunn. "Sensory processing in children with and without autism: A comparative study using the short sensory profile." *American journal of occupational therapy* 61, no. 2 (2007): 190–200.

Treffert, D. A. "*Islands of genius: The bountiful mind of the autistic, acquired, and sudden savant.* Jessica Kingsley Publishers, 2010.

Tufvesson, Catrin, and Joel Tufvesson. "The building process as a tool towards an all-inclusive school. A Swedish example focusing on children with defined concentration difficulties such as ADHD, autism and Down's syndrome." *Journal of housing and the built environment* 24, no. 1 (2009): 47–66.

Ulrich, Roger. "View through a window may influence recovery." *Science* 224, no. 4647 (1984): 224–225.

Ulrich, Roger S. "Effects of gardens on health outcomes: Theory and research." In C. C. Marcus and M. Barnes, *Healing gardens: Therapeutic benefits and design recommendations* (pp. 27–86). New York: John Wiley & Sons, 1999.

Ulrich, Roger S. "Effects of healthcare environmental design on medical outcomes." In *Design and health: Proceedings of the second international conference on health and design* (pp. 49–59). Stockholm, Sweden: Svensk Byggtjanst, 2001.

Ungerer, Judy A., and Marian Sigman. "Symbolic play and language comprehension in autistic children." *Journal of the American Academy of Child Psychiatry* 20, no. 2 (1981): 318–337.

University of Illinois College of Agricultural, Consumer and Environmental Sciences. "Green environments essential for human health, research shows." ScienceDaily. www.sciencedaily.com/releases/2011/04/110419151438.htm (accessed November 11, 2015).

U.S. Equal Employment Opportunity Commission. "Facts about the Americans with Disabilities Act." The U.S. Equal Employment Opportunity Commission, 2008.

U.S. Department of Education, Office of Special Education Programs. "Individuals with Disabilities Education Act (IDEA) Data." Retrieved March 21, 2008, from https://www.ideadata.org/index.html.

Van Bourgondien, Mary E., Nancy C. Reichle, Duncan G. Campbell, and Gary B. Mesibov. "The environmental rating scale (ERS): A measure of the quality of the residential environment for adults with autism." *Research in developmental disabilities* 19, no. 5 (1998): 381–394.

Van Bourgondien, Mary E., Nancy C. Reichle, and Eric Schopler. "Effects of a model treatment approach on adults with autism." *Journal of autism and developmental disorders* 33, no. 2 (2003): 131–140.

Van Hover, Stephanie D., and Elizabeth A. Yeager. "'Making students better people?' A case study of a beginning history teacher." In *International social studies forum* (vol. 3, pp. 219–232). Information Age Publishing Inc., 2003.

Verghese, Preeti. "Visual search and attention: A signal detection theory approach." *Neuron* 31, no. 4 (2001): 523–535.

Vogel, Clare L. "Classroom design for living and learning with autism." *Autism Asperger's digest* 7 (2008).

Volkmar, Fred R., Rhea Paul, Ami Klin, and Donald J. Cohen, eds. *Handbook of autism and pervasive developmental disorders, diagnosis, development, neurobiology, and behavior.* Vol. 1. John Wiley & Sons, 2005.

Wagner, Cheryl. "Planning School Grounds for Outdoor Learning." *National clearinghouse for educational facilities* (2000).

Waldron, Nancy L., and James McLeskey. "The effects of an inclusive school program on students with mild and severe learning disabilities." *Exceptional children* 64, no. 3 (1998): 395–405.

Walker, Morton. *The power of color.* Avery Publishing Group, 1991.

Watling, Renee L., Jean Deitz, and Owen White. "Comparison of sensory profile scores of young children with and without autism spectrum disorders."*American journal of occupational therapy* 55, no. 4 (2001): 416–423.

Weimer, Amy K. *Motor impairment in Asperger Syndrome: Evidence for a deficit in proprioception.* No publisher information, 1999.

Weimer, Amy K., Amy M. Schatz, Alan Lincoln, Angela O. Ballantyne, and Doris A. Trauner. "'Motor' impairment in Asperger syndrome: Evidence for a deficit in proprioception." *Journal of developmental & behavioral pediatrics* 22, no. 2 (2001): 92–101.

Weiss, Margaret P., and John Lloyd. "Conditions for co-teaching: Lessons from a case study." *Teacher education and special education: The journal of the teacher education division of the council for exceptional children* 26, no. 1 (2003): 27–41.

Welch, Polly, Valerie Parker, and John Zeisel. *Independence through interdependence: Congregate living for older people.* Office of Policy and Planning, Department of Elder Affairs, 1984.

Wells, A. *Emotional disorders and metacognition: Innovative cognitive therapy.* Chichester, UK: John Wiley & Sons Ltd., 2000.

Wells, Nancy M., and Gary W. Evans. "Nearby nature a buffer of life stress among rural children." *Environment and behavior* 35, no. 3 (2003): 311–330.

Westin, A. F. *Privacy and freedom.* Atheneum, NY, 1967.

White, Robert W. "Motivation reconsidered: The concept of competence." *Psychological review* 66, no. 5 (1959): 297.

Whitehouse, Sandra, James W. Varni, Michael Seid, Clare Cooper-Marcus, Mary Jane Ensberg, Jenifer R. Jacobs, and Robyn S. Mehlenbeck. "Evaluating a children's hospital garden environment: Utilization and consumer satisfaction." *Journal of environmental psychology* 21, no. 3 (2001): 301–314.

Whitemyer, David. "The future of evidence-based design." *International interior design association.* 2010. See http://www.iida.org/content.cfm/the-future-of-evidence-based-design (accessed January 17, 2014).

Williams, Emma. "Who really needs a 'theory' of mind? An interpretative phenomenological analysis of the autobiographical writings of ten high-functioning individuals with an autism spectrum disorder." *Theory & psychology* 14, no. 5 (2004): 704–724.

Williams, Emma, Alan Costall, and Vasudevi Reddy. "Children with autism experience problems with both objects and people." *Journal of autism and developmental disorders* 29, no. 5 (1999): 367–378.

Wilson, E. O. *Biophilia.* Harvard University Press, 1984.

Winterbottom, Mark, and Arnold Wilkins. "Lighting and discomfort in the classroom." *Journal of environmental psychology* 29, no. 1 (2009): 63–75.

Woodcock, A., D. Georgiou, J. Jackson, and A. Woolner. "Designing a tailorable environment for children with autistic spectrum disorders." *The Design Institute, Coventry School of Art and Design, Coventry University, UK.* n.d.

World Health Organization. "Preamble to the Constitution of the World Health Organization as adopted by the International Health Conference." [Official Records of the World Health Organization, no. 2, p. 100.] New York, 1946. pp. 19–22.

Zeisel, John. *Inquiry by design: Environment/behavior/neuroscience in architecture, interiors, landscape and planning.* New York: WW Norton & Company, 2006.

Zeisel, John, and Martha Tyson. "Alzheimer's treatment gardens." In *Healing Gardens: Therapeutic benefits and design recommendations* (pp. 437–504). New York: John Wiley & Sons, 1999.

Zuo, H., T. Hope, M. Jones, and P. Castle. "Sensory interaction with materials." In *Design and emotion* (pp. 223–227). CRC Press, 2004.

Index

Please note that page numbers relating to figures will be in italics followed by the letter 'f', while numbers indicating tables will be in the same format but contain the letter 't'.

T - #0190 - 191020 - C232 - 279/216/11 - PB - 9780367030469